Managing Inclusive Education

Managing Inclusive Education: From Policy to Experience

Edited by

Peter Clough

P·C·P

Paul Chapman
Publishing Ltd

Paul Chapman Publishing Ltd
A SAGE Publications Company
6 Bonhill Street
London EC2A 4PU

SAGE Publications Inc.
2455 Teller Road
Thousand Oaks, California 91320

SAGE Publications India Pvt Ltd
32, M-Block Market
Greater Kailash-I
New Delhi 110 048

British Cataloguing in Publication Data

A catalogue record for this book is available from the British Library

ISBN 1 85396 411 5
ISBN 1 85396 393 3 (pbk)

Library of Congress catalog card number

Typeset by Dorwyn Ltd, Rowlands Castle, Hampshire
Printed and bound in Great Britain by Athenaeum Press, Tyne & Wear

A B C D E F   3 2 1 0 9 8

Contents

Preface

Contexts of the book

This book started life only three years ago as a series of key readings for a postgraduate course called 'Managing Special and Inclusive Education'; this title reflected what we, as editors, saw as a period of transition from the 'special' (and segregated) practices of only twenty or so years ago, through the (more) integrative developments of the 1980s, towards a much wider discourse about inclusive education. Its present form – and title – reflect our own development as a group of colleagues working together.

In its present form, the collection represents a number of statements about – and 'snapshots' of – a series of emerging practices. This sort of collection brings together many different professional voices, reflecting a myriad principles, practices and interests. Although there might be some broad consensus about inclusive education discernible in the chapters which follow, it will also be seen that there is a variety of competing definitions and aspirations at work. This is, of course, one of the legacies of 'special' education; for practitioners and policy-makers alike, it has become a ground of contested aims and values, and these will be evident in this collection – not least in the different forms of language which are used to address what are basically the same phenomena. Some writers in this collection can clearly no longer tolerate an unproblematised notion of 'special' – and its deficit-driven lexicon – whilst others are still grappling with the 'given' terminology of 'special education' terminology to make a radical transition to inclusive education.

In any event, for all this, this is undoubtedly an era of change. Perhaps outwardly not a lot may appear to have changed in the recent years: the distribution of 'segregated' and 'integrated' schools has altered little and legislation for social justice is – at best – still only a promise. But for all that, there *is* a newly distinct movement of ideas and passions within the teaching and research communities of 'special' education; there can be no doubt that *inclusion* – as an immanent idea if not yet a set of established practices – is finding its moment. And it is more than a buzzword, much more than a politician's cypher, for its unique provenance is the vast weight of experience of the collective human rights and – particularly – disability movements.

In this sense, 'special' education is coming into a sort of 'third age', and its moral and political sponsors are no longer to be found in the academic disciplines which have so far justified this or that provision, but in the voice of a consumer movement. What might be called the 'first age' of 'special' education was formed through the patronage first of medical and then of psychological conceptions of deficit or abnormality, and a basically segregative regime was established. This gave way to some extent – in rhetoric if not in widespread practice – to a 'second age', licensed by sociological understandings of the relative and interactive nature of difficulties, and hence broadly integrative policies.

But in its origin as a movement, 'inclusion' owes less to academic disciplines – though there are many accounts, like this, which partially appropriate it – than to arguments about human rights, and in the daily lived political activity which seeks to establish them. It is in this sense that – unlike integration, which is essentially assimilative – inclusion is truly radical, for it appears to seek a profound social change which actually 'celebrat[es] difference in dignified ways . . . [For] education for all . . . involves a serious commitment to the task of identifying, challenging and contributing to the removal of injustices' (Barton, 1997, p. 234).

Organisation of the book

The book is organised around a series of key questions, which structure the various chapters. Each chapter also includes a number of study activities which are generally intended to help reflection and frequently to enable readers critically to relate ideas under discussion to their own professional contexts. Each chapter concludes with suggestions for further reading on the topic.

In the introductory chapter, I point up some of the policy changes which characterise the move from segregative through integrative to inclusive education, dwelling in particular on the role of curriculum and resources in realising inclusion. Still with an eye on special and inclusive provision, Hugh Busher in Chapter 2 provides answers to the basic question: 'What is educational management exactly?' – first of all for the newcomer to management studies, then in a critical review of some different approaches and the values and ideologies which underpin them. In Chapter 3, Derrick Armstrong considers 'What traditions of policy and practice have led us to where we are?' and provides a detailed examination of the history of management of special education. Felicity Armstrong then asks in Chapter 4 'To what extent does the school's delivery of the curriculum produce or prevent the occurrence of learning difficulties?' This question leads to the exploration of the role of curriculum policies and practices in the realisation of learning difficulty.

In Chapter 5, Alan Marsh asks 'How can teachers/schools best access the resources statutorily available to meet the needs of their exceptional students?' The chapter examines how funding policies variously affect the ways in which instances of learning difficulty can be met within LEAs and schools. Finally in this section, Len Barton addresses in Chapter 6 the question 'Can inclusive education compete in the market?'

The second section of the book is more directly concerned with practitioner accounts of inclusive practices. In Chapter 7, Elaine Herbert explores ways in which the incidence of learning difficulties can – and arguably should – be not only the role but also the duty of early years management; the key question here is 'How early should inclusion start?' Caroline Roaf in Chapter 8 addresses the question 'What can – and what *must* – the special educational needs co-ordinator do?' in a critical assembly of both policy requirements and the practitioner experience of attempts to deliver those demands. Drawing on her own experience again, in Chapter 9 Caroline critically explores the possibilities for collaboration between the many agencies involved in defining and meeting SEN. The key question is: 'How can we best bring together different professional interests in the interest of the student with learning difficulties?' In parallel with this chapter, Martin Desforges in Chapter 10 considers 'What can – and what *must* – we expect of local educational authorities in their provision of centrally organised support services?' This case-based chapter uses various data to problematise LEA commitment to inclusive policies. In the final chapter, Cathy Nutbrown gives a response to the book based on her view of children's rights and her own experience of 'managing to include'.

Of a number of recent publications which tell of the personal experiences of segregative and exclusive education systems, Pippa Murray and Jill Penman's collection, *Let Our Children Be* (1996), is a powerful collection; and Jill's own poem, 'When you look at my child' ends with a parent's observation that, as teachers and researchers – and editors of academic writing – we should do well always to bear in mind:

> Don't you understand that
> The comments you make about my child
> Tell about yourself
> And not about him?
>
> And the needs we discuss
> Are yours
> And not his.
>
> When you look at my child.
>
> *Peter Clough, Sheffield 1998*

References

Barton, L. (1997) Inclusive education: romantic, subversive or realistic?, *International Journal of Inclusive Education*, Vol. 1, no. 3, pp. 231–42.

Murray, P. and Penman, J. (1996) *Let Our Children Be*, Parents with Attitude, Sheffield.

Acknowledgements

Most of the chapters in this book were developed as teaching materials following discussion between Derrick Armstrong, Felicity Armstrong and Peter Clough; the present edition owes much to Felicity's earlier and judicious editing work. Most of the original papers have been substantially rewritten to reflect policy developments in general, and our commitment to the emerging importance of the inclusive principle; I thank all the authors who worked to tight deadlines to realise this project.

As Course Secretary, Tracey Haslam supported the team with characteristic warmth and efficiency, and saw the text through several drafts to its final form. Further support is gratefully acknowledged from Tina Cartwright and Jean Booker of the university's Education Research Centre. Finally I should like to acknowledge the many critical comments of our students, who have helped to give the text the shape it has today.

List of Contributors

Derrick Armstrong is a lecturer in education in the Division of Education at the University of Sheffield. His current interests are in the history of special educational policy, and in particular the way in which policy–practice negotiations articulate different social constructions of 'learning difficulties' in relation to the life experiences of those so labelled. His previous books include *Power and Partnership in Education*, which was awarded the 1995 National Association for Special Educational Needs Academic Book Prize, and *The Assessment of Special Educational Needs: Whose Problem?* written with David Galloway and Sally Tomlinson.

Felicity Armstrong is a lecturer in the Division of Education at the University of Sheffield. She is Director of the UK MEd programme in inclusive education and a member of the Inclusive Education Research Group. She has particular interest in policy and equality issues in education and the questions raised by crosscultural research. Her publications include with P. Potts, F. Armstrong and M. Masters (1995) *Equality and Diversity in Education: Learning, Teaching and Managing Schools* and *Equality and Diversity in Education: National and International Contexts*, both Routledge.

Len Barton is founder and editor of the international journal *Disability and Society*. He is interested in the politics of disability and crossnational perspectives on inclusion.

Hugh Busher is Senior Lecturer in the School of Education, University of Leicester, where he works with colleagues in the EMDU and school improvement groups to focus on the cultural and political dimensions of leadership, management and policy-making in schools as organisations. He is Chair of the British Education Management and Administration Society's publications committee and a series editor for the books it publishes with Paul Chapman. His most recent publication, co-edited with Rene Saran, was *Managing Teachers as Professionals in Schools* (BEMAS/Kogan Page, 1995).

Peter Clough worked in all phases of public education before moving to the University of Sheffield. His teaching and research interests are in experiences of special and inclusive education – of students, parents, teachers, researchers and others. With Len Barton, he co-edited *Making Difficulties: Research and the Construction of SEN* (1995) and *Articulating with Difficulty: Research Voices in Inclusive Education* (1998), both Paul Chapman Publishing.

Martin Desforges worked as a secondary schoolteacher in England and Nigeria before training as an educational psychologist. He worked in Sheffield LEA as an educational psychologist for many years, before becoming associate tutor to the educational psychology training course at the University of Sheffield. He is currently a lecturer in education at the University of Sheffield. His publications include *Infant Index* (1995), *Baseline Plus* (1997) and *Baseline Assessment* (1998).

Elaine Herbert worked in home settings alongside families and their pre-school children with possible special educational needs for twelve years, reinforcing her belief that to maximise the effectiveness of early intervention programmes, it is essential to work closely with parents and other colleagues. Despite early retirement from the LEA in 1996, she has been busy working on a part-time basis at the Institute of Education, Warwick University and as a registered nursery education inspector. She has undertaken research on the needs of fathers of children with special needs. She is married with two sons. Her interests include her family, theatre and good food.

Alan Marsh taught in primary, secondary and special schools before taking up a post as a chartered educational psychologist with Lancashire County Council. He is presently completing a PhD thesis 'Formula funding and special educational needs' with the Centre for Education and Management at the Open University.

Cathy Nutbrown began her career as a teacher of young children and has since worked in a range of settings and roles with parents, teachers and early childhood educators. Her research interests include children's early learning and development, their literacy, assessment, children's rights and work with parents. She is currently Co-ordinator of the Sheffield University–LEA REAL (Raising Early Achievement in Literacy) project. Her publications include *Threads of Thinking – Young Children Learning and the Role of Early Education* (PCP, 1994), *Respectful Educators – Capable Learners: Children's Rights in Early Education* (PCP, 1996) and, recently, *Recognising Early Literacy Development – Assessing Children's Achievements* (PCP, 1997).

Caroline Roaf has been a special needs co-ordinator in Oxfordshire secondary schools since 1979. She studied for the master's degree in rights in education at the London Institute of Education. During 1993–4 she held a part-time lectureship in the School of Education at Oxford Brookes University. She is currently concluding a doctorate on factors contributing to successful interagency co-operation for young people in difficulty, particularly those whose needs are such that no single agency can accept sole responsibility. From 1989–1994 she was convenor of the Oxford City interagency project 'Children and Young People in Difficulty' (supported from 1992 by the Joseph Rowntree Foundation and findings published as *Social Care Research* 68, 1995). She contributes regularly to books and journals on special educational needs and was co-editor, with Hazel Bines, of *Needs, Rights and Opportunities* (Falmer, 1983).

Abbreviations

AEN	additional educational needs
AWPU	age-weighted pupil unit
DES	Department of Education and Science
DFE	Department for Education
DfEE	Department for Education and Employment
DOE	Department of the Environment
EBD	emotional and/or behavioural difficulties
EPIs	educational priority indices
FSME	free school meals entitlement
LEA	local education authority
LMS	local management of schools
LMSS	local management of special schools
LSA	learning support assistant
MLD	moderate learning difficulties
NARE	National Association for Remedial Education
NASEN	National Association for Special Educational Needs
NCAs	National Curriculum assessments
OFSTED	Office for Standards in Education
PMLD	profound/multiple learning difficulties
SATs	standard assessment tasks
SEN	special educational needs
SENCO	special educational needs co-ordinator
SIE	special and inclusive education
SpLD	specific learning difficulties
SSA	standard spending assessment

1

Introduction: What's Special About Inclusion?

PETER CLOUGH

Introduction

This book examines the management of educational services for all children, though particularly for those understood to have learning difficulties. Clearly, provision for children with SEN has, in the past two decades, been continuously affected by major policy changes with regard to the funding and management of schools and colleges. Changing contexts in the management of SIE are in many respects similar to the developments in all other compulsory education settings. Special education occurs within the same policy contexts as all state education, and is subject not only to the same structures but also to many of the same impositions, opportunities, dilemmas and conflicts. For all in education, the recent years have seen the following trends:

- the increasingly explicit politicisation of educational structures and processes;
- wide and deep-ranging development of legislation which increases the regulation and control of education through central policies;
- the elaboration of systematic inspection processes and criteria;
- the devolvement of certain areas of responsibility (most importantly, funding) to schools;
- the consequent 'marketisation' of schooling;
- the complication and – sometimes – conflict of the 'rights' of children; of parents; and of the consumer generally;
- the increasing separation – both within schools and in the broader institutions which maintain them – of managers from professionals; and
- the development of an accountability ethos which effectively promotes instrumentalism within the curriculum.

All compulsory state schooling takes place within a broadly common statutory context, and therefore management developments in special education will have many features in common with those in other 'non-special' settings. What may be most noticeably different are the additional requirements and practices which must be managed within the school in order to meet a wide spectrum of need within a framework of rights. However, there may be differences not so much in structure as in culture of practice, differences which have important implications for managing a truly inclusive system.

Is there something 'special' about the management of special education?

Regulation of special education

In many ways, one could say that the changes highlighted above are in fact all the more noticeable in special schooling, since the regulation of education for children with significant learning difficulties was traditionally notably – and sometimes notoriously – open to local and hence widely varying interpretation. The basis on which decisions were made about appropriate schooling for students with learning difficulties could vary tremendously from one LEA to the next, according to the traditions of practice which had determined a certain pattern of provision. It has often been noted – and borne out by DfEE statistics – that whether children with learning difficulties attend special schools or not still sometimes depends more on where they live than on their learning needs. The *Code of Practice* (DfEE, 1994) sought to address the identification and standardisation of provision for pupils with SEN and, more recently, the green paper (DfEE, 1997) further developed the theme of equalising opportunity for all children.

Curriculum change

A much more noticeably radical change, however, is in the area of the curriculum. In the old dispensation, the greater part of what went on in special schooling was a matter for schools – and frequently individual teachers – to decide. The curriculum could be as arbitrary as were many of the decisions which had led to a child's particular placement – though it must be acknowledged that this was also an opportunity for creative teachers to enable individual children to flourish. Now, of course, a statutory National Curriculum affects – if only by technical default – the education of all learners, and the degrees of freedom open to teachers in their selection of curricula are considerably more limited.

The culture of 'special' education

The greatest change, however – as a consequence of the above features – is arguably in the culture of special schooling. Effectively as cultures unto themselves, special schools and 'special' departments in mainstream schools were surely distinctive by nature of a broadly child-centred philosophy. This distinction – relatively unhindered by regulation – could issue in practices which were more accountable to a notion of individual difficulty than to the statutory demands of policies. To be sure, there were some poor or rankly 'bad' practices which did little to extend either the children themselves or any cause of inclusiveness. In some cases, the curricula on offer could vary in precisely these terms between the extremes of daily, sometimes quixotic and situation-sensitive improvisation in some settings to the rigour of an instrumental learning form organised by an often poorly – though surely benignly – understood behaviourist psychology. In any event, teaching intentions were regulated – and mediated – more by implicit traditions of professional practice and personal preference than by any explicit, mandatory, and essentially externally imposed requirement.

The introduction of statutory funding, and curricular and assessment frameworks brings this culture of child-centred education to a crisis, since the organising principle of management becomes one of accountability to structures hierarchically far removed from the immediate and daily needs of any child (though they are surely intended to guarantee the meeting of such needs).

Issues of equality

The Education Act 1981 – and other legislation like it in other countries – was essentially liberal and egalitarian. It recognised:

- the manifest inequalities in society, and therefore in its educational system;
- the determining effects which particular forms of schooling and particular curricula have on a student's ability to take his or her place in his or her society; and
- the stigmatising effects of school failure both directly on the self-esteem and dignity of the individual and on his or her access to the job market.

In these respects the Act reflected broader concerns in social policy with the effects of social class, race, gender, sexual orientation, marital and domestic status and so on. In an attempt to maximise opportunities for students with learning difficulties, the Act sought as far as possible to minimise any stigmatising effects of 'being different'. As a piece of liberal legislation it *sought* to promote a pluralistic society which valued the different strengths and contributions of its citizens.

For students with learning difficulties, this meant most particularly the provision of access to the same institutions and the same curricula as other learners; to use a phrase from US legislation, it calls for education *in the least restrictive environment*. However, it must be emphasised that whilst liberal and egalitarian in intention, the Act was *enabling* rather than *prescriptive*. It did not, for example, make funds available to create the conditions which would facilitate integration, or adequately train teachers to work within such a system. It left LEAs to struggle to interpret and implement the spirit of the legislation or not, as they chose. The result is wide geographical variation in provision. Further, the Act created a massive bureaucratic nightmare with statementing procedures, which have been exploited by some LEAs – which have delayed processes in order to manage minimal resources for support – and diverted the time of educational psychologists from working with children to complex assessment tasks and report writing.

The changes which schools and LEAs are occupied with are very complex, and they depend as much on the education of attitudes as on structural rearrangement. Of course, change itself does not happen simply, immediately and unilaterally, but is a much more awkward, less predictable and often painful affair. For the constructions of the accepted, traditional culture are deeply embedded in how schools and support services alike typically operate, and how they are organised in traditions of practice. In any event, the new culture is surely taking a hold as schools and services wrestle to define a role sensitive to their traditional concerns but delimited by new funding, regimes of inspection, accountability (and other) regulation. These developments are reshaping special education in the same moment as they reconstruct mainstream schooling and have seen over the last thirty or so years at least some movement along a line which runs from 'special' – that is, more or less segregative – education to integrative education. What is happening now, however, whilst historically continuous with these developments, is something much more radical, and it is necessary here to rehearse something of the fundamentally distinct and distinctive demands of an inclusive programme.

Moments and meanings of inclusion: the UNESCO Salamanca Statement (1994)

Representatives of 92 governments and 25 international organisations met in Salamanca, Spain, in 1994 to form the 'World Conference on Special Needs Education'. A bold and dynamic statement was agreed on the education of all disabled children. The statement called for inclusion to be – quite simply – the norm. The conference further adopted a new 'Framework for Action', which would require all children to be accommodated in ordinary schools, regardless of their physical, intellectual, social, emotional, linguistic or other conditions; according to the framework, national and local policies should stipulate that disabled children attend the neighbourhood school 'that would be attended if the child did not have a disability' (p. 17).

The statement insists on providing education for all children, young people and adults 'within the regular system'. It says:

> Regular schools with this inclusive orientation are the most effective means of combating discriminatory attitudes, creating welcoming communities, building on an inclusive society and achieving education for all; moreover, they provide an effective education to the majority of children and improve the efficiency and ultimately the cost-effectiveness of the entire education system.
>
> (CSIE, 1995, p. 8)

This multinational commitment to include has national, local and personal implications. It requires families of children with learning difficulties, their schools, LEAs and governments to manage – together – to include children as a first option. But in this multinational urge *for* inclusion lies the danger of physical *inclusion* but curricular and emotional *exclusion* unless children are included for and of themselves, by teachers who are professionally and personally equipped to provide appropriate education for all. For inclusion is about a radical deal more than physical location. For Barton (1997, p. 234), amongst others, inclusive education is about responding to diversity:

> it is about listening to unfamiliar voices, being open, empowering all members and about celebrating 'difference' in dignified ways. From this perspective, the goal is not to leave anyone out of school. Inclusive experience is about learning to live with one another . . . it is about how, where and why, and with what consequences, we educate *all* pupils . . . [and] involves a serious commitment to the task of identifying, challenging and contributing to the removal of injustices.

In school terms, this agenda becomes a function of the curriculum. Managing inclusive education is in its essence a curricular task, for whatever else educational managers may do, their ultimate justification is the management of learning. Such a view of learning, curriculum and inclusion needs expanding.

Inclusion: a curriculum problem ·

The way schools are organised, what they teach, how it is taught – and the host of other features that make up the school curriculum – are expressions of how a wider society is organised, of what it values (and of how in the past it has come to value these things). And at the level of curriculum content specifically, what is taught is a deliberate selection which in one way or another seeks to answer the questions: what do we want learners to know and for what purpose?

School curriculum is a selection from culture; the relevance of any curriculum determines what individuals achieve in terms of personal and cognitive growth, whether and how they make sense of and contribute to the culture in which they live. But – as has often been observed – channels of communication largely determine what may pass along them, and different channels lead to different outcomes. There is something deceptive about the statement of the Warnock Committee (DES, 1978, p. iii) that 'The purpose of education for all children is the same; the goals are the same. But the help that individual children need in progressing towards them will be different.'

It is clear that purposes and goals may be separated from effects and outcomes by a wide variety – in type and quality – of help; and these purposes and goals will be differentially realised. Thus the 'old' curricula of special education – whilst ostensibly guided by a common broad, liberal principle of mass compulsory education – very clearly produced a different sort of student as a result of the process. The traditional curriculum of special education served largely to reinforce the separateness of students with learning difficulties, not least by cutting them off from the common curriculum which is an expression of the culture in which we commonly live.

For these reasons there are very good grounds for insisting on a curriculum for all; for insisting, that is, that a *National Curriculum should exclude no one*. Such a statement is not without its problems!

A curricular approach to learning difficulty

Emphasising the *relativity* of problems, the Fish Report (ILEA, 1985, p. 1) urged a view of handicap relative to the contexts in which children and young people are educated, and is unequivocal in its recognition of the local conditions and conceptions of SEN: 'Most [learning difficulties] can only be defined precisely by individual schools in terms of the flexibility of their approach to individual differences.' More pointedly, the report affirmed (*ibid.*): 'Attitudes towards pupils and students judged to be less successful learners, and the curriculum, methods and materials offered to them, are particularly important in determining the extent to which many special educational needs arise.' There are good reasons for putting a consideration of curriculum at the centre of learning difficulties issues and practice. Some of these are obvious, others less so, but in each case there are logical grounds for insisting on the curricular nature of learning difficulties. The main arguments are as follows:

1) Special needs are not noticed in a vacuum; they appear against a background of 'normal' ability and performance which gives them relief; they are noticed because the students fail to meet the requirements of a given curriculum. They are ways of locating and describing the points of mismatch between individual understanding and performance on the one hand, and the notional demands of a given curriculum on the other. They are inevitably norm-referenced, and the norms which give them their distinctness are in the *first* instance those of the

given curriculum. However, we have not in the past typically admitted and considered this background; to be sure, the child's engagement with the curriculum tells us something about him or her, but it also tells us a great deal about the curriculum. Thus we have tended to reify a notional disability rather than attend to the broader and much more elusive curricular data of which any given failing is an abstraction. Let us say, finally, then, that *learning difficulties only occur in specific and describable contexts, though too often we generalise the difficulty and fail adequately to describe its context.*

2) The curriculum, as a set of aims, objectives, teaching plans and so on is generally conceived and expressed as something whole, general, explicit and communicable, whereas the acts of learning which make sense of that given curriculum are by their very nature partial, tacit and frequently difficult to articulate. This is of course true for all learners, whatever their notional ability; but it is particularly relevant in the case of students with SEN, whose learning is more manifestly 'imperfect'. *In this respect the 'special needs' case serves to remind us of the gaps which always and inevitably exist between curricular projections and learning context.* A conception of the curriculum which at least recognises those gaps is not only prepared for instances of special need but also sees them as routinely continuous with all learning processes.

3) Apart from the growing body of evidence pointing to the close correlation of learning and behavioural difficulties with aspects of curriculum organisation, *it must logically be the case that failure to learn reflects a failure to teach.* We would negate the whole teaching enterprise if we did not accept some responsibility for its outcomes, and it remains at least logically true that a child who fails is one for whom a successful teaching method and curriculum has not been found or maximised.

4) As an extension and partial explanation of the last point, we can say that most curricula elevate the cognitive-intellectual domain above the aesthetic-creative, the physical-motor, the social-interpersonal and so on. Such high-status curricula, valuing and rewarding a particular form of thinking, typically provide the basis for defining the student with learning difficulties; or, put simply, *the elevation of particular kinds of knowledge produces students who fail.*

Taken together these arguments call for an inclusive teaching organisation which is sensitive to individual learners and learning styles; this in turn means the careful assessment of learners, the critical appraisal of curricula and the evaluation of one's own teaching. In this way, a more effective 'matching' of the resources and deficiencies of learners and curricula is possible, and the potential for school failure is reduced.

Thus, what we would call a *curricular approach to learning difficulties* can be seen to depend on three main themes, of *needs*, of *relativity* and of *responsibility* (Clough, 1989).

Entitlement and the curriculum

The move to a needs-orientated organisation of special education has in many societies taken on momentum, and its effects are variously visible. But the debate about appropriate policies has not stood still, and towards the end of the 1980s a number of critiques emerged which questioned the moral and political desirability of a needs-led system; the term 'special educational needs' was seen itself as problematic, and repeatedly prompted consideration of the points at which a school's characteristic concern for *individual* needs becomes its attention to exceptional and hence *special* ones. In terms of rights, is there – should there be – any essential difference between schools' structural support for individual and special needs? On what grounds should individuals receive attention particular to their perceived needs?

The original idea of handicap implied that there was something 'wrong' with the individual; this was replaced by the idea of 'need', but still located with the individual; but then the idea of 'rights' or 'entitlement' shifts the locus from the individual into communities and asks 'What can, but more so, *must* the community (and particularly the educational one) do for and with these differences *as a matter of right?*'

The question of what 'rights' children have is clearly culturally and historically determined, and there can be few enduring and transcendental entitlements when fundamental human rights themselves cannot be categorically and universally agreed. Nevertheless, teachers in all educational systems worthy of the name could probably agree within broad parameters that – all thing being equal – children do share certain rights to be educated. Of course, 'things' are *not* 'equal', and shortly after such broad agreement the necessary process of qualification would soon reveal the cultural assumptions and beliefs that subtend the differences between cultural systems, and which lead to concomitantly differentiated 'rights'. However, the concept (of rights or entitlements) does add a new dimension to the argument about how children's learning difficulties might be conceptualised and provision organised around them. Roaf and Bines (1989) write at length about the virtues of 'Rights' as a basis for developing special education policy and practice (and are quoted at some length here for the careful detail of their argument); thinking about special education in terms of political and legal rights, they say:

> 'Rights' as a basis for developing special education policy and practice would seem to have a number of advantages. As Kirp (1983) has suggested, comparing British and American special education policies and legislation, thinking about special education in terms of political and legal rights makes one reappraise resource allocation, relationships among the affected parties, the level and amount of dispute and the very conception of handicap. In respect to resource allocation, for example, the American structure of rights does not formally treat resource limits as constraining what can be provided. Whereas the British

approach weighs the interests of special and ordinary children, the American orientation on rights places the burden of adjustment on the ordinary school. The greater disputes engendered by a rights approach, including increased litigation, may make for a more dynamic policy and lead school authorities to offer more than would otherwise have been provided. In respect to the disabled themselves, rights should encourage a stronger definition and assertion of self and interests, reducing professional power and paternalism. When rights legislation is explicitly linked with other civil rights, special education also becomes part of the larger struggle for equity. Race or gender dimensions of being 'special' can then also be raised.

Rights would also seem to encourage a more careful and objective distribution of resources. It avoids the dangers of relativism and localism. It can potentially identify and secure not only type and amount of provision but also placement, policy, practice and curriculum, for example the least restrictive environment as in the USA. 'Rights' would seem to strengthen the social justice element in opportunity to raise broader social as well as educational issues.

To regard children considered to have special educational needs as children whose rights are being infringed in some way would very substantially alter the status not only of children themselves, but also of special teachers and others who work in the educational hierarchy. For Bandman (1973), rights 'enable us to stand with dignity, if necessary to demand what is our due without having to grovel, plead or beg'. Lack of dignity and respect is all too often associated with 'having a need'. As Freeman (1987, p. 300) argues

> Children have not been accorded either dignity or respect. They have been reified, denied the status of participants in the social system, labelled as a problem population, reduced to being seen as property. Too often justice for the young has been trumped by considerations of utility, or even worse, of convenience.

The emergence of children's rights as an important social and political issue is thus to be welcomed. However, as with needs and opportunity, there are difficult issues in the rights approach to be faced by educators. Currently, there is more concern to protect children or professional interests than to protect children's rights. Further, in order to develop rights we need to identify groups and must ask whether entitlement presumes categories. This may well seem contradictory to special needs teachers who have been exhorted to abandon categories.

We also have to consider whether a rights approach can be flexible enough to accommodate individuals with particular configurations of needs and therefore rights. In addition, there is the issue of what should be the basis of rights and how they can best be implemented. If we use legislation, there is the potential problem of too much litigation. On the other hand, just focusing on political discussion and change may be too long-term. There is also the question of how to balance the rights of some against the rights of others, given finite resources.

Each of the terms which have been used to characterise the issues of this chapter is problematic; for example – as Roaf and Bines conclude – the rights of some are bound to conflict at some point with the rights of others; and can there ever be a real equality of opportunity? Would that require a positive discrimination, and if so on what grounds? And might one individual's needs actually go against the needs of his or her community or society? These and many other questions take on a new poignancy when set in the context of real policy decisions: when, that is, decisions have to be taken about how to allocate resources, and on what schedule of priorities. It is at such a time that moral decisions about entitlements and opportunities and needs frequently have to give way to arguments conditioned by finite resources and 'common sense'. It is the case that such questions are often posed by those who are fundamentally opposed to the pursuance (or recognition) of children's rights (Lansdown, 1996), and such difficult questions should not be justification for lack of action in seeking solutions. It is in the contexts of real policies that our problematic terms take on hues of meaning and degrees of usefulness.

Curriculum and learning

Research into classroom learning over the last few years has moved away from a model of learning which saw the learner as a passive recipient of taught materials, transmitted often indifferently with the hope that something would 'stick'. In the 1970s particularly, learning was increasingly seen as something dynamic, which happens because individuals have particular intentions, purposes and motivations. In this view, what the learner brings to a task from past experience, and how that task is presented become all important. And equally important is the understanding that individuals learn differently – they have different styles, rhythms and paces of learning according to their different interests. This of course means that some will develop understanding more rapidly than others, and that teaching must allow for this. It also means that the potential for *later* learning must be respected in teaching plans and school organisation. Learning is a life-long series of events, and to *fail* (or be failed) at an early stage in formal education may close down on subsequent opportunity for development.

These views apply obviously to learners whose more marked learning difficulties exclude them from the mainstream of education, and who therefore follow exceptional – and usually dilute – patterns of schooling and curricula (if they follow any at all). But they apply equally in the 'ordinary' classroom, for all students, including the apparently high-achieving. The real point of value of such insights into individual learning is the demand they make for sensitive teaching and curricula which can prevent or minimise learning difficulty. The report of the Commission on Social Justice (1994) included goals for *lifelong learning*, its third goal being 'high achievement for every young person'. The report (*ibid.*, p. 131) stated: 'An education system appropriate to the demands of the twenty-first century must be designed to establish a foundation of knowledge and skill for all children and to nurture the particular talents of each child. But that is exactly what our system is failing to do.'

National Curriculum: problems and possibilities for inclusion

Perhaps the biggest source of difficulty for teachers and schools is balancing needs with entitlements, especially where these entitlements are not merely notional but statutorily required to be met. Teachers are required at the same time to provide a curriculum which is individually needs-relevant but within the spirit and the letter of collective policy requirements. Curricula have always been a means of exclusion; they have always been the means by which, ultimately, this group of students is separated from that. Decisions about 'ability' based on psychometric or other forms of assessment lead ultimately to decisions about what can and should be studied. Such decisions themselves reach deep into political ideology, for the curriculum is and always has been a selection from culture for particular ends. Of course, this seemed to be more glaringly the case with the introduction of the National Curriculum, an explicitly political agenda, but it is so in any culture and in any time. What and how we choose to teach and to which students are vital determinants of the part which those students are able to play in shaping a society's development.

For these reasons, a National Curriculum must obviously be a curriculum for *all* as of *right*. We must clearly take care, however, that our commitment to such inclusiveness does not serve to exclude meeting needs which no subject-driven conception of curriculum can entertain. The task for all special educators is clearly one of finding the right balance.

Conclusion: balancing resources?

Throughout this book themes will occur and recur, but all pervading – if not always explicit – will be issues of teacher skills, attitudes and available resources – again an issue of balance. I wish to end this chapter with a brief tale from part of my own recent research. This highlights what I see as a key element in understanding the dynamics of teachers' perspectives on inclusive policies and practices – and thus the prospects for an inclusive future in our schools.

In 1991 I carried out a survey of nearly 1,000 mainstream teachers' perspectives on SEN, in 16 secondary schools, divided equally among four English LEAs (Clough, 1991). One LEA – let us call it Largeshire – stood out startlingly. In Largeshire, almost one half of the teachers were clearly committed to inclusive policies. In the other three LEAs, a significantly smaller number – between one quarter and one third – of the sample of teachers positively endorsed integrative, fully comprehensive schooling.

Each of the four LEAs had explicitly articulated integration policies; each had undertaken some extra SEN-focused initiative; each had an elected, advisory and administrative staff wholly committed to integrative principles. By and large the pattern of institutional distribution of students with SEN was common throughout each of the four LEAs. So, given the broad similarities between the LEAs, how is this difference explained?

What chiefly distinguished Largeshire was that it put its money – and considerably more of it – where its mouth was, and whilst all four LEAs demonstrated vigorously written and stated policies, Largeshire's were more visibly *enacted* (Macdonald, 1981, p. 103). Resources were clearly attached to the development of supportive structures, *for both students and staff*. Importantly, these included not only generous staffing of in and out-school support teams but also financial inducements to adopt broadly inclusive structures, such as mixed-ability teaching across the curriculum.

Teachers' attitudes to exceptional children are very closely correlated with the success or otherwise of integrative/inclusive policies; for it is, in the end, teachers who 'realise' policy and who have the job of 'realising' statutory curricula. However there is growing evidence of a further, triangular link between teacher attitudes, the policies within which they work and the resources which are attached to realising these policies (Clough, 1998).

Research over the last thirty years shows three enduring trends in terms of teachers' tolerance of learning difficulties in mainstream settings:

1) The more teachers work within inclusive settings, the more sympathetic they become to working with a wider range of achievement. Segregated settings maintain suspicion and even fear, whilst exposure demystifies prejudice and diminishes resistance to exceptional children.
2) Whilst the legislation may have done away with the notion of 'handicap', mainstream teachers' views are frequently shaped by a 'categorical' notion of learning difficulty, and there is a marked 'hierarchy of tolerance'. This ranges from the most positive attitudes towards children with (certain forms of) physical disability, to high resistance to children with EBD.
3) Positive attitudes to inclusive education are directly linked to the resources which are attached to policies. These attitudes 'shrink' in keeping with diminishing resources.

This last point in particular is important if inclusive policies are to have an impact on special (or 'specialist') education. Far from overhauling SEN policies of the last twenty years, the most recent UK governmental indications remain very much in the spirit of both the Warnock Report of 1978, and the Education Act 1981. This is a 'Good Thing', in that the need for such inclusive moves are unchanged twenty years on, and the Green Paper (DfEE, 1997) seeks to address these enduring concerns; it may be a 'Bad Thing', however, if the bill which eventually issues from consultation has teeth like those of the 1981 Act.

Estelle Morris (at the time of writing, Parliamentary Under Secretary of State) put the case for inclusive education as justified 'morally, educationally and socially' (*TES*, 24 October 1997), and at this level of argument there are probably few who would disagree with the broad aspirations of such policies. However, as is often noted, the 1981 legislation was in most respects essentially *enabling* rather than prescriptive, and permitted across England and Wales a wide variety of interpretation, as LEAs devoted resources differently to address the same problems. These different levels of resourcing directly affect how mainstream teachers react to learners with SEN.

In 1997 I repeated my survey in the four Largeshire schools, and the results are again startling. In two of the schools, there was no discernible change in positive attitudes to inclusion; in the other two, positive responses were down by nearly one quarter. There have been no significant changes in personnel or other significant factors in any of the schools – *excepting one*: the two schools maintaining relatively positive attitudes to mainstreaming provision have each obtained grant-maintained status – and the funding that goes with it. These schools have been able to sustain their resourcing of a properly supported, integrative SEN system. The other two schools, conversely, have struggled to maintain their integrative systems with diminished resources, and with genuine regret are capitulating to a system which appears to resource an exclusive – rather than inclusive – principle.

I say 'with genuine regret' because I know these schools well; I spent hundreds of hours among their pupils, classrooms and staff in 1990–1, and saw at close hand the fine detail of their lived commitment to integrative systems. Some six years later I see the same teachers reaching for justifications to exclude the same pupils whose interests they were vigorously supporting, often against their own instincts and professional training – *but with proper resources*. One school's head of history who had been a key player in her school's development of its inclusive system told me in interview:

> I teach a subject which is . . . finally non-negotiable in content, I mean in examinable content, and . . . I suppose in the way it has to be learned. And taught. So if I'm going to succeed . . . personally, that is, and professionally and if the school's going to succeed in the [local press] I've got to go for the more academic, haven't I? And that means just not having the kids who can't make it in the class.

From my experience of this teacher, this is not the limited view of the élitist, credentialist subject specialist. It is rather that of a dedicated teacher with a realistic sense of the point at which her own limited resources can stretch no further.

Such a view is not to be confused with the reaction to inclusive policies of at least one of the UK teacher unions, whose arch public horror does not speak for the moral and political will for inclusion of a majority of teachers. But it should remind the architects of any anticipated legislation that, without properly resourced support, this inclusive initiative may well prove at best empty if elegant rhetoric; at worst a further alienation of the teaching profession.

References

Bandman (1973) Do children have any natural rights? *Proceedings of the 29th AGM of the Philosophy of Education Society*, pp. 234–42, London, Philosophy of Education Society.

Barton, L. (1977) Inclusive education: romantic, subversive or realistic? *International Journal of Inclusive Education*, Vol. 1, no. 3, pp. 231–42.

Clough, P. (1989) Bridging the gap between special and 'mainstream' education: a curriculum problem, *Journal of Curriculum Studies*, Vol. 21, no. 3, pp. 327–38.

Clough, P. (1991) *A Survey of Teachers' Perspectives on SEN Policy and Practice*, SUERC, Sheffield.

Clough, P. (1998) Work in progress: a replication of Clough (1991) (in preparation).

Commission on Social Justice (1994) *Social Justice: Strategies for National Renewal*, Vantage, London.

CSIE (1995) *International Perspectives on Inclusion*, Centre for Studies on Inclusive Education, Bristol.

DES (1978) *Special Educational Needs: Report of the Committee of Enquiry into the Education of Handicapped Children and Young People (the Warnock Report)*, HMSO, London.

DfEE (1994) *Code of Practice on the Identification and Assessment of SEN*, HMSO, London.

DfEE (1997) *Excellence for All Children: Meeting Special Educational Needs*, HMSO, London.

Freeman, M. (1987) Taking children's rights seriously, *Children and Society*, Vol. 1, no. 4, pp. 229–319.

ILEA (1985) *Educational Opportunities for All? (The Fish Report)*, ILEA, London.

Kirp, D.L. (1983) Professionalism as a policy choice: British special education in comparative perspective, in Chambers, J.B. and Hartman, W.T. (eds) *Special Education Policies: Their History, Implementation and Finance*, Temple University Press, Philadelphia, PA.

Lansdown, G. (1996) The United Nations Convention on the Rights of the Child – progress in the United Kingdom, in Nutbrown, C. (ed) *Respectful Educators – Capable Learners: Children's Rights in Early Education*, Paul Chapman Publishing, London.

Macdonald, I. (1981) Assessment: a social dimension, in Barton, L. and Tomlinson, S. (eds) *Special Education: Policy, Practices and Social Issues*, Harper and Row, London.

Nutbrown, C. (ed) (1996) *Respectful Educators – Capable Learners: Children's Rights and Early Education*, Paul Chapman Publishing, London.

Roaf, C. and Bines, H. (eds) (1989) *Needs, Rights and Opportunities*, London, Falmer Press.

UNESCO (1994) *The Salamanca Statement and Framework for Action on Special Needs Education*, UNESCO, Paris.

Section 1

From policy . . .

2

Educational Leadership and Management: Contexts, Theory and Practice

HUGH BUSHER

Introduction

Management is about helping people singly or in groups to get things done to meet predefined purposes. These purposes may be generated by a group of people with which a manager is working or be identified by the organisation in which people work and managers supervise. Such a definition makes visible two different ideologies of management: that of the manager or leader as servant of the group, an ancient tradition that has many religious antecendents, and that of the manager as representative of institutional authority and so as an agent of control. While the former may be visible in collegially run and professionally staffed organisations such as general medical practices, the latter is most commonly seen in hierarchically organised business and industry. What seems to distinguish the former from the latter is that in the former, the purposes and practices of work are predominantly derived from expert knowledge. This is used to meet best the needs of the clients whom the organisation serves through a face-to-face relationship with them. In the latter, the major concern is with making a profit from distant customers, although this will also require a high-quality product or service to be created and delivered.

In education, teachers and their leaders or managers draw on their pedagogical expertise, made up of their subject knowledge and their expertise in education practice, to legitimate their actions with students and other people with interests in education. However, the purposes of schools in the UK in the 1990s are largely defined by bodies external to a school, such as central and local government, or by foundation bodies for independent schools. Headteachers or principals are expected to implement these purposes, including the requirement on state schools at least to break even financially since the introduction of LMS (Education Reform Act 1988). Consequently, in schools there may be a tension between the teachers' authority, based on expert knowledge, and their desire to act in certain ways, and the bureacratic authority of a headteacher and other leaders, derived from their administrative positions, which they use to help a school meet the purposes imposed upon it.

This chapter, then, looks briefly at how schools and colleges are managed in a variety of different contexts and how those contexts influence the internal workings of educational institutions. In doing so, the chapter suggests that a careful distinction has to be made between leadership and management. To gain a sophisticated view of educational organisations which will effectively guide practice, it suggests that managers and leaders have to look at schools through at least four different perspectives or lenses.

Managing in contexts

Management, then, is about working with people in particular contexts. These may be categorised as contexts of values; of policy at local and national levels; of resources; of markets (quality assurance and consumer or client choice); of technology (what may or can be created or produced); and of communities. These different contexts interact with each other. For example, school leaders and managers have to serve and work with a variety of external and internal constituencies: meeting the needs of current and future students; meeting the needs of varied local social groups and communities; meeting the requirements of local and central government regulations; working within the resources available; and working with the staff available. These contexts also intimately influence the internal decision-making processes of schools. Glatter (1997) suggests that this interaction has been overlooked for too long in understandings of internal school management processes. For example, the location of a school in a community with a particular socioeconomic profile will have considerable influence on both the academic performance of its students and on the school's relationships with students and parents (e.g. Willis, 1977).

In turn this raises questions about what are the appropriate social and educational values to be created and sustained in an educational institution. Some of these focus on issues of equity and equality of opportunity. They are enacted in part through a curriculum differentiated to meet the needs of a wide range of students. Since the late 1980s in England and Wales, there has, for example, been a growing pressure on schools and

LEAs to integrate more fully those children with identified SEN into mainstream state schooling. Millward and Skidmore (1998) argue that the Education Act 1993 and the 1994 *Code of Practice on the Identification and Assessment of Special Educational Needs* (DfEE, 1994) have increased the emphasis on and the opportunity for ethical and inclusive practice towards all students. In their survey of 99 LEAs in England and Wales education officers expressed great support for the *Code of Practice* because it put in place a clearly defined structure and process of assessment of student need to guide the work of schools and LEAs in managing inclusive education. Prior to 1994 such clarity had not, they argued, existed as an overall system.

The policy context in which schools and colleges operate is of considerable importance to how they are managed internally. Bell (1996) has attempted to construct a model to show the dynamics of this. For example, the establishment of LMS in England and Wales under the Education Reform Act 1988 brought major changes in the relationships between LEAs and schools (Maclure, 1989). Amongst other things it weakened the ability of LEAs to support equally every type of student in all its schools and colleges, not least because such a large proportion of LEA funding had to be distributed to schools. On the other hand this empowered schools to take resource-based decisions on how to implement the curriculum to meet best the needs of their local students.

In turn, this raises questions about another key area of the context for management decisions: the use of resources. These are essentially questions of opportunity cost, i.e. of opportunities forgone if a certain line of action is pursued. For example, allocating resources to one group of pupils must, necessarily, mean depriving others of those resources, at least for the time being, and the impact of that deprivation on pupils' personal, social and educational development has to be weighed by teachers in their pedagogical decision-making. Although LEA officers may welcome the 1994 *Code of Practice* (Millward and Skidmore, 1998), anecdotally teachers in many schools complain about the time and effort it requires to implement it. Some wonder if teachers before 1994 did not make equally accurate judgements of need and much more quickly on the basis of their professional experience.

As well as being empowered by central government policy, schools are also subject to central control by government. In 1992 a process of quadrennial review by inspection teams was implemented for all schools in England and Wales. These are supervised by OFSTED to hold schools to account for the quality of work they carry out with their pupils. This is intended to guarantee to parents and the state that schools are giving good value for the money spent on them. As Thomas (1996) points out, these inspections are carried out according to explicit criteria which define whether or not school practice is effective at classroom and whole-school level. To do this, inspectors scrutinise the schemes of work that teachers create, observe teachers at work in the classrooms and collect evidence from parents about their views of a school. The inspectors then produce a report to a school's governors and ask them to draw up an action plan to meet any weaknesses they have discovered. Headteachers are left to help staff to cope with the stress and worry they suffer through the inspection process.

Another aspect of this control represents the technology context of schools. It is the prescription of a National Curriculum under the Education Reform Act 1988. Although this was revised in 1997 by the Dearing Review, in 1998 the Secretary of State for Education and the Environment gave guidance on how primary schools should relax their implementation of it to allow more time for students to focus on literacy and numeracy. Teachers, then, have had to cope with both imposed massive change and repeated change in the curriculum in the decade up to 1998, and headteachers and middle managers have had to help staff to cope with that creatively. Ozga (1995), among others, has argued that this has led to a major diminution of teacher autonomy and professional competence.

The operation of the National Curriculum, although designed to create for students an entitlement and equity of access to knowledge, in fact faces teachers with ethical dilemmas. For example, under the 1993 Act certain pupils who are statemented for special education are allowed to avoid the full National Curriculum. Apart from the obviously discriminatory implications of this, it also raises fundamental management problems of how to implement inclusive educational policies in schools and colleges. One of the easiest ways to differentiate curriculum provision is through segregated classes, but this may neither make efficient use of resources – i.e. discriminates against those students not in the smaller classes – nor provide students with equal social opportunities.

At a local level, state schools and colleges are intertwined with their communities. Busher (1989; 1992) chronicled some of the diverse ways in which the views and actions of people in the local communities of schools influenced the internal processes of those schools on a daily basis. Apart from the influence of school governors as agents of particular local community groups, parents have a vital interest in what takes place in schools and how the educational processes are carried out. The legitimacy of this interest is recognised through government requirements on schools to publish to parents and others a wide variety of information. At a more detailed level, pupils daily bring into schools the perspectives and aspirations of local communities, as do those other members of local communities who are employed in schools on whatever basis.

The impact of these local communities on school performance is taken into account by LEAs when they construct value-added measures of school performance. Richmond (1996) reports on how LEAs use crude measures of social deprivation, such as the numbers of pupils in a school on free school meals, to weight their comparisons of one school's achievements in public examinations against those of other schools in an LEA's area. Gray and Wilcox (1995) suggest that measures of added-value for schools give a more accurate view to parents of the real impact of teachers' practice on the learning of pupils than do central government league tables, introduced in 1992, which compare schools' raw examination results with each other. These added-value measures take account of students' past performances as a baseline against which to measure current performances. Such performances have long been known to be heavily influenced by social factors.

Activity 2.1

To what extent do factors in the external context of a school affect the quality of its students' performance? What evidence do you have or would you look for?

Leadership for the effective management of education

Much of the argument in this section hinges around the nature of staff in schools and colleges. So it considers what might constitute effective leadership and management for professionally qualified staff or staff who regard themselves as vocationally committed to their occupation. Sergiovanni (1994) suggested that because of the pervasiveness of the latter view amongst staff in schools and colleges, these institutions should be analysed as communities rather than as contractually based organisations. Busher and Saran (1995) found that many support staff held similar vocational or quasi-professional views of their work as did teachers.

Not all processes of management can be described as educational. Autocratic styles of leadership which demand obedience from followers, however they are coerced, do not fit into notions of educational or transformational leadership which Blase and Anderson (1995) might recognise. The latter style is one which invites participants to share in decision-making and in creating and enacting the key values of an organisation. It is sometimes referred to as collaborative leadership.

However, not all collaborative leadership is transformational. It ranges from corporate styles to co-operative ones (Busher and Saran, 1995) or from contrived collegiality to real collegiality (Hargreaves, 1994). While the former keeps decision-making power largely in the hands of leaders and managers, whatever processes of consultation may be undertaken, the latter envisages a major delegation of power, within an agreed framework of decision-making, to those responsible for enacting practice. Telford (1996) defines only this latter as collaborative leadership. This she envisages as incorporating particular values and beliefs of shared approaches to decision-making by teachers and headteachers.

Persistance by people in either the corporate or collegial styles of leadership is likely to produce institutions with sharply contrasting cultures. The corporate is likely to lead to staff developing a cynical view of the influence they wield through consultation and an instrumental view of their work. Staff are likely to perceive that the scope of their professional knowledge (Mortimore, 1993) is undervalued by senior staff in the interests of executive expediency. Stoll and Myers (1998) suggest that only a collegial style of leadership will raise the morale of staff and promote enthusiasm through senses of empowerment and real influence in decision-making.

The distinction here between leadership and management is of some importance since the processes of leadership relate to how one person inspires others and helps them to develop a sense of shared values and purpose (Brighouse, 1991). The quality of management complements these, enacting them through planning, organising, co-ordinating, monitoring and evaluating the work of the other people who are engaged in the particular project or activity. Sergiovanni (1984) presents a different conceptualisation of the leadership process, saying that leaders have to engage with five different aspects of an organisation. The processes listed above he incorporates into a technical aspect. In addition, to give effective leadership, a person must engage with a human aspect of relationships amongst people; an educational aspect of curriculum construction, support and development; a symbolic aspect to communicate and gain commitment to a school's purposes; and a cultural aspect to establish shared values and beliefs. Although Telford (1996) supports the division between symbolic and cultural aspects, other authors, such as Bolman and Deal (1991) regard these two as one aspect which focuses on the creation, portrayal and enactment of values and beliefs.

If it is important to distinguish between leadership and management, it is also important to do so between management and administration, since the terms 'management' and 'administration' are used differently in the USA and the UK. In the UK, the administration of a school refers to how it sustains its social and physical structures through bureaucratic processes. One aspect of this focuses on how agreed decisions are implemented efficiently through secretarial work, or work carried out by teachers, such as lesson-planning and record-keeping. Another aspect focuses on how the flow of relevant communications and information is sustained, such as the ways in which information is made available to and collected from people. A third aspect concerns the support and guidance given to pupils, staff and parents about how a school operates and how that is made visible to them. It will include the production of artifacts such as handbooks and timetables. A final aspect focuses on the efficient allocation of resources, including the uses and care a school makes of its grounds and premises.

Activity 2.2

What qualities of leadership have you observed, and in what contexts, which have generated the greatest enthusiasm and commitment from a leader's colleagues?

The final sections of this chapter suggest four perspectives or lenses through which leaders and managers need to survey their organisations if they are to construct effective and sophisticated understandings to guide their practice. These are the perspectives which individual people hold of the school in or for which they work; the cultural perspective which people develop jointly to create their view of their place of work; an understanding of the organisational structures which influence and contain the ways in which people work; and an analysis of how power flows and is used by people to enact their visions and educational values.

Managing with people

In schools and colleges people can be classified into three main groups: support staff (e.g. secretaries, bursars, technicians, cleaners); teaching or academic staff (including senior staff who may do little teaching); and students. This view of students construes them as part of an educational organisation who contribute to that organisation's social construction and processes. This view is in tune with the findings of researchers such as Ruddock and Wallace (1995) on the impact on and understandings of school processes which students have. In contrast, a market-orientated or total quality model of education (e.g. West-Burnham, 1992) views students as internal customers, directly or by proxy through their parents. Employers might be viewed as external customers of a school. Gray (1991) suggests that it is problematic where the border is drawn between people who are in a school's community and those outside it. For example, many parents identify closely with a school, at least so long as their children attend it.

The complexity is that people in educational organisation play many parts both within a school and outside it. These different roles interact with each other. For example, at one and the same time students of a school are both members of its community, and help to shape and change it, and the people whom a school serves and for whose changing needs schools and colleges have to change. Staff, too, occupy a complexity of roles. The teacher who is both subject leader, form tutor and school governor is but one example. Furthermore there are many support staff who identify themselves quite strongly with a school or college (Busher and Saran, 1995), despite some of them being employed only on part-time contracts.

Rational approaches to how people construct their understandings of their work, such as role theory, are helpful in locating a person in his or her organisational structures but fail to explain adequately the variety of interpretations of that role which emerge from both the role incumbent and the other people in the role set. Nor does it explain the variety of roles which each person plays in the formal and informal organisation of a school or college (Hoyle, 1986). The inter-relationship between teachers and their pupils is complex and often transcends bald contractual defini- tions of what teachers are supposed to do.

Greenfield (1993) argues forcefully that people invent and reinvent their own identities, whether or not they acknowledge that process, tak- ing account of factors such as their socioeconomic background, their gen- der, their religious affiliations, and their ethnic and regional backgrounds, as well as their personal qualities. For example, people who become subject specialist teachers are likely to draw on the knowledge structures of their subject to define their preferred methods of teaching and learning. These are likely also to shape people's views of what to emphasise in a school's curriculum and in the intellectual development of pupils. As teachers gain promotion at work or families at home, their views and emphases in their work are likely to change. Busher (1992) suggested that teachers' approaches to work were affected by a variety of self-identified professional, organisational, personal and social interests.

How people construct their professional identities will shape the way they respond to the demands of leaders and managers. For example, those teachers whose self-identities emphasise their work with students are unlikely to be greatly excited at the prospect of being further involved in managing the school as an organisation, even if that is what external contexts such as the Education Reform Act 1988 encourages. Both Hoyle and John (1995) and Strain (1995), along with many others, point out how the nature of teaching as a profession has changed since the late 1980s in the UK to incorporate a stronger emphasis on working with clearly de- fined roles and accountabilities in organisational structures. On the other hand those teachers who conceive of themselves as 'extended profes- sionals' (Hughes, 1973) and take a holistic view of educational and organ- isational processes may welcome such greater involvement.

To manage people effectively, then, it is necessary to understand how they construe themselves and their activities in a school. Bush (1986) describes this as an individual or subjective view of educational organisations. For managers, then, such perspectives of organisations complement an understanding of organisational structures, and the or- ganisational cultures which people create to facilitate their preferred ways of working.

Managing the culture

People do not work in isolation. Even when teachers go into a classroom to teach, although there may be no other adults present there are usually lots of other people, pupils, with whom they will develop particular ways of working. Part of that development will include the creation of a particular 'ethos' or culture. Galton *et al.* (1980) found twelve different styles of working by teachers in primary school classrooms.

Teachers also develop cultures of working with other staff both in a school as a whole and within individual departments in a school or college. Telford (1996) and Lodge (1998) emphasise the importance of leaders managing organisational cultures in such a way as to create a positive climate for change and improvement. Indeed, Stoll and Fink (1998) point out how some schools fail to change because of the culture generated in them. Hoy *et al.* (1991) point to the importance of organisations having healthy cultures or climates to enable people to work together effectively. Blase and Blase (1994) suggest, from their research, that this includes a belief that people prefer to perform to the best of their ability in their work, a reversal of the X theory popularised by McGregor (1960).

None the less, culture is difficult to define. Loosely it can be described as the way people choose to do things in a particular location – institution or community. However, Bennett (1995) rightly points out the dangers of interpreting such definitions to mean that the culture of an organisation or of a department within it is static. It changes as relationships change between staff, students and community members and as people join or leave. It focuses on the values purveyed through an organisation's practices: the degree of trust between people; the extent to which people can discuss openly their differences; the extent to which people are included in or excluded from decision-making (a measure of collegiality); the extent to which senior staff are available to or prepared to listen to other staff and students; and the degree to which organisational processes are rule bound or needs/tasks driven.

These intangible but important qualities manifest themselves through what Smircich (1983, p. 344) calls 'cultural artifacts', such as rituals, legends and ceremonies. How people respond to such artifacts indicates how they are responding to the values being purveyed through them. So, how students and teachers respond to a school assembly, a ceremony, taken by a headteacher is an indication of their attitudes to the values conveyed through the assembly and to the way in which the headteacher leads the school. As with any such ceremony, the actions and language used in it are ritualised and mythic. So, important guides to the culture of a school are both the language used in talking about particular events or people and the stories that are told to illustrate success or failure. The work of Deal and Kennedy (1982) and Morgan (1986) elaborates these ideas.

Samier (1997) suggests that the culture of a school is often regarded as a dimension of its informal organisation. In the same way Hoyle (1986) claims that micropolitical processes are predominantly confined to the informal aspects of organisational life, a view which the research of Busher (1992) challenges. Since an organisation's culture permeates every aspect of how people work together in it, it is perhaps overly mechanistic to sustain the division between formal and informal aspects of an organisation too strongly. It lends weight to the view of Wallace (1997) that using different perspectives on organisations in combination with each other creates more powerful insights into how people work with each other.

Managing structures and power

Schools' organisational structures are visible in the administrative structures and hierarchies of departments and meetings cycles, and in the curriculum structures of how subjects are taught and how pupils are grouped. These are influenced and shaped by changes in schools' policy contexts and understandings of how subject knowledge should be structured. Within a school, the educational philosophies and values (and whims!) of senior staff, especially those of the headteacher, will have considerable influence on the administrative and curriculum practices to which teachers and students have to adapt.

This focus on the structural elements in a school's organisation is often referred to as a systems perspective. It explores how these elements relate to each other and how communications and coherence are sustained between them. It also considers how effectively a school or college operates to meet its purposes. So, for example, it could help senior staff in a school evaluate how effectively its pastoral care system linked with its system of keeping academic records in order to track and support changes in student performance. Such a view is less concerned with how individual staff and students relate to and make sense of the organisational structures within which they work.

On the other hand this perspective is concerned with how people are helped or coerced into fitting in with the structures and purposes of an organisation. Through this, then, leaders and managers can consider how to appraise staff and institute staff development to meet identified school needs. Similarly questions of people's conditions of service as well as of their allocation to particular work also form part of this area. This perspective is sometimes referred to as human resources management (Hendry, 1995), although Bottery (1992) challenges how far it allows for consideration of the ethics of working with people or provides adequate recognition of the heterogeneity of individual people.

There is, however, another way of construing how the organisational structures of schools work. These structures can be perceived as the outcomes of past debates about how power should be distributed and resources allocated and knowledge structured in different ways (Foucault, in Ball, 1990), i.e. they, too, are social constructions rather than 'naturally occurring' features. This political perspective is closely linked to how people develop organisational cultures to purvey their values through creating networks with other people (Blase and Blase, 1995; Wallace, 1997). In this perspective lie considerations of how and where people bargain, with whom they negotiate, with whom they form alliances, what constitutes legitimate and non-legitimate interests in particular situations, and what forms do power, authority and resources take. Authors such as French and Raven (1968), Bacharach and Lawler (1980), Busher (1992) and Blase and Anderson (1995) identify a range of sources of power which different people use over, through and with other people in pursuit of their organisational or professional interests as much to build collaboration as to prosecute conflict.

It is mistaken, then, to view a political perspective as only focusing on conflicts in educational institutions. Importantly, however, and unlike the other perspectives or lenses for looking at organisations referred to in this chapter, it does acknowledge that conflict is normal in groups of humans and a way through which differences can be aired and resolved openly (Blase and Anderson, 1995; Stoll and Myers, 1998). Nor, as Ball (1989) argues, are management and political activity two discrete fields. As Bennett (1995) points out, power is an important resource for leaders and managers, which other people can use too if they can gain access to it.

Conclusion

There is a variety of different typologies of perspectives on organisations which can be used to make sense of organisational processes. Hughes (1990) made an extensive survey of several of these typologies, pointing out that there was no one dominant paradigm in the field of education management at that time. However he noted that the focus on the cultural and human interactive aspects of organisations had, since the mid-1970s, challenged in a major way the pervading perspective on schools as organisational systems.

This chapter has used one such typology to discuss in some detail how a school's processes can be defined through the perspectives of individual people; through a cultural lens focusing on the symbolic interactions of people; and through an analysis of a school's structural or formal processes. The fourth perspective in this typology is a political one that focuses on how power is used by everybody, not just senior staff, to try to gain access to the resources they need to enact their educational and social values. This perspective can also encompass the activities of pupils, parents and other stakeholders in a school, too, all of whom hold and want to enact particular views on education. It can also help leaders and teachers to understand issues of disempowerment and disaffection if some students' educational or social needs are not being adequately met. It is, therefore, a lens which is of vital importance to complement the other three perspectives outlined in this chapter.

While it may be difficult for leaders and managers in schools and colleges to find the time to carry out sophisticated analyses of how staff and pupils work in their institutions, use of these four perspectives will help them identify a range of clues and explanations for why people act in the way they do and baulk at changing their practices to meet changes in the internal and external environment of schools and colleges.

Activity 2.3

Choose a particular problem or situation in an educational institution that you know. Consider how the four different perspectives referred to here can cast complementary lights on it, allowing somebody to manage it more effectively.

Suggested further reading

Gray, J. and Wilcox, B. (eds) (1995) *Good School, Bad School: Evaluating Performance and Encouraging Improvement*, Open University Press, Buckingham.

Greenfield, T. and Ribbins, P. (eds) (1993) *Greenfield on Educational Administration*, Routledge, London.

Stoll, L. and Myers, K. (eds) (1998) *No Quick Fixes: Perspectives on Schools in Difficulty*, Falmer Press, London.

References

Bacharach, S. and Lawler, E. (1980) *Power and Politics in Organizations*, Jossey-Bass, San Francisco, CA.

Ball, S. (1989) Micropolitics versus management: towards a sociology of school organisation, in Walker, S. and Barton, L. (eds) *Politics and the Processes of Schooling*, Open University Press, Milton Keynes.

Ball, S. (ed) (1990) *Foucault and Education: Disciplines and Knowledge*, Routledge, London.

Bell, L. (1996) Educational management, some issues of policy and practice, Inaugural professorial lecture, mimeo, Liverpool John Moores University, 14 February.

Bennett, N. (1995) *Managing Professional Teachers: Middle Managers in Primary and Secondary Schools*, Paul Chapman Publishing, London.

Blase, J. and Anderson, G. (1995) *The Micropolitics of Educational Leadership*, Cassell, London.

Blase, J. and Blase, J. (1994) *Empowering Teachers: What Successful Principals Do*, Corwin, Thousand Oaks, CA.

Blase, J. and Blase, J. (1995) The micropolitical orientation of facilitative school principals and its effects on teachers' sense of empowerment, paper given at the AERA annual conference, San Francisco.

Bolman, L.G. and Deal, T.E. (1991) *Reframing Organizations: Artistry, Choice and Leadership*, Jossey-Bass, San Francisco, CA.

Bottery, M. (1992) *The Ethics of Educational Management*, Cassell, London.

Brighouse, T. (1991) *What makes a good school?* Stafford: Network Educational Press.

Bush, T. (1986) *Theories of Educational Management*, Harper and Row, London.

Busher, H. (1989) Making sense of reality: a case-study of one teacher reflecting on her practice, in Lomax, P. (ed) *The Management of Change, BERA Dialogues 1*, Multilingual Matters, Clevedon.

Busher, H. (1992) The politics of working in secondary schools: some teachers' perspectives on their schools as organisations, unpublished PhD thesis, University of Leeds, School of Education.

Busher, H. and Saran, R. (eds) (1995) *Managing Teachers as Professionals in Schools*, Kogan Page, London.

Deal, T.E. and Kennedy, A. (1982) *Corporate Cultures: The Rites and Rituals of Corporate Life*, Addison Wesley, Reading, MA.

Dearing (1993) *The National Curriculum: the Final Report*, Schools' Curriculum Assessment Authority, London.

DfEE (1994) *Code of Practice on the Identification and Assessment of Special Educational Needs*, DfEE, London.

French, J. and Raven, B. (1968) The bases of social power, in Cartwright, D. and Zander, A. (eds) *Group Dynamics, Research and Theory*, Tavistock Press, London.

Galton, M., Simon, B. and Croll, P. (1980) *Inside the Primary School Classroom*, Routledge, London.

Glatter, R. (1997) Context and capability in educational management, *Educational Management and Administration*, Vol. 25, no. 2, pp. 191–2.

Greenfield, T. (1993) Against group mind: an anarchistic theory of organisation, in Greenfield, T. and Ribbins, P. (eds) *Greenfield on Educational Administration*, Routledge, London.

Gray, L. (1991) *Marketing Education*, Open University Press, Buckingham.

Gray, J. and Wilcox, B. (eds) (1995) *Good School, Bad School: Evaluating Performance and Encouraging Improvement*, Open University Press, Buckingham.

Hargreaves, A. (1994) *Changing Teachers, Changing Times: Teachers' Work and Culture in the Postmodern Age*, Cassell, London.

Hendry, C. (1995) *Human Resources Management*, Butterworth-Heinemann, Oxford.

Hoy, W.K., Tarter, C.J. and Kottkamp, R.B. (1991) *Open Schools/Healthy Schools*, Corwin, Newbury Park, CA.

Hoyle, E. (1986) *The Politics of School Management*, Hodder & Stoughton, London.

Hoyle, E. and John, P. (1995) *Professional Knowledge and Professional Practice*, Cassell, London.

Hughes, M. (1973) The Professional-as-Administrator: the case of the secondary school head, in Peters, R.S. (1973) *The Role of the Head*, Routledge, London.

Hughes, M. (1990) Institutional leadership: issues and challenges, in Saran, R. and Trafford, V. (eds) *Research in Education Management and Policy*, Falmer Press, London.

Lodge, C. (1998) What's wrong with our schools? Understanding 'ineffective' and 'failing' schools, in Stoll, L. and Myers, K. (eds) *No Quick Fixes: Perspectives on Schools in Difficulty*, Falmer Press, London.

Maclure, S. (1989) *Education Reformed* (2nd edn), Hodder & Stoughton, London.

McGregor, D. (1960) *The Human Side of Enterprise*, McGraw-Hill, New York.

Millward, A. and Skidmore, D. (1998) LEA responses to the management of special education in the light of the *Code of Practice, Educational Management and Administration*, Vol. 26, no. 1, pp. 57–66.

Morgan, G. (1986) *Images of Organizations*, Sage, Beverly Hills, CA.

Mortimore, P. (1993) School effectiveness and the management of effective teaching and learning, *School Effectiveness and School Improvement*, Vol. 4, No. 4, pp. 290–310.

Ozga, J. (1995) Deskilling a profession: professionalism and the new managerialism, in Busher, H. and Saran, R. (eds) *Managing Teachers as Professionals in Schools*, Kogan Page, London.

Richmond, J. (1996) Quantitative measures of secondary school performance using school-level data, *Educational Management and Administration*, Vol. 24, no. 2, pp. 151–62.

Ruddock, J., Chaplain, R. and Wallace, G. (1995) *School Improvement: What Can Pupils Tell Us?* David Fulton, London.

Samier, E. (1997) Administrative ritual and ceremony: social aesthetics, myth and language use in the rituals of everyday organisational life, *Educational Management and Administration*, Vol. 25, no. 4, pp. 417–36.

Saran, R. and Busher, H. (1995) Working with support staff in schools: relationships between teachers, governors and other staff, in Busher, H. and Saran, R. (eds) *Managing Teachers as Professionals in Schools*, Kogan Page, London.

Sergiovanni, T. (1984) Leadership and excellence in schooling, *Educational Leadership*, Vol. 41, no. 5, pp. 4–13.

Sergiovanni, T. (1994) *Building Community in Schools*, Jossey-Bass, San Francisco, CA.

Smircich, L. (1983) Concepts of cultural and organisational analysis, *Administrative Science Quarterly*, Vol. 28, no. 4, pp. 339–58.

Stoll. L. and Fink, D. (1998) The cruising school: the unidentified ineffective school, in Stoll, L. and Myers, K. (eds) *No Quick Fixes: Perspectives on Schools in Difficulty*, Kogan Page, London.

Stoll, L. and Myers, K. (eds) (1998) *No Quick Fixes: Perspectives on Schools in Difficulty*, Falmer Press, London.

Strain, M. (1995) Teaching as a profession; the changing legal and social context, in Busher, H. and Saran, R. (eds) *Managing Teachers as Professionals in Schools*, Kogan Page, London.

Telford, H. (1996) *Transforming Schools through Collaborative Leadership*, Falmer Press, London.

Thomas, G. (1996) The new schools' inspection system: some problems and possible solutions, *Educational Management and Administration*, Vol. 24, no. 4, pp. 355–69.

Wallace, M. (1997) Combining cultural and political perspectives for analysing interaction in educational management settings: the best or worst of both conceptual worlds? Paper given at the second of the ESRC seminar series 'Redefining educational management', Cardiff, October.

West-Burnham, J. (1992) *Managing Quality in Schools*, Longman, Harlow.

Willis, P. (1977) *Learning to Labour: How Working Class Kids get Working Class Jobs*, Saxon House, Farnborough.

3

Changing Faces, Changing Places: Policy Routes to Inclusion

DERRICK ARMSTRONG

Introduction

The twentieth century has seen remarkable growth in the provision of educational services and facilities throughout the world. One aspect of this growth has been the expansion of 'special education' systems for disabled children and children with learning difficulties. The special education 'phenomenon' is not something confined to the developed world. In developing countries, too, access to educational opportunities for all children is increasingly being advocated and 'inclusive' education raised in policy debates. Responsibility for education has principally been taken on by the state, though private, and especially denominational schools, have played an important part. In many countries, the rationale for the provision of education has been one that directly links economic and social development to the education and training of the potential workforce.

The argument that economic development is dependent upon investment in systems of education for training the potential workforce with appropriate skills has been called the 'human capital' theory of education, but the linear relationship that is suggested between educational investment and economic productivity is far from straightforward. For instance, is economic development the consequence of investment in education and training, or is investment in education and training a social outcome of economic development? This is a complex question which goes well beyond the scope of this chapter. However, there are aspects of the question that are very relevant to an understanding of the growth worldwide of special systems of education for disabled children and adults and/or children and adults with learning difficulties. Is the provision of educational services for these children designed to include them into the labour market or is the provision of these services a humanitarian outcome, made possible by the economic prosperity of nation-states?

Investment in education and training increases the pool of available labour by equipping the potential workforce with the skills that are necessary to take advantage of opportunities for economic development based upon technological advance. Where the existing labour force is fully employed investment in new sources of labour becomes necessary to maximise the opportunities for economic growth. Hence, at times of labour shortage, the pool of labour is extended to those previously excluded from productive work – for instance the employment of women during the Second World War.

The problem with human capital theory is that where demand for labour begins to exceed supply, labour becomes more expensive and investment in technology, rather than labour, offers a more efficient return on capital. Under these conditions, the education and training of the 'disabled' may come to mean something quite different. Oliver (1990, p. 47) has argued that

> The idea of disability as individual pathology only becomes possible when we have an idea of individual ablebodiedness, which is itself related to the rise of capitalism and the development of wage labour . . . Under capitalism . . . disabled people could not meet the demands of individual wage labour and so became controlled through exclusion.

Thus the category of disability, far from having a fixed meaning linked to physical, sensory or intellectual impairments, is actually a fluid and ever-changing category system for sorting people according to their economic value in the labour market. The development of capitalism brought into being the bureaucratic systems necessary to administer this system (Stone, 1985).

The expansion of special systems of education for disabled people is often characterised as 'benevolent humanitarianism' (Tomlinson, 1982). From this perspective the reform of education to include disabled children has been guided by moral concerns. However, Stone (1985) suggests a less spiritual, less moral, understanding of this benevolence. She maintains that all societies function through the 'distributive principle' under which goods and services produced within a society are distributed through work (be that working capital or labour). Yet for those unable to work for whatever reason at any given historical conjuncture a distributive system based on 'need' is also required. The precise nature of this will vary enormously but whether it be organised around the 'workhouse', 'welfare' or 'welfare to work' is not the point. The point is that the system of categorisation in use at any given time and in any country operates as a mechanism for controlling the distribution of goods and services to those excluded from the mainstream system of 'value' under capitalism – the exchange value of labour.

The origins of special education and the management of the 'abnormal'

Foucault (1967) demonstrated how, from the middle ages to the end of the eighteenth century, insanity and idiocy were part of everyday life, and 'fools and mad men walked the streets'. By the beginning of the nineteenth century the industrialising discipline of the factory system had led to the 'mad' and the 'defective' being perceived as a threat to the new social order and consequently requiring confinement and treatment. At first this confinement was part of a more general confinement of the poor and the unemployed in the workhouses but as these also became increasingly regimented the presence of 'defectives' interrupted the smooth functioning of forced labour. The introduction of asylums for 'defective' poor children was intended largely to remove these troublesome children from the workhouses.

In a short time cultural understandings of 'idiocy' were transformed. This can be shown by the terms employed. The term 'cretin' derives from the French word *chrétien* (Christian) and is testimony to the fact that in early times the severely handicapped were cared for by religious communities. Yet as the social and cultural organisation of societies was transformed by capitalism 'cretins' became 'mental defectives' whose 'genetic mutation' was attributed to the unfortunate result of inappropriate breeding on the part of defective parents.

As the century progressed the work of Charles Darwin exerted a great influence on those concerned with the management of the 'defective' and the 'useless'. His 1859 book *On the Origin of Species* was seen by many as an indicator of how far scientific understanding had progressed. By providing a direct relationship between human beings and other animals, with terminology denoting survival of the fittest and natural selection, Darwin's theories of evolution were used to justify arguments in favour of controls over the breeding of those considered 'defective'.

The views of an eminent theorist around this period highlight the impact of Darwinism on intellectual thought:

> The feeble-minded are a parasitic, predatory class, never capable of self-support or of managing their own affairs . . . they cause unutterable sorrow at home and are a menace and danger to the community. Feeble-minded women are almost invariably immoral, and if at large usually become carriers of venereal disease or give birth to children who are defective as themselves . . . every feeble-minded person, especially the high-grade imbecile, is a potential criminal . . . the unrecognised imbecile is a most dangerous element in the community.
> (Fernald, 1912, in a lecture given to the Massachusetts Medical Society, cited in Sarason and Doris, 1969, p. 42)

Social Darwinism provided a rational and powerful ideology within which the control of 'mental defectives' could be efficiently devised. The perceived scientific authenticity provided by this framework of understanding appealed to 'a society dominated by a relatively small elite of property owning . . . individuals who welcomed any opportunity to justify their newly-acquired wealth, status and power. It was quickly adapted from the biological domain to apply to human societies' (Barnes, 1991, p. 19).

In England the Idiots Act 1886 introduced a distinction between 'lunatics' and 'idiots', providing for the placement of 'idiots' in a registered hospital or institution. The subclass of 'imbeciles' was recognised as a group less defective than idiots. Meanwhile, attention was being given to a further group of 'high-grade defectives' or 'feeble-minded' children. By the end of the 1880s the 'feeble-minded' were regarded as an educational and economic problem and the notion that special schooling for this group would benefit the state was one that was formally recognised by the Elementary Education (Defective and Epileptic Children) Act 1899.

The identification, and refinement in classification, of 'defective' children must be seen in the context of wider socioeconomic and political change. The industrialisation of the means of production and the attendant urbanisation of social life that characterised nineteenth-century England led to the 'discovery' of the 'mental defective' and a eugenicist drive to control defective populations in the interests of social progress. The eugenicist Goddard (1914), for instance, recognised that what constituted 'mental deficiency' was relative to different societies and historical periods. None the less, he held the view that 'progress' revealed the deficiencies of moral, physical and mental degenerates: 'the persons who constitute our social problems are of a type that in the past and under simpler environments have seemed responsible and able to function normally, but for whom the present environment has become too complex so that they are no longer responsible for their actions.' (p. 70) The regulation of economic activity in factories required controlled and disciplined workers ordered by the time and space of the production process as the 'hands' of machines.

Yet educational reform was not simply directed by the functional demands of dominant economic and political interests. Its goals and methods, as well as its organisation and curriculum were highly contested both by those who saw education as a way of raising political consciousness in the struggle for social inclusion based upon the citizenship of common ownership and human rights, and by those with a more modest political agenda of reform centred around the principle of compassion for the unfortunate.

In addition, the expansion of education to include the children of the urbanised working class during the last two decades of the nineteenth century presented teachers and school managers for the first time with the full variety of children's needs and conditions (Sutherland, 1984). In the 1880s the endeavour to impose discipline in the factories was reconstructed, through the system of 'payment by results', in the new training ground of the industrial working class – the schools. This system was linked to an instructional code based upon the assumption that children 'of ordinary health and intelligence who attend school with fair regularity' could all progress at the same rate. The continued expansion of compulsory education and the regulation of teachers' work under the code placed ever greater pressure upon the capacity of the ordinary school system to cope. Many schools reacted by creating a standard 0 taught by pupil-teachers into which fell children who could not cope with the curriculum in the ordinary class.

From this point on arguments were put forward in favour of 'feeble-minded' children being accommodated within a special school sector (Shuttleworth, 1888) and that this sector should be managed by the school boards and not by voluntary bodies (Charity Organisation Society, 1893). In 1891 the London School Board had been the first to open three experimental schools for 'special instruction' in the poorest areas of the city and children were placed on the nomination of their headteachers. Before admission each child was examined by a committee consisting of a school inspector from the School Board, the board's medical officer and the headteacher of the receiving school. By 1896, 900 children were attending 24 special schools in Bradford, Birmingham, Nottingham, Bristol and Brighton as well as London.

Calls for an expanded special education sector continued until the beginning of the First World War. The highpoint of this campaign came with the Mental Deficiency Act 1913 which required LEAs to ascertain those children aged 7–16 who were mentally defective. The only children to be excluded from these proposals were those who were identified as incapable of benefiting from education in a special school, which today would have been those identified as having severe learning difficulties. In the period following the First World War, however, the proposed expansion of the special education sector did not take place. In the period from 1914 to 1939 the number of children in schools for the mentally defective had increased by no more than 4,000 from 13,563 to less than 17,000. In large part the failure to implement the 1913 Act was the outcome of the postwar recession.

The Wood Committee, which reported in 1929, estimated there to be 300,000 mentally defective persons in England, giving a mean incidence of 8.56 per 1,000 (in every 100 mental defectives it was estimated that there would be 5 idiots, 20 imbeciles and 75 feeble-minded children). It was argued that existing special schools were catering for no more than one sixth of feeble-minded children who were seen as being able to benefit from an education. Moreover, it was suggested that no proper provision was being made for an even larger number of children (some 10 per cent of the population) who did not technically meet the criteria for certification as feeble-minded. Under existing legislation this group could not be admitted to special schools because they were not mentally defective despite their exclusion from education in the ordinary school (Board of Education and Board of Control, 1929). The recommendation of the Wood Committee was that certification of the feeble-minded should be abolished so that the feeble-minded and the retarded could be catered for in one comprehensive system. The abolition of certification would, it was believed, lead to the removal of the stigma of attendance at a special school for the feeble-minded whilst at the same time extending educational provision to a much wider group of children hitherto denied access to educational opportunities.

Inconsistencies between the number of children as a proportion of the population identified as mentally deficient and the number of adults similarly labelled reflect the fact that educational criteria were being invoked. In other words, 'educability' was proposed as the criterion of mental deficiency rather than medical factors (Duncan, 1938). Thus, moves to extend the special school system of this period cannot be understood simply in terms of the exclusion of troublesome children from mainstream. It also constituted an inclusionary project. Yet, despite the attempt to support the inclusion of these children the underlying organisational response to the 'problem' of mental deficiency remained that of segregation and control, precisely because the extension of educational opportunity was envisaged as being provided in a separate system.

The economic circumstances of the interwar period meant that the recommendations of the Wood Committee did not impact upon legislative reform until the Education Act 1944. Yet, the tensions contained in the report between the educational goals of provision and the use of special educational provision as a tool of social control and exclusion were to become ever more prominent in the growth and development of special educational services. These tensions reflect both the continuity, and the persisting contradictions, of special education policy in the UK: namely, that the introduction and expansion of the special school sector have encouraged and promoted social inclusion through access to educational opportunities otherwise denied, whilst at the same time doing so through structures that exclude significant numbers of children from mainstream.

Postwar educational reform and a new age of partnership

The years following the end of the Second World War witnessed wide-ranging social reform. Education was at the centre of the reform movement as evidenced by a new philosophy of social inclusion embodied in the Education Act 1944. Education was seen as a key to change in society, by reformers who saw it as the catalyst and vehicle for realising their aspirations for the masses, and by those at the forefront of the new economic revival who saw it as the means of preparing a skilled and motivated workforce. The 'inclusive' character of these reforms is suggested by what McCulloch (1994, p. 93) has described as 'education as a civic project':

> 1944 could be read as the high-water mark of education as a civic project in this country. Educational reform was seen not only as a means of achieving equality

of opportunity, but also as a way to enhance citizenship. This project involved a strong sense of the power of education to foster social solidarity and cohesion.

However, McCulloch goes on to argue that although the reforms of the 1940s pursued a strongly civic goal, they lacked the means to achieve this goal, contradicted as it was by the tripartite divisions of 'academic', 'technical' and 'vocational' education that lay at the heart of the 1944 Act. The special education project of 'education for all' suffered the same fate.

The introduction of compulsory post-elementary education for all children established the principle that all children are educable and therefore that their educational needs should be met within the school system. This was a profoundly inclusive policy but it also had consequences that encouraged the growth of separate forms of provision for the disabled. This reflected a fundamental contradiction in the philosophy of the Act itself. While the Act introduced the principle of 'education for all' it organised this universal education on the basis of a differential understanding of children's needs. Separate provision for the disabled, therefore, was seen in precisely the same way as was separate 'academic', 'technical' and 'vocational' education. The failure of the tripartite system to challenge the hierarchies of social and economic power and privilege embedded within it was similarly reflected in the criticisms subsequently directed at special education and its system of categories.

The Handicapped Pupils and School Health Regulations (Ministry of Education, 1945) identified 11 categories of handicapped pupil, later amended to 10 (Ministry of Education, 1959). Local authorities were empowered to request a formal certificate of ascertainment from a school medical officer where a child was identified as suffering from a condition described by one of the categories of 'disability of mind or body'. Following 'ascertainment' the child would be placed in a special school. 'Ascertainment' was not actually a requirement for special school placement. Section 34 of the Education Act 1944 was explicit in stating that formal ascertainment was only needed when an LEA wished to impose attendance at a special school against parental wishes. None the less, local authorities very often ascertained all children placed in special schools:

> This served to emphasise the separate nature of special education, with an implicit assumption that 'special' education could only be provided in schools or classes recognised by the DES as efficient for the education of children with a particular category of handicap. The formality helped to ensure that transfer from special schools to the mainstream was a rare event.
>
> (Galloway, 1985, p. 29)

In consequence, the Education Act 1944 reinforced the division between ordinary and mainstream schools and in so doing emphasised the stigma of special education. Similarly, the curriculum in special schools was generally restricted to a simple vocationalism that was often little more than a caricature of the secondary modern curriculum.

The impact of Plowden

While the 1944 legislation extended educational provision to all children (with the exception of those deemed to be 'severely subnormal'), children with SEN continued to be seen as different from other children by virtue of their impairments and decisions about these children were framed by the character of individual impairments rather than by any broader principle of educational entitlement. Some twenty years later this view of SEN was to become increasingly outmoded. The Plowden Report (CACE, 1967) was particularly important in pointing to the significance of social and environmental factors upon educational achievement. It also suggested how schools could compensate for social and economic deprivation through an infusion of resources and a more flexible approach to individual learning needs.

The report concluded (*ibid.*, para. 161) that

> special need calls for special help . . . We ask for 'positive discrimination' in favour of such schools and the children in them, going well beyond an attempt to equalise resources. Schools in deprived areas should be given priority in many respects . . . The justification is that the homes and neighbourhoods from which many of their children come provide little support or stimulus for learning. The schools must provide a compensating environment.

The Plowden Report was also significant in that it rejected the idea that educational 'handicap' arises from individual deficits. This view was to have important consequences for the future of special education in Britain. Although lacking the depth of analysis needed to explain how social institutions, including the education system, themselves create and reinforce the social and economic disadvantages which can undermine the pursuit of learning and educational success, it was, none the less, an analysis which acknowledged that there should be a collective responsibility towards those individuals who experienced learning difficulties in their education.

The Plowden Report has come in for much criticism (Acland, 1980) and has been the focus of the 'new right's' reaction against progressivism in education. It placed an emphasis upon the value of education as an agent of social change which is at least questionable and which ignores the wider social and economic context of deprivation and its reproduction. Moreover, its assumptions about professional judgement disregard the way in which professional interests may be advanced through the creation of 'needy' client groups who are subsequently disenfranchised on the grounds that they lack the knowledge to exercise power rationally. Yet, the Plowden Report represented a milestone in educational thinking and one which continued to influence policy-making in the UK until the emergence of neoliberalism in the 1980s.

The Warnock Report

Despite the philosophy encapsulated in the Plowden Report, it was some time before a policy shift towards these principles could be detected in the special education field. Just as the principle of tripartitism in the 1944 Act had ultimately perpetuated discrimination and privilege, despite the underlying goal of enhancing citizenship, the expansion of a fourth stream of separate special education for those who could not manage in, or would not be managed by, the secondary modern sector, led to the growth of an efficient, if educationally dubious, system for managing the 'useless'.

That this mechanism was ultimately concerned with bureaucratic rather than educational management is well illustrated by Tomlinson's (1981) study of the assessment of children identified as 'educationally subnormal'. Tomlinson showed how the procedures for categorising educational needs in terms of 'handicap' were the product of different and competing professional interests. Assessments tended to be based on assumptions that were rarely made explicit by the professionals. These were derived from professionals' perceptions of their own professional roles and interests rather than from any 'objective' assessment of the child's needs. The system of categorisation served in practice to reinforce the 'expertise' of professionals whilst operating as a bureaucratically convenient, if crude, mechanism for rationalising the redistribution of resources encouraged by the civic project of the 1944 Act.

The Warnock Committee was set up in response to a growing disenchantment with the 1944 framework. It had wide-ranging influence upon the subsequent development of special educational policy and practice. Not all the report's recommendations were translated into legislation although nearly twenty years after publication of the report its influence can still be seen in the area of special education policy (witness the *Code of Practice* on the assessment of SEN – DfEE, 1994).

The recommendations of the Warnock Report included:

1) Abolition of categories and their replacement by a generic concept of SEN that emphasised educational criteria (not medical).
2) Acknowledgement that up to 18 per cent of children experiencing learning difficulties in mainstream schools do so because of SEN.
3) Placing emphasis upon multiprofessional assessment and of maximising parental involvement in the assessment and decision-making processes.
4) Extension of special needs assessment procedures and provision to include children of preschool age.

5) Extension of special educational provision to take account of the needs
   of young adults in further education.

The Warnock Report clearly identifies schools as a context within which
children's educational needs may be created. This is significant because it
implies that the educational needs of a child may vary according to factors occurring within the school attended. Thus, it is argued by Warnock
that

> some handicapping conditions, particularly behavioural disorders, may be
> brought about or accentuated by factors at the school, such as its premises,
> organisation or staff. In such cases, assessment may need to focus on the institu-
> tion, the classroom setting or the teacher as well as the individual child and his
> family if it is to encompass a full consideration of the child's problems and their
> educational implications. This needs to be borne in mind by all who take part in
> assessment.
>
> (DES, 1978, p. 59)

The report also laid the foundations for a new approach to parental
involvement in special education assessments. The challenge for professionals was seen to be that of developing multiprofessional procedures
that could also facilitate the contribution of parents as partners. However,
if partnership is to be effective parents must have the same rights as
professionals to information that is used in decision-making about their
children's needs. Yet, as Mittler and Mittler (1982) have argued, the concept of 'partnership' suggests a sharing of power as well as expertise but
in practice the parent–professional relationship may be primarily built
upon a model of 'involvement' containing an implicit assumption of professional expertise and control. In so far as the Warnock Report did not
concern itself with these subtleties its recommendations may be seen as
rather naive.

Kirp (1983) has suggested how the apparent naiveté of the Warnock
Report was underpinned by a belief in professional benevolence based
upon the professional's role as 'expert' working on behalf of an ever-
expanding clientele towards an agreed common goal. Yet the economic
context in which this managerial model of 'consensus' was located is
highly relevant. Whereas the model may match the demands placed on
professionals during periods of economic growth and social reform, it is a
model that is subject to increasing tensions during periods of social and
economic upheaval and dislocation when resources are more scarce and
more aggressively fought over.

The Warnock Report does need to be seen within the overall context of
an attempt to construct a more rational framework for identifying and
dealing with children failing in or failed by the mainstream school system. In this respect, the recognition by Warnock that up to 18 per cent of
children in the mainstream sector may have SEN at one time or another
and that these needs can and should be addressed using the resources

normally available to those schools is highly significant. Indeed it could be seen as far more significant in its implications than the recommendations made with regard to the 2 per cent of children considered to have exceptional needs such that special schooling would be required.

From 1981 to the present day

The Education Act 1981 took up many of the recommendations of the Warnock Report, establishing a new framework for managing special education assessment and decision-making. In particular, categories of 'handicap' were abolished and replaced by a generic concept of 'special educational needs'. 'Special needs' were assumed to be educational and not medical and to exist on a variable continuum. Section 1(1) of the Education Act 1981 refers to a child as having SEN 'if he has a learning difficulty which calls for special educational provision to be made for him'. This will be the case where he or she 'has a significantly greater difficulty in learning than the majority of children of his age; [or] he has a disability which either prevents or hinders him from making use of educational facilities of a kind generally provided in schools' (Education Act 1981, Sec. 1(1))

The significance of this was twofold. First, the assumption of a necessary link between 'impairment' and educational need was rejected. Needs would be identifiable by an assessment of learning needs in context. Thus, the resources available within a particular school, the curriculum and its delivery, and the skill of teachers, as well as factors in the wider community impacting upon opportunities and achievement were all relevant factors. Secondly, these needs might vary both across different contexts and across time. The identification of 'special educational needs' was not to lead to a life-long labelling but rather to a flexible procedure for managing intervention and resources. This was reinforced by the introduction of procedures for annual review of statements of SEN. This framework was subsequently restated and strengthened in the Education Act 1993, supported by the *Code of Practice on the Identification and Assessment of Special Educational Needs* (DfEE, 1994), and introduced in response to demands for more careful and consistent monitoring procedures prior to the initiation of any formal assessment of a child's needs.

According to Oliver (1988) the definition of 'needs' adopted by recent legislation continues to perpetuate a within-child model by focusing upon how the child's needs can be *met* within the context of his or her schooling rather than upon how those needs are *created* by those situations (including the interactions that take place within them). Galloway and Goodwin (1987) have similarly argued that reference to a child's needs may actually refer to something the teacher wants to be provided on the child's behalf. Moreover, they claim that concern over the progress or behaviour of an individual child 'may be little more than a *post hoc* rationalization of the teacher's absolutely reasonable concern about the progress of other children' (*ibid.*, p. 17).

Fulcher (1989) has criticised the 1981 Act for its retention of a 'discourse on disability'. She argues (*ibid.*, p. 167) that the 1981 Act 'defines special education as provision; in the context of a state apparatus this means resources in general . . . The Act establishes a generalist discourse and provides a basis for negotiating over and focusing on, resources rather than examining the educational and social context in which particular "needs" might emerge.' Whilst the definition of 'needs' in any given situation may arise from negotiations taking place between people with differing and, sometimes, conflicting interests (those of teachers, parents, other pupils, the LEA and the LEA's professional advisers, for example), the Act ignores the role of conflicting interests in the construction of individual needs, focusing solely upon the needs of the child once present. Consequently, the child's needs become the focal point for parallel negotiations between all interested parties over the allocation of resources. Yet this may inhibit the development of a theoretical framework within which the interplay of interests and needs can be examined (Armstrong and Galloway, 1992a; 1992b). The development of an appropriate framework revolves around three questions:

1) Under what conditions is educational disadvantage or 'failure' reconceptualised as 'special educational needs'?
2) Whose needs are defined at that point?
3) How does the power to define the needs of others affect the way the issue of 'special educational needs' is understood?

The 1981 and 1993 legislation treats these questions as unproblematic. The fundamental role of categorisation as a tool for managing resources is ignored. Yet the upsurge in statements of SEN in the 1990s, particularly for 'moderate learning difficulties' and 'emotional and behavioural difficulties', suggests that struggles around these questions impact strongly upon the construction of policy as practice, and in ways not necessarily intended by those who formulated the original policy statements. Whereas the logic of replacing categories of handicap with a general and relativistic concept of SEN would be to move towards curricular responses rather than organisational or bureaucratic responses, in practice categories are frequently recreated both as a resource management mechanism by LEAs and as a tool for prizing additional resources out of the system by schools and, increasingly, by organised parent groups.

Although criticised by some for failing to address the issue of rights and entitlement, the most significant challenge to the Warnock philosophy has in fact come from the political 'right'. Looking back from the mid-1990s, the Warnock Report may appear to have been an anachronism, even before it was published. The fact that it was commissioned by Margaret Thatcher, the incumbent Secretary of State for Education in 1974, is not without irony. Postwar optimism about the potential of education for engineering social reform had already begun to splutter, even before James Callaghan's (1976) call for a Great Debate challenged belief in a society guided by the rationality of professional technocracy and benevolence. By 1981 a new era had already begun in which much of the responsibility for Britain's alleged lack of industrial competitiveness was laid squarely at the door of those who championed the postwar consensus and the civic project.

This ideological shift impacted on special educational provision in two ways. First, resources became more hotly contested. As resources were shifted from local authorities to schools under the provisions of LMS there was a significant reduction in LEA-managed support services. Yet a lack of financial regulation and accountability in respect of schools' non-statemented SEN budgets has led to concerns that the overall budget allocated for special education within the mainstream sector is effectively being reduced as schools divert this money towards other areas. Ironically, government commitment to drastic reductions in public expenditure has resulted in more pressure being exerted for access to the greatly reduced resources retained by LEAs. Thus, the number of statements for SEN (together with the additional resources that followed them) continued to rise at a significant rate throughout the 1980s and 1990s (Norwich, 1994). In consequence LEA professionals, such as psychologists, have been placed more than ever into the front line of budgetary control – managing resources rather than learning.

Second, the professional ethic of service came under increasing pressure as the agenda for reform in education shifted away from that set by the liberal theories of consensus which had underpinned the philosophy of the Warnock Report. These were now replaced by a new orthodoxy of consumer-driven market forces (Cox *et al.*, 1986; White, 1988). The reforms of the new regime struck at the heart of teachers' professional autonomy as a 'schools failure' discourse replaced the humanitarian benevolence of the postwar 'special needs' discourse (Galloway *et al.*, 1994). Teachers were held responsible for and publicly blamed for the failure of pupils to achieve standards set by government.

The devolution of resources from LEAs to schools gave control over financial planning to a new managerial bureaucracy within schools, but it was accompanied by the centralisation of policy-making in the hands of the DfEE and the Treasury. External pressures were brought to bear on schools and teachers to adopt pupil selection and financial policies to maximise their competitiveness in the marketplace. A major policy objective has been to make the delivery of professional services subject to the discipline of the marketplace, with consumer (parental) choice becoming the arbiter of quality. In these circumstances schools have found themselves under pressure to divert resources away from children with SEN (unless those resources are protected by a statement) towards those whose success is likely to enhance the academic reputation of the school. Moreover, the very presence of large numbers of children with special needs in mainstream schools, particularly where those needs arise from learning and/or behaviour difficulties, may be seen as harmful to a *school*'s performance on National Curriculum tests when compared with other schools in the locality. This is a powerful force for exclusion.

In response to these pressures new policy initiatives centred upon 'inclusive' schooling have been advanced. In the UK the election of a Labour government in 1997 has encouraged a move away from a 'schools failure' discourse and towards a 'school improvement' discourse in official policy statements. This is premissed upon an objective of 'excellence' for all. Thus in his Foreword to the government's recent green paper on special education, the Secretary of State David Blunkett emphasises the theme that the underlying principle of inclusion is that of improving achievement: 'Good provision for SEN does not mean a sympathetic acceptance of low achievement. It means a tough-minded determination to show that children with SEN are capable of excellence. Where schools respond in this way, teachers sharpen their ability to set high standards for *all* pupils' (DfEE, 1997, p. 4). The impact of these proposals remains to be seen but it is interesting that the language used to talk about 'inclusion' remains that of the market (the saleability of achievement) rather than of the social inclusion of difference and diversity. A political programme for social and economic inclusion centred upon the value of educational achievement in the marketplace resurrects the human capital theory of education and training while doing little to challenge the inequalities that underpin the exclusion of those with limited exchange value in the marketplace of employment. Moreover, there is a danger that the rhetoric of inclusion advanced as written policy will disguise the financial imperatives that are reining in the redistribution of goods and services according to 'need'. In other words, the irony here may be that 'inclusive' education becomes the rhetoric which legitimates the withdrawal of an inclusive, if imperfect, system of social welfare, itself based on recognition of the diversity of needs and the diversity of people's contributions to social life.

Conclusion

This chapter has sketched a history of the traditions that have been important in the development of inclusive policies and practices in the field of special education. The history of special education has at one and the same time been a history of inclusion and a history of exclusion. It is homogeneous neither in terms of its function nor in terms of its impact. In consequence it is important that these concepts are treated with great caution if they are to be more than rhetorical and therefore analytically useful for exploring the management of SEN.

Different strands are clearly discernible within the history of education and, more importantly, can be seen to cut across different policy positions. Thus, the management of special needs within the mainstream may in some situations represent a wider policy agenda of inclusivity, yet in different contexts may reflect an attempt to restrict the availability of resources for children who are educationally disadvantaged by arrangements within the mainstream system. Likewise, categorisation may be used to constrain and control but it has also provided a mechanism for redistributing resources according to need, within a system of economic imperatives which make inclusion on the basis of the celebration of diversity unworkable. Thus, the history of special education has in many ways been a compromise, but it is a pragmatic compromise that is the outcome of an ongoing struggle.

If by 'inclusion' we mean the accessing of educational opportunities then there is evidence to support the claim that special education systems were developed not simply to manage difference but to extend opportunities. If, on the other hand, we concur with Barton (1997, p. 234) that 'it is about listening to unfamiliar voices, being open, empowering all members and about celebrating "difference" in dignified ways', the struggle for inclusion remains far from won. There were and are many pressures within the system that encourage the use of special educational procedures to exclude troublesome children and special schools as a means of managing those children once excluded.

Activity 3.1

Talk to someone who attended a special school before 1981:

- What experiences does he or she recall?
- What impact has the experience had on his or her life subsequently?

Activity 3.2

What special schools are there in your local area? How long have they existed? Have they always been of the same type?

Activity 3.3

What proportion of children attend special schools in your local authority? How has this changed in the last twenty years? Where will you find this information?

Acknowledgements

This chapter arises out of research undertaken with a grant (R000221555) from the Economic and Social Research Council on 'Special Education and the Life Histories of People with Learning Difficulties'. The Research Council's support is gratefully acknowledged.

Suggested further reading

Ball, S. (1994) *Education Reform: A Critical and Post-Structural Approach*, Open University Press, Buckingham.
Daniel, D.M. (1996) 'Education, or care and control?': the development of provision for mentally handicapped children in England and Wales, 1870 to 1914 – an examination of legislation, reports, theory and practice, *History of Education Society Bulletin*, Vol. 57, no. 1, pp. 17–29.
Hurt, J.S. (1988) *Outside the Mainstream: A History of Special Education*, Routledge, London.

References

Acland, H. (1980) Research as stage management: the case of the Plowden Committee, in Bulmer, M. (ed) *Social Research and Royal Commissions*, Allen & Unwin, London.
Armstrong, D. and Galloway, D. (1992a) On being a client: conflicting perspectives on assessment, in Booth, T., Swann, W., Masterton, M. and Potts, P. (eds) *Policies for Diversity in Education*, Routledge, London.
Armstrong, D. and Galloway, D. (1992b) Who is the child psychologist's client? Responsibilities and options for psychologists in educational settings, *Association for Child Psychology and Psychiatry Newsletter*, Vol. 14, no. 2, pp. 62–6.
Barnes, C. (1991) *Disabled People in Britain and Discrimination: A Case for Anti-Discrimination Legislation*, Hurst & Co., London.
Barton, L. (1997) Inclusive education: romantic, subversive or realistic? *International Journal of Inclusive Education*, Vol. 1, no. 3, pp. 231–42.
Board of Education and Board of Control (1929) *Report of the Joint Departmental Committee on Mental Deficiency (the Wood Committee)*, HMSO, London.
Callaghan, J. (1976) Speech by the Prime Minister, the Rt Hon. James Callaghan MP, at a foundation stone laying ceremony at Ruskin College, Oxford, on Monday, 18 October (press release).
Central Advisory Council for Education (CACE) (1967) *Children and their Primary Schools (the Plowden Report)*, HMSO, London.
Charity Organisation Society (1893) *The Epileptic and Crippled Child and Adult. A Report on an Investigation of the Physical and Mental Condition of 50,000 School Children, with Suggestions for the Better Education and Care of the Feeble Minded Children and Adults*, Swan-Sonnenschein, London.
Cox, C., Douglas-Home, J., Marks, J., Norcross, L. and Scruton, R. (1986) *Whose Schools?*, Hillgate Group, London.
DES (1978) *Special Educational Needs (the Warnock Report)*, HMSO, London.
DfEE (1994) *Code of Practice on the Identification and Assessment of Special Educational Needs*, DfEE, London.

DfEE (1997) *Excellence for all Children: Meeting Special Educational Needs*, HMSO, London.

Duncan, J. (1938) *Mental Deficiency*, Watts & Co., London.

Foucault, M. (1967) *Madness and Civilization: A History of Insanity in the Age of Reason*, Tavistock Press, London.

Fulcher, G. (1989) *Disabling Policies: A Comparative Approach to Educational Policy and Disability*, Falmer Press, London.

Galloway, D. (1985) *Schools Pupils and Special Educational Needs*, Croom Helm, London.

Galloway, D. and Goodwin, C. (1987) *The Education of Disturbing Children: Pupils with Learning and Adjustment Difficulties*, Longman, London.

Galloway, D., Armstrong, D. and Tomlinson, D. (1994) *The Assessment of Special Educational Needs: Whose Problem?* Longman, Harlow.

Goddard, H.H. (1914) *Feeble-Mindedness: Its Causes and Consequences*, Macmillan, New York.

Kirp, D.L. (1983) Professionalism as a policy choice: British special education in comparative perspective, in Chambers, J.B. and Hartman, W.T. (eds) *Special Education Policies: Their History, Implementation and Finance*, Temple University Press, Philadelphia, PA.

McCulloch, G. (1994) *Educational Reconstruction: The 1944 Education Act and the Twenty-First Century*, Woburn Press, Ilford.

Ministry of Education (1945) *Handicapped Pupils and School Health Service Regulations* (Statutory Rules and Orders no. 1076), HMSO, London.

Ministry of Education (1959) *The Handicapped Pupils and Special Schools Regulations* (Statutory Instrument no. 365), HMSO, London.

Mittler, P. and Mittler, H. (1982) *Partnership with Parents*, National Council for Special Education, Stratford-upon-Avon.

Norwich, B. (1994) *Segregation Statistics*, CSIE, London.

Oliver, M. (1988) The social and political context of educational policy: the case of special needs, in Barton, L. (ed) *The Politics of Special Educational Needs*, Falmer Press, London.

Oliver, M. (1990) *The Politics of Disablement*, Macmillan, London.

Sarason, S.B. and Doris, J. (1969) *Psychological Problems in Mental Deficiency*, Harper & Row, New York.

Shuttleworth, G.E. (1888) The education of children of abnormally weak mental capacity, *Journal of Mental Science*, Vol. 34, no. 7, pp. 80–4.

Stone, D. (1985) *The Disabled State*, Macmillan, London.

Sutherland, G. (1984) *Ability, Merit and Measurement: Mental Testing and English Education 1880–1940*, Clarendon Press, Oxford.

Tomlinson, S. (1981) *Educational Subnormality: A Study in Decision-Making*, Routledge & Kegan Paul, London.

Tomlinson, S. (1982) *A Sociology of Special Education*, Routledge & Kegan Paul, London.

White, P. (1988) The new right and parental choice, *Journal of Philosophy of Education*, Vol. 22, no. 3, pp. 195–9.

4

Curricula, 'Management' and Special and Inclusive Education

FELICITY ARMSTRONG

Introduction

This chapter is about the idea of 'curriculum', how it relates to teaching and learning, recent policy developments and the struggle for an equitable education system for all. Questions will be raised concerning the possible difficulties and tensions which arise in the complex intermeshing of policy, curriculum, difference and ideology, during a period in which an emerging agenda for inclusive education is tested against other agendas and discourses relating to selection, competition and 'choice'. Selection or exclusion of pupils on the basis of class, culture, disability or difference have no place in the management, organisation and curricula of an inclusive school ethos which 'is characterised by curricula that meet the educational needs of the full range of children' (Lewis, 1995, p.37).

In this chapter, inclusion is not perceived as a technical problem about increasing the numbers of children and young people in ordinary schools by providing lifts, ramps, extra staff or even smaller classes (although all these are important). Booth (1996, pp. 34–35) explains that he thinks of integration or inclusion in education as involving two processes;

> the process of increasing the participation of pupils within the cultures and curricula of mainstream schools and the process of decreasing exclusionary pressures. To attempt the first without the second is self-defeating. Pupils included under one category may be excluded under a different label. Exclusion, like segregation, can be conceived of as *the process of decreasing the participation of pupils in the cultures and curricula of mainstream schools*. Exclusion affects all pupils who are devalued by, and in, mainstream school.

The question of how to develop inclusive curricula in the face of the increasing regimentation of schools, students and teachers – a process set in motion under successive Conservative governments and continued under New Labour – poses particular challenges. In practice, the daily problems and opportunities which face teachers committed to inclusive teaching are complex ones. It is important for all those involved in educational research, planning, policy-making and practice to listen to the voices of all students and to the arguments put forward by disability groups and representatives of other marginalised groups in the community. There is also a need to study, question and learn from classroom practice in ordinary schools (Ainscow, 1997). Only then will it be possible to develop creative responses within schools and colleges which recognise the richness and diversity of human experience in the local communities whose interests they should serve.

Defining curriculum

The question of what should be taught in schools has provided a focus for political, religious and philosophical debate since the very early days of formal education and the setting up of grammar schools in the fifteenth and sixteenth centuries (Armytage, 1964). In contrast, the possible wider meanings and definitions attached to the notion of 'the curriculum' (or 'curricula') is an area which, historically, has not always received the attention from educationalists which it deserves, although there have been important periods in which such questions have been regarded as critical. The Plowden Report (DES, 1967), James Callaghan's 'Ruskin Speech' in 1976 and the Cockcroft Report (DES, 1982) characterise such periods.

Since the 1960s, a period of questioning and change in society, the purpose of education and what is taught in schools have become the focus for intense critical debate in the UK. This has been fuelled by wider debates concerning the economy, technology, culture and the kind of society we live in. Inevitably this raises highly political and contentious issues concerning equality, power and social relationships.

Traditional definitions of the curriculum, resonant with the introduction of the National Curriculum and SATs (standard assessment tests) in England, reflect the view that it is concerned with specifying and producing particular targets, performances and behaviours in students which are explicit and testable according to certain narrowly defined criteria.

In contrast with this view Carr (1993, pp. 5–6) describes 'curriculum' as 'not a description of subject matter but a set of proposals indicating how this subject matter is to be organised, the educational purposes it serves, the learning outcomes it is intended to achieve and the methods by which such outcomes are to be evaluated'. Similarly, Stenhouse (1975, cited in Rudduck and Hopkins, 1985, pp. 77–8) argued that the behaviourist model of curriculum ignored knowledge about the ways in which learning takes place, misunderstood the nature of knowledge, blurred 'the ethical and political problems associated with the control of education, its aspirations and its individualization' and did not 'adequately face the multi-variate situation of the classroom'. This quotation (from a lecture given nearly twenty-five years ago) reaches to the heart of the questions we are still concerned with in this book.

One starting point for this chapter is the argument that the curriculum is 'made' (or produced) at many levels in society, including at the levels of formal policy-making at national and local government levels, as well as through the working and reworking of policy by teachers, advisers, local communities and pupils themselves through practice.

'Curriculum' is understood as being at the centre of what happens in schools and colleges and the values and views of the world they represent and transmit through their structures, cultures and practices. There are enormous differences between schools and colleges which can be explained, at least partly, by differences in the way the purposes of education are understood. The curriculum, how it is organised and delivered, to whom and in what contexts, is pivotal in the processes and planning involved in the management of schools and colleges:

> The curriculum, as Musgrave (1972) has noted, 'stands analytically at the centre of the process whereby any society manages its stock of knowledge.' It is the distribution of different kinds of knowledge and skill through the curriculum to different groups of children or the withholding of certain kinds of knowledge that largely determine their future status, social and occupational, in society. Those who are involved in curriculum decisions thus have great power.
>
> (Tomlinson, 1982, p. 135)

Two important ideas about curriculum emerge from this argument. One is the notion of *curriculum as an agent for social control* through the transmission of social and cultural values (or 'symbolic capital'). The other is the related notion of *power as residing in those involved in making decisions about curriculum*. These ideas turn upside down a traditional view of curricula as neutral 'bodies-of-knowledge' requiring delivery through commonly accepted classroom practices. The term 'curriculum' is often used in England as synonymous for, or interchangeable with, the term 'national curriculum'. This can be understood within the context of the enormous changes which have taken place in the ways in which the curricular requirements for all pupils are understood, planned for and delivered since the phased introduction of the National Curriculum in England and Wales following the Education Reform Act 1988 (ERA).

Much of the literature on teaching and learning largely ignores complex issues surrounding the nature and purpose of curriculum policy-making and focuses on descriptive accounts of curriculum legislation and guidelines for implementation. Surprisingly, government policy and guidance documents relating to special education devote little attention to a discussion of curriculum. The government's green paper *Excellence for All Children: Meeting Special Educational Needs* (DfEE, 1997), for example, skirts around the real issues involved in curriculum, teaching and learning, focusing on 'target-setting', 'assessment' and the implementation of the *Code of Practice*. Those wanting guidance on approaches to differentiation and classroom practice are referred, in the green paper, to other publications by the Qualifications and Advisory Authority (QCA). The exclusion of a full discussion of curriculum issues in the green paper is a 'missed opportunity' because curriculum and pedagogy are of major interest and concern to all teachers, especially within the context of a consultation document which is presented as contributing to development towards inclusive schools.

Activity 4.1

Think about the school or college in which you work. How would you describe its culture and ethos? To what extent does the broad curriculum in your school or college include or exclude some groups of students? What factors contribute to the processes and mechanisms which include or exclude students?

Curriculum and difference: policy, curriculum and special education

The development of special education, the proliferation of categories of disability and the emergence of related structures, processes and practices within the social and economic transformation of society during the nineteenth and twentieth centuries, have been discussed in the previous chapter by Derrick Armstrong. He argues that the history of special education 'has at one and the same time been a history of inclusion and a history of exclusion' and that historically 'special education systems were developed not simply to manage difference but to extend opportunities'.

Both these purposes have been apparent in the way the content and context of curricula have been understood in special education. The setting up of special schools, units and classes and the planning of the content and experience of teaching and learning have been 'egalitarian' in the sense that their humanitarian purpose has been to open up opportunities to those who were traditionally excluded from formal education. At the same time, the focus on particular impairments and the social construction of 'needs' that are deemed to arise from them have been realised and confirmed through the imposition of different curricula and teaching.

Tomlinson, writing at the beginning of the 1980s, commented on the high degree of autonomy and lack of accountability enjoyed by special schools (Tomlinson, 1982). Historically, there was no specified curriculum for any schools, including special schools, apart from the area of religious education. Special schools frequently focused on 'treatment' rather than academic skills and much of the 'curriculum' was in fact embodied in therapeutic responses to specific disabilities. Headteachers and teachers in special schools had enormous control over what happened in their schools and classrooms, including the management of the provision and deployment of resources, the organisation of pupils for learning and what was taught in classrooms. Tomlinson (*ibid.*, pp. 146–7) argued:

> The goals of the special school curriculum are 'non-goals' in that there is no pressure to prepare children for examinations, to make them literate, or even, despite lip-service paid to the idea, to move children back into normal schools or classes . . . the kind of pressures concerning educational standards and school preparation for employment . . . have so far by-passed special education. With no public pressure concerning exams or standards, the need for accountability concerning the special school curriculum has largely been removed from practitioners.
>
> A [further] possible reason for the greater control and decreased accountability in special education has been the development of a powerful special education pressure group, comprising a variety of professionals and practitioners in special education who manage to define special education in their own terms and as their business and deflect too much outside scrutiny.

Historically, this view of special educators has been legitimated by the clearly delineated physical and social spaces they occupy in the educational system and by practices such as the payment of additional allowances as apparent recognition for the peculiar 'special' characteristics needed for their work.

A further legitimation of the power and autonomy traditionally enjoyed by professionals in special education is the status and peculiarity of the language associated with special education, firmly rooted in the medical model of disability and learning difficulty. The pseudo-medical terminology often used by professionals in relation to the children and young people with whom they work marks out a particular, exotic and separating territory which legitimates the development and the sustaining of different curricula. In this sense, the culture and curriculum of special education have exercised a 'management' role in legitimating and harmonising all the other structures, procedures and practices associated with special education. These arguments have traditionally been equally true for remedial or 'special needs' departments within, or units attached to, ordinary schools, as they have been for physically segregated environments such as special schools.

Integration and change

During the last twenty years, the education system in the UK has been the subject of massive legislative changes and debate. To some extent, the whole educational landscape is in a period of apparent realignment and transformation, and the structures and principles underpinning special education have been, and continue to be, part of this process. During this period the subject of 'integration' has been at the heart of debate about change surrounding the education of disabled children and young people and those referred to in more general terms as having 'special educational needs'.

The publication of the Warnock Report (DES, 1978) and the Education Act 1981 opened up to debate and scrutiny the principles and practices of an education system which confined large numbers of children and young people to segregated schools away from their peers and local communities. If segregation was not acceptable, what changes were needed to bring more disabled students and those segregated because of their learning difficulties, into ordinary schools? This question was being posed at a time when the populations and character of schools had already undergone enormous change over the previous twenty-five years.

Planning for the integration of children from special schools into ordinary schools often focused on the perceived abilities, disabilities and potential of students themselves and on the question: which students would benefit from integration? This has led to individual arrangements being made for students deemed suitable for integration, ranging from weekly visits on a half-time to full-time basis, supported placement, special classes and units attached to ordinary schools. Frequently, 'integrated' students have been assigned the status of 'visitors' rather than full members of a school community, and have not had access to the full mainstream curriculum. This focus on the perceived abilities and shortcomings of students as a criterion for integration has its roots in an individual deficit model of disability and difference and is the antithesis to inclusive education, the 'strong' version of which argues that schools and colleges should transform themselves into community schools and colleges to which all learners are welcomed as a right and on an equal basis.

Such a transformation involves letting go of deeply rooted assumptions about the kind of 'special' individualised teaching required for students identified as 'having SEN', and refocusing on what ordinary classroom teaching and learning can offer. Ainscow (1997, p. 4) argues for such a change of focus, based on his research in school:

> Recently, as part of a study, I watched a Year 7 geography class in an urban comprehensive school . . . The teacher began the lesson by explaining, 'This is the first of a series of lessons about the USA.' He went on to say that before they opened their books he wanted to know what the class already knew about this subject. Immediately lots of hands went up and within minutes the blackboard was full of information . . . Sitting on the front row was James, a student who has Down's syndrome. Next to him was a classroom assistant who, for what use he was at this stage of the lesson, might as well not have been there. James raised his hand and, when called on by the teacher, said, 'They have yellow taxis.'

In this case, the teacher was using a familiar tactic to *warm up* his class by using questioning to draw on existing knowledge, prior to introducing new material. It is an approach which many teachers use. Certainly it is not *special education* but nevertheless, it proved to be a means of facilitating the participation of members of the class, including one who is seen as needing permanent adult help.

This perspective suggests that it is necessary to question assumptions about the necessity of 'support' allocated by adults to individual learners and to ask whose interests it serves. Innovative ways of encouraging the learning of all students need to be explored.

Differentiation, curriculum and difference

During the 1980s the questions of integration, 'special needs', curriculum, teaching and pedagogy were linked to the discussion and development of innovative approaches to classroom practice in response to student diversity in general. The notion of differentiation was central to this debate.

'Differentiation' in its diverse forms is inextricably bound up with content, processes and structures relating to the curriculum both in its broad and narrow interpretations. The whole question of how school systems and those working within them recognise, identify and respond to differences between pupils is made more complex by an absence of common agreement about what the purposes and outcomes of teaching and learning should be.

The current debates going on under 'New Labour' about what should be taught and how are examples of this.

The concept of 'differentiation' has been particularly associated with the planning and delivery of what is taught (i.e. the 'narrow' curriculum). The Education Act 1981 which, it was believed, would bring more pupils with disabilities and learning difficulties into ordinary schools, provided an impetus for change. A further influence has been the introduction of the notion of 'entitlement' for all – or nearly all – to a broad and balanced curriculum, strengthened by the Education Reform Act 1988. These developments have brought questions of how teachers respond to individual differences, levels of attainment, perceived ability and interests, to the forefront of the debate about teaching and learning.

Another, historically more firmly established, level at which differentiation has always taken place is through the processes by which pupils are directed along different channels through assessment and selection practices. These have been determined by social factors such as social class and levels of wealth and realised through a highly differentiated education system offering different kinds of schools, curricula, assessment and forms of accreditation to different social groups. Needless to say, young people have emerged from this highly stratified educational system with highly differentiated educational experiences and qualifications. Whatever the value of these to the individual, the public value placed on different kinds of education has been made bleakly apparent in terms of the expectations and destination of school leavers and, in spite of professed greater uniformity in what is taught and how it is assessed, this is still the case at the close of the 1990s.

Curriculum and policy-making 1981–98

Educational policy-making and change affect diverse groups of learners, even when a particular policy or Act of Parliament appears to be focused on just one group or one area of education. The Education Act 1981 in England and Wales touched thousands of ordinary schools, not just provision and practices for learners identified as having SEN in segregated schools. As classrooms became increasingly diverse and discourses of 'need', then 'entitlement' took a hold, LEAs and schools struggled to develop often innovative curricula responses to these changes. Increasing numbers of students in schools were identified as 'having special educational needs' and this process was given an impetus by the statementing procedure, often activated because a statement secured additional resources for special provision or support for students who experienced difficulties. The Education Reform Act 1988 introduced a National Curriculum and other measures designed to raise standards through increasing consumer choice, including open enrolment, LMS and grant-maintained status (GMS). This Act, while invoking students' rights to a common curriculum amid a discourse of entitlement and choice, increased competition between schools, thus increasing differences between them (Harris, 1994). Power over what is taught in schools from ages 5 to 16 became centralised in central government and the role of LEAs in education was greatly reduced. The introduction of SATs and the publication of league tables further emphasised differences between schools, placing on public display the 'achievements' in public examinations of individual schools and students. The *Code of Practice on the Identification and Assessment of Special Educational Needs* (DfEE, 1994), introduced following the Education Act 1993, imposed on all schools procedures for the assessment, identification and management of 'special educational needs'. Thus, not only has the curriculum become subjected to the control of central government, but the management of the 'SEN policy' of every school is also now regulated by legislation. Although the *Code of Practice* virtually ignores the question of the curriculum and teaching and learning, it imposes regulations which are legally binding and which schools must follow. The tightening of the regulatory hand of central government over education has transformed the experience of teaching and learning for many students and teachers.

In her ethnographic study of teachers' views and attitudes on integration, Vlachou (1997, p. 167) found that

Children with special educational needs were in danger of experiencing a higher degree of exclusion within ordinary classrooms because of the mechanization of the teaching act, which reinforced a restrictive notion of learning, a specific image of children and a linear process of development. While political rhetoric talks about 'entitlement' in a broad and balanced curriculum, teachers talk about stronger external pressures to 'fit children in a specific system'. Teachers' struggles to avoid doing so represented their opposition to such political directives.

These 'struggles' refer to the mediation by teachers of an imposed curriculum by government and represent a grassroots reworking of policy which will be discussed in the following sections.

The curriculum and social reproduction

At the beginning of this chapter we looked at some definitions of the term 'curriculum' which argued that, far from being to do with 'subject matter' and the transmission of syllabuses in different, clearly identifiable disciplines, 'curriculum' is concerned with the ways in which different kinds of knowledge and the values which underpin them are transmitted by schools in ways which sustain and promote differences between pupils.

Two important aspects of curriculum were identified relating to its role in social control and the transmission of social and cultural values and, secondly, to the power invested in those who make decisions about curriculum in schools and colleges.

These observations clearly relate to the reproductive role of the curriculum and the structures and practices which surround it. Schools and colleges, it is argued, reproduce and sustain differences in class, culture and perceived ability by processes of assessment and selection based on a curriculum which recognises and privileges certain values and forms of knowledge over others.

In 'reproduction' theory,

> schools are considered to reproduce both the forces and the relations of production in the interests of the capitalist class. The first schools 'achieved' by providing different classes and social groups with the knowledge and skills they needed to occupy their respective places in a labour force stratified by class, race and gender. As for the relations of production, these were reproduced mainly through the maintenance and development of a 'legitimate' ideology and set of behaviours and patterns – in the service of the dominant culture and its ideological interests.
>
> (Sultana, 1989, p. 288)

It is within this context that we need to understand the nature and role of 'curricula' in the UK, and in particular the imposition of the National Curriculum (with its emphasis on national (i.e. 'British') culture and identity). In addition, an understanding of the reproductive role of the education system in the UK renders the notions of equality and inclusion more powerful and more sharply defined because they fundamentally challenge the 'dominant culture and its ideological interests' with which they are in direct opposition:

> Schools process both knowledge and people. In essence, the formal and informal knowledge is used as a complex filter to process people, often by class; and at the same time, different dispositions and values are taught to different school populations, again often by class (and sex and race). In effect, for this more critical tradition, schools latently recreate cultural and economic disparities, though this is not what most school people intend at all.
>
> (Apple, 1990, p. 34)

This complex, filtering process is achieved through all kinds of formal and informal mechanisms. An informal mechanism might include the attitudes of teachers or other pupils towards pupils in bottom sets or from so-called 'minority' cultures. Formal mechanisms are more easily identifiable and include testing and selection (SATS and GCSEs, for example), the organisation of pupils into different groups for learning, the publication of league tables and OFSTED reports.

Curriculum and educational practice

If we accept a view of curriculum as being at the centre of educational practices and as playing a key part in reproducing and sustaining dominant cultural values and existing relationships between different groups in society, the role of the curriculum in relation to pupils who experience difficulties in learning is crucial. Disabled children and young people and those who experience difficulties in learning, for whatever reason, are themselves part of an educational system which tests and selects according to normative criteria. Many will be subjected to more frequent and more diverse forms of testing and assessment than their peers because of the way in which their difficulties are perceived and understood by professionals. This additional testing and assessment itself becomes a part of students' curricula and is embedded in the transmission of messages concerning how people are ranked and valued, and what counts as knowledge and skills. The curriculum, then, acts as an agent for managing people and controlling and ordering different social groups. It forms an integral part of the management of educational structures and practices.

Of course, many other groups experience exclusion and marginalisation through the structures and processes of the education system and these are well documented. Examples of such groups include young women and girls (Murphy, 1989; Weiner, 1994), students from families of different cultural origins (Mac An Ghaill, 1988; Gilborn, 1990), students from poor families, disabled students, students who experience difficulties in learning (Souza, 1995), students whose families are from the travelling community, students who are HIV positive (Russell, 1992), students from non-standard family units, and students who have a parent in prison or with a prison record. The idea of inclusive education challenges all practices which exclude any group, regardless of the category or label assigned to them.

The degree to which different groups are 'selected out' or discriminated against through the curriculum will depend, not only on 'top-down' policies adopted by government and LEAs but also policies as they are interpreted and enacted by teachers and others in individual schools and college communities.

Curriculum and 'reproductive' pedagogy

Policy-making through practice

The ways in which different kinds of knowledge are selected and de-selected and placed in a hierarchical relationship to each other are one aspect of the reproductive curriculum. Another is through pedagogy. Like 'knowledge', pedagogy is never neutral. The conscious and unconscious practices adopted by teachers themselves embody and convey meanings and messages about teachers' opinions and expectations of their students and how they should be valued. These practices are part of the way in which knowledge and access to it is 'filtered' and managed through setting and banding and classroom organisation.

Teachers make choices in the pedagogies they adopt (and hence the curriculum offered) based, in part, upon their perceptions and expectations of the students they teach. The findings of a study carried out in Portugal which aimed to relate the underachievement of large numbers of pupils in the sciences with sociological variables suggested that:

> *the realised 'competence' of the teacher is strongly related to the school context where he/she teaches.* It is that social context which makes teachers develop courses with a low or high level of abstraction to match what they consider to be attributes of the school population they encounter. A working-class school and/or a school in the country acts selectively on the conceptual level of the teaching so as to produce a reduced conceptual demand and focus of the pedagogic practice . . .
>
> We believe that *teachers who make a very low level of conceptual demand have failed to understand the sociological implications* of the transmission–acquisition process they are promoting. Their pupils, already disadvantaged when entering the school, will be more so in the process of selection which takes place both inside and outside the school.
>
> (Domingos, 1989, p. 365)

The ways teachers differentiate between students through teaching expectations relates to the second of the two ideas pulled out at the beginning of the chapter relating to the location of power with those involved in making decisions about curriculum. Decisions – or 'policy' – are made at many levels and while government in England and Wales has imposed a National Curriculum and national testing on teachers and students, there are still enormous differences between schools in ethos and organisation and between teachers in terms of the kinds of pedagogies they adopt.

The fact that educational systems are 'reproductive' of existing class relationships and dominant values in society does not mean that the transmission of these relationships and values is mechanical or not open to mediation and contest. The contested nature of curriculum, for example, is recognised by students and teachers in many schools and by their local communities and fundamental changes in emphasis and the development of creative pedagogies can bring about a shift in control over the curriculum and over what is taught. Such shifts of control are outcomes of struggles over policy on the part of 'actors' (students, teachers, advisers, parents . . .) in particular 'arenas' (classrooms, meetings, etc.). This notion, argues Fulcher (1993, pp. 129–30),

> dissolves . . . distinctions between theory, policy, practice – arguing against the top-down model of policy and the idea of implementation – and putting policy in a wider model of social life as social practice, in which we seek to achieve our objectives, deploying discourse as both tactic and theory about an aspect of the social world we want to influence, and engaging in *struggle*, in *political states of play* [or] . . . 'contests'.

If we understand 'management' as the enactment of policy, or *as* policy, Fulcher's argument against the 'top-down' model of policy and against 'the idea of implementation' is empowering because it relocates policy enactment within the ordinary arenas of schools and classrooms in which the key actors are the people who occupy them – teachers, pupils, parents, etc. Teachers, then, make policy and are managers in their own classrooms.

This argument presents us with contradictions and tensions between the reproductive role of education and the possibility of subverting the normative, reproductive curriculum and claiming some of the curricular space in schools by those who work in them. These 'contradictions', these 'tensions', occur at the points at which the struggles themselves are situated. The curriculum, including teaching and assessment, provides a major arena for such struggles. An example, below, of creative curricular development in response to student diversity illustrates the importance of school cultures in mediating teaching and learning.

Alperton High School

Alperton High School in London welcomes students from many different cultural backgrounds, many of whom speak a language other than English at home and some of whom have only recently arrived in England, some as refugees (Armstrong, 1995). Alperton is committed to equal opportunities and inclusion for all students and this is realised through the school organisation, culture and social relations based on principles of equity and human justice. Students are not categorised and sorted into sets for learning according to perceived ability, and teachers and students work together to make the curriculum relevant to students' diverse experiences and interests as far as possible. They have developed ways of working which are collaborative and recognise differences as a matter of course. The curriculum is an arena – or space – which students and teachers are shaping and filling with their own personal, social and cultural knowledge in ways which challenge the standard expectations of the National Curriculum. Difficulties arise when 'policy' at school and classroom level encounters 'policy' at the 'top-down' level of government legislation. The areas at which confrontations take place relate to the imposed, narrow selections of knowledge in the National Curriculum and assessment, and the consequences of the introduction of league tables and competition between schools which all exert regulatory pressure upon the curriculum and organisation in schools.

Chris Searle (1996, p. 43), writing about another inner-city school, Earl Marshall School in Sheffield during the time when he was headteacher there, described teachers' struggles with the effects of the imposed National Curriculum whose

> central concept – that of a state-licensed corpus of knowledge handed down through government 'orders' to teachers for 'delivery' in the classroom – is effectively de-skilling teachers, attacking their instinct to be creative and original at the point of sharing and imparting knowledge. Such a concept is a daily disincentive to imaginative and stimulating teaching. Of course, teachers are conductors of knowledge but they are also its constructors and interpreters in the process of teaching and learning in the classroom between their pupils and themselves.

The examples above suggest that teachers and pupils can – and do – intervene in the process of teaching and learning from beyond the boundaries of the National Curriculum to include rich sources of knowledge and culture derived from their own lives and experiences. Of course, it is not always the case that students and teachers see themselves as engaged together in a common struggle.

Making schools more equitable, finding ways of standing up to exclusions and discrimination, inevitably involves a battle. Teachers and students, parents and members of local communities are all 'actors' in the contests which take place. What is the usefulness of understanding theories of 'reproduction' and theories of 'resistance' to teachers working in schools? What relationship do these ideas have to the management of the curriculum and special and inclusive education? The answer lies perhaps in Sultana's article (1989, p. 288) in a quotation taken from Viegas Fernandes: 'the more sophisticated our knowledge is of the ways in which schools carry out their social and cultural reproduction, "the easier it will be to define the spaces of possible intervention, the potentialities and limits of resistance to that reproduction".'

Activity 4.2

Write some notes on how the teaching and learning in your school or college could be made 'more inclusive'. Are there some aspects of the culture of teaching and learning which are particularly resistant to change? If so, discuss the reasons for this.

   Is there any relationship between pedagogy and policy-making by central government?

Conclusion

In this chapter it has been argued that the curriculum in schools and colleges is an integral part of the management and governance of education and, through processes of selection and exclusion, part of the wider management of social groups and their relative positions in society. Of course, there is the related major question of how teaching and learning is managed in schools in terms of practice and this is part of the wider issue of how exclusions and inequalities in society as a whole can be challenged and reduced. There is a need to focus more intently and with greater openness on how learning takes place in ways which include all students and to place greater emphasis on theorising curriculum and pedagogy. Teachers and students routinely theorise about the experience of teaching and learning in their daily lives and, as insiders, can provide a source of knowledge and experience which has been greatly neglected in recent years by researchers and policy-makers. Collaborative school and college-based research, involving teachers and students as researchers, is a necessity if new possibilities, new practices, within inclusive cultures, are to be opened up.

Suggested further reading

Potts, P., Armstrong, F. and Masterton, M. (eds) (1995) *Equality and Diversity in Education. 1. Learning, Teaching and Managing in Schools*, Routledge, London.

Tomlinson, S. (1982) *A Sociology of Special Education*, Routledge & Kegan Paul, London.

Vlachou, A.D. (1997) *Struggles for Inclusive Education*, Open University Press, Buckingham.

References

Ainscow, M. (1997) Towards inclusive schooling, *British Journal of Special Education*, Vol. 24, no. 1, p. 4.

Apple, M. (1990) *Ideology and Curriculum* (2nd edn), Routledge, New York.

Armstrong, F. (1995) Equality of access: language through the curriculum, in Potts, P., Armstrong, F. and Masterton, M. (eds) *Equality and Diversity in Education. 1. Learning, Teaching and Managing in Schools,* Routledge, London.

Armytage, W.H.G. (1964) *Four Hundred Years of English Education,* Cambridge University Press, Cambridge.

Ball, S.J. (1994) *Education Reform: A Critical and Post-Structural Approach,* Open University Press, Buckingham.

Blyth, E. and Milner, J. (eds) (1996) *Exclusion from School: Inter-Professional Issues for Policy and Practice,* Routledge, London.

Booth, T. (1996) Stories of exclusion: natural and unnatural selection, in Blyth, E. and Milner, J. (eds) *Exclusion from School: Inter-Professional Issues for Policy and Practice,* Routledge, London.

Callaghan, J. (1976) Speech by the Prime Minister, the Rt Hon. James Callaghan MP, at a foundation stone laying ceremony at Ruskin College, Oxford, 18 October (press release).

Carr, W. (1993) Reconstructing the curriculum debate: an editorial introduction, *Curriculum Studies,* Vol. 1, no. 1, pp. 5–6.

DES (1967) *Children and their Primary Schools: A Report of the Central Advisory Council for Education (England) (the Plowden Report),* HMSO, London.

DES (1978) *Special Educational Needs: Report of the Committee of Enquiry into the Education of Handicapped Children and Young People (the Warnock Report),* HMSO, London.

DES (1982) *Mathematics Counts: Report of the Committee of Inquiry into the Teaching of Mathematics in Schools (the Cockcroft Report),* HMSO, London.

DfEE (1994) *Code of Practice on the Identification and Assessment of Special Educational Needs,* DfEE, London.

DfEE (1997) *Excellence for all Children: Meeting Special Educational Needs,* HMSO, London.

Domingos, A.M. (1989) Influence of the social context of the school on the teacher's pedagogic practice, *British Journal of Sociology of Education,* Vol. 10, no. 3, pp. 351–66.

Gilborn, D. (1990) *'Race', Ethnicity and Education,* Unwin Hyman, London.

Harris, S. (1994) Entitled to what? Control and autonomy in school: a student perspective, *International Studies in Sociology of Education,* Vol. 4, no. 1, pp. 57–76.

Lewis, A. (1995) *Children's Understanding of Disability,* Routledge, London.

Mac An Ghaill, M. (1988) *Young, Gifted and Black: Student–Teacher Relations in the Schooling of Black Youth,* Open University Press, Milton Keynes.

Murphy, P. (1989) Gender and assessment in science, in Murphy, P. and Moon, B. (eds) *Developments in Learning and Assessment,* Hodder & Stoughton, London.

Musgrave, P.W. (1972) Social factors affecting the curriculum, in Hughes, P.W. (ed) *The Teacher's Role in Curriculum Design,* Angus & Richardson, London.

Potts, P., Armstrong, F. and Masterton, M. (eds) (1995) *Equality and Diversity in Education. 1. Learning, Teaching and Managing in Schools,* Routledge, London.

Rudduck, J. and Hopkins, D. (eds) (1985) *Research as a Basis for Teaching: Readings from the Work of Lawrence Stenhouse,* Heinemann, London.

Russell, P. (1992) Affected by HIV and AIDS: cameos of children and young people, in Booth, T., Swann, W., Masterton, M. and Potts, P. (1992) *Learning for all 1: Curricula for Diversity in Education,* Routledge, London.

Searle, C. (1996) The signal of failure: school exclusions and the market system of education, in Blyth, E. and Milner, J. (eds) *Exclusion from School: Inter-Professional Issues for Policy and Practice,* Routledge, London.

Slee, R. (ed) (1993) *Is there a Desk with my Name on it? The Politics of Integration*, Falmer Press, London.

Souza, A. (1995) My experience of schooling, in Potts, P., Armstrong, F. and Masterton, M. (eds) *Equality and Diversity in Education. 1. Learning, Teaching and Managing in Schools*, Routledge, London.

Stenhouse, L. (1975) A view of curriculum design: the objectives model: some limitations (from 'Teacher development and curriculum design', a paper given at a curriculum conference, University of Trondheim, Norway).

Sultana, R.G. (1989) Transition education, student contestation and the production of meaning: possibilities and limitations of resistance theories, *British Journal of Sociology of Education*, Vol. 10, no. 3, pp. 287–309.

Tomlinson, S. (1982) *A Sociology of Special Education*, Routledge & Kegan Paul, London.

Viegas Fernandes, J. (1988) From the Theories of Social and Cultural Reproduction to the Theory of Resistance, *British Journal of Sociology of Education*, Vol. 9, no. 2, pp. 169–80.

Vlachou, A. (1997) *Struggles for Inclusive Education*, Open University Press, Buckingham.

Weiner, G. (1994) *Feminisms in Education*, Open University Press, Buckingham.

5

Resourcing Inclusive Education: The Real Economics

Alan Marsh

Introduction

... whose eyes glazed over when the question of funding and finance was raised.
(Robin Squire, MP, giving evidence as the Parliamentary Under Secretary of State (DFE) to the House of Commons Education Committee 'A Common Funding Formula for Grant-Maintained Schools', 2 March 1994)

The profile of 'the question of funding and finance' in the area of special and inclusive education (SIE) has been raised significantly in recent years. Changes have occurred to the funding of SEN since the implementation of the Education Reform Act 1988, LMS and local management of special schools (LMSS). No longer is officer discretion permissible to allocate extra staff to schools where they judge the needs to be greatest. Although resourcing special educational provision in the days before LMS was a comparatively simple matter (Fish and Evans, 1995), it was not without its own problems (e.g. Audit Commission, 1992a; House of Commons, 1993). A central theme throughout the chapter will be the national and international concern about the escalating costs of providing for pupils with SEN (e.g. Wolman and Parrish, 1996; TES, 1997).

As part of LMS and LMSS, every LEA has had to construct a formula for calculating school budgets and make plans to give control over those budgets to school governing bodies. According to the government, LMS is designed to give those in tune with a school's needs the authority and the money to manage that school. It is also seen as about ensuring that all schools are equitably funded. In both these ways, LMS is meant to be a protection for schools against the impositions of bureaucratic LEAs which are viewed as often wasteful and sometimes misdirected (Lee, 1992). However there is a lack of strong theoretical arguments and empirical evidence on how delegated budgeting improves the quality of teaching and learning as claimed by the government – although one is on stronger ground in claiming that local management is more cost-efficient than the previous system (Levačić, 1995).

The main aim of this chapter is to provide an overview of the funding arrangements for SIE in England and Wales. Scotland has a separate education system under Scottish legislation and Northern Ireland has its own version of English and Welsh legislation (MacKinnon *et al.*, 1996). It will be proposed that a well designed formula can be a key instrument of policy. The chapter will consider how funding policies variously affect the ways in which instances of learning difficulty can be met within LEAs and schools. It will address the question: 'How can teachers/schools best access the resources statutorily available to meet the needs of their exceptional students?' Initially the chapter will explore the definition, identification and measurement of SEN, often referred to as the wide currency of the 20 per cent and the 2 per cent. Reference will be made to the purposes and principles (e.g. simplicity, efficiency, equity and effectiveness), which underlie additional funding for SIE. It will be shown that different methods of resource allocation for SIE will better meet certain principles than others. The funding arrangements taken by LEAs will be analysed and the advantages and disadvantages of each will be indicated. The conclusion will focus on the problems a number of LEAs are experiencing in controlling the costs of special educational provision.

Formula funding of schools in England and Wales

The Education Act 1988 has been described as the most important piece of educational legislation in the UK since 1944. LMS is a key policy of this Act and has brought radical changes to the way schools are run and how resources are allocated both within mainstream and special schools. Underpinning the statutory detail of LMS are two fundamental principles:

- allocating resources to schools on an equitable basis, and
- giving schools considerably greater autonomy in the management of those resources.

(DfEE, 1994b, para. 1)

A number of commentators have described the trend of decentralisation as a growing feature of school systems throughout the western world (e.g. Hill *et al.*, 1990). The rationale behind this trend is the observation that there has been a considerable growth in centralised administration. Several national governments and their agencies have come to the view that too many decisions were located at a distance from the place of learning. This has led to initiatives taking place and later national policies and guidelines being formulated in The Netherlands, the USA, Australia, New Zealand, England and Wales. Formula funding was proposed by LMS as an alternative method of resource allocation to the three main systems of historic funding, bidding and officer discretion described by Knight (1993).

Devising an acceptable formula for pupils with non-statemented SEN has been one of the most difficult and politically sensitive tasks for LEAs.

The task has become all the more arduous as serious tensions exist between the Education Act 1981 and the Education Reform Act 1988 (Wedell, 1988). The definition of SEN in the 1981 Act marked a change from a 'within child' view to an 'interactive' view. In other words special educational needs are the outcome of the interaction between the resources and deficiencies within a child and the resources and deficiencies within the environment (Goacher *et al.*, 1988). A main tenet of LMS is the emphasis on the individual pupil as the main unit of resource, which sits uncomfortably with the 'interactive' view of SEN.

It is now reasonable to assume that all LEAs will have considered methods of identifying pupils with SEN but without statements for their LMS formulae. It is interesting to note that in the original Isle of Wight scheme in 1990, the LEA estimated that the incidence of non-statemented SEN was reasonably constant between all schools. Thus a specific allocation for special needs in the formula was deemed unnecessary. In 1996–7 the London Borough of Newham was the only LEA not to allocate any additional resources for non-statemented SEN but by the following year they had changed their stance and had begun to use *Code of Practice* assessment stages (DfEE, 1994a).

What are the implications of funding arrangements for inclusive education? If mainstream schools perceive a relative lack of funds to meet the needs of pupils with SEN, will they put pressure on the LEA to initiate a statutory assessment in order to gain a statement of SEN and perhaps a special school placement? Norwich (1994) has reported that there was a small increase in special school placements in 1992. However the green paper on SEN, *Excellence for all Children* (DfEE, 1997b), uses more recent statistics and reports that: 'Across the country as a whole some 98,000 pupils are educated in maintained or non-maintained special schools, a number which has been virtually constant throughout the 1990s' (*ibid.*, p. 45, para. 5). In percentage terms, the special school population has reduced marginally from 1.28 per cent in 1991 to 1.20 per cent in 1997 whereas pupils with statements in mainstream primary and secondary schools have doubled from 0.82 per cent in 1991 to 1.64 per cent in 1997. The overall rise in the number of statements has had the effect of increasing SEN budgets. The issue of budget control has been given emphasis by the *SEN Initiative* (Coopers and Lybrand/Society of Education Officers, 1996) and will be discussed further in the conclusion of this chapter. Let us first consider whether pupils with non-statemented SEN in mainstream schools are being funded with 'adequate' levels of funding.

The average amount of the funding delegated to schools by LEAs for pupils with SEN but without statements is only 3.6 per cent (the range is from 10.4 to 0.0 per cent) (Marsh, 1997). This figure would appear to be low if compared to the 20 per cent allocated by central government to LEAs in the standard spending assessment (SSA). Although the government has never claimed that the allocation for additional educational needs in the SSA should actually be 'earmarked' or spent on additional educational needs (AEN), the question has to asked why the particular amount of 20 per cent is in the SSA formula in the first place. On the other hand the government might claim that the AEN component in the SSA includes the differential costs involved in producing and maintaining statements as well as pupils with SEN but without statements. This point raises the general issue of accountability which has been re-emphasised by the white paper *Excellence in Schools* (DfEE, 1997a, Chap. 3, 'Standards and accountability'), having been previously noted by the Audit Commission (1992a; 1992b; 1994) and by Coopers and Lybrand/Society of Education Officers (1996).

It might be reasonable to assume that LEAs which allocate a 'high' percentage on AEN in their own formula would expect a lower percentage of overall statements and perhaps even a greater commitment to the principle of inclusion. However there is no correlation, either positive or negative, between the amount of budget allocation for AEN and the percentage of statements ($r = 0.01$) (Marsh, 1996), and there is a negative correlation ($r = -0.30$) between the amount of budget allocation for AEN and the proportion of overall statements within mainstream schools. At 1996 the three LEAs with the best performance with regard to inclusion of pupils with SEN were Cumbria (90 per cent of pupils with statements are educated in mainstream schools), Cornwall (85 per cent) and Newham (84 per cent) (Audit Commission, 1997). However these LEAs spend very different amounts on AEN: Cumbria 3.3 per cent, Cornwall 1.1 per cent and Newham 0.0 per cent. Clearly it is too simplistic to assume that LEAs which put relatively large amounts of money within the non-statemented SEN component of the formula will be any more successful at meeting the needs of pupils with SEN and/or implementing a policy of inclusive education.

Activity 5.1

Obtain a copy of your school's LMS budget statement:

- What is the allocation for AEN? Find out in exact terms how your LEA formula works for SEN with reference to your school. Do you think the formula is clear, simple and predictable? Can you suggest methods of improving the formula for SEN?
- Should LEAs ask schools to account for how they allocate resources to provide for the special educational needs of pupils? Outline the case for and against.

The 20 per cent and the 2 per cent

In any discussion of SEN it is important to remember the relative and interactive nature of SEN and the background to the wide currency of the

20 per cent and the 2 per cent which are reinforced by the *Code of Practice* (DfEE, 1994a, para. 2.2).

A concise summary to the use of the percentage cut-offs is provided by Gipps *et al.* (1985). These authors remind us that Burt (1921, p. 167) postulated: 'Mental deficiency must be treated as an *administrative* rather than as a psychological concept' and 'for administrative purposes the only satisfactory definition of mental deficiency is a percentage definition based on the amount of existing accommodation.' As the special schools of London in the 1920s could accommodate only 1.5 per cent of the child population, then this is where Burt advocated that the cut-off should be set.

A number of commentators have questioned the use of the 18 per cent and 20 per cent figures. In 1978, HMI argued that up to 50 per cent of pupils in Scottish schools could be said to have learning difficulties (SED, 1978). Dessent (1987, p. 21) also questions the notion of the 20 per cent:

> If 'specialness' is judged in terms of educational failure and if educational success is synonymous with the possession of examination credentials – why stop at 20 per cent? Warnock's 20 per cent is but a short step from the '40 per cent' of pupils who leave our secondary school system with no negotiable qualifications after twelve years of compulsory schooling.

In 1992 the school performance tables (DFE, 1992) quoted 35 per cent of Y11 pupils who did not achieve at least one GCSE at grades A–C. Galloway *et al.* (1994, p. 14) feel that the 20 per cent is really a political compromise based on statistical artifact, which illustrated the scale of the problem without necessarily implying the need either for excessive additional resources or for radical redefinition of current educational priorities.

Although the 2 per cent statement figure is still used in official publications, there is now strong evidence that the 'one child in fifty' is an underestimate of current practice. A study by Evans *et al.* (1994) indicated an increase in the demand for statements and less willingness on the part of schools to make provision for pupils with SEN from within their own resources. The green paper (DfEE, 1997b) makes reference to the average percentage of statements in England as 2.8 per cent. Although this figure is at variance with one published by the Audit Commission (1997) – i.e. 3.4 per cent – it still provides further evidence of the growth of statements.

It is clear that a number of LEAs are experiencing considerable difficulties in identifying, assessing and controlling the costs of SEN. Concern has been expressed that the system of providing statements is in danger of collapse (*TES*, 1995). Indeed Mary Warnock has even questioned the need for continuing with statements (House of Commons, 1993; Visser and Upton, 1993).

As the number of statements increases and the resources expand to provide for these pupils, then there are consequent reductions in other budget areas (e.g. in the amount distributed through the pupil led age-weighted pupil unit (AWPU)). This point is given priority by Birmingham and Nottinghamshire LEAs:

> It is important that most provision for special educational needs continues to be made through general schools' funding and that a greater percentage is not identified through statements for such provision to be determined by the LEA . . . It should be remembered that the resources allocated for the production and provision of statements draw their funding from the same overall budget as schools funding through AWPU. Thus large numbers of costly statements will tend to reduce schools' funding and damage the curriculum differentiation and preventative measures being pursued by schools.
> (Birmingham LEA *SEN Handbook*, criteria for statutory assessment, p. 2)

> The Education Committee wishes to emphasise it is the needs of the child, and not whether or not the child has a statement, that decides on additional resourcing. The processes for allocation of additional funds for SEN, through the formula, through Mainstream Support Groups (MSGs) and through support services ensure that available funds are spent on children and not on costly administrative statementing procedures, where these are unnecessary.
> (*Platform for Progress*, Nottinghamshire Education Committee's policy statement on special educational needs, p. 7)

Activity 5.2

Find out how many pupils have statements of SEN within your school and also the type of their learning need, i.e. moderate learning difficulties (MLD), specific learning difficulties (SpLD), emotional and/or behavioural difficulties (EBD), etc. Is the overall percentage in your school more or less than expectation considering proxy indicators and area/county averages? If your school's percentage of pupils with statements appears to be 'out of line' then consider some of the factors which may have had an impact.

Obtain a copy of your LEA's published criteria for deciding to make a statutory assessment of SEN. How many of the current pupils with statements in your school would meet the criteria? If your LEA does not have published criteria can you suggest what these should be for MLD, SpLD and EBD?

The purposes of additional funding for SEN

This section will consider the two main purposes for providing additional funding for SEN – first, to raise educational achievement because the resourcing needs of gaining access to the curriculum are greater for pupils with various degrees of learning difficulty. This purpose could be defined in terms of improving effectiveness or providing a focus on outcomes. Secondly, to compensate for social disadvantage experienced outside school – this might be regarded as an equity argument. Whatever the purpose of additional resourcing there is the over-riding political and economic issue of constraining the growth of public spending which includes minimising administrative costs. A theoretical framework can be used to undertake an assessment of local management, against the criteria or principles of efficiency, effectiveness, equity, accountability and choice (Levačić, 1989; 1995).

The purpose of additional funding also determines a number of further funding considerations. If the purpose is for equity reasons then the use of social disadvantage data to fund schools might be justified on the grounds that this readily available information is well correlated with educational achievement data. In addition it might also be thought by policy-makers that social disadvantage needs to be compensated for independently of educational achievement. However if the purpose of additional funding is for effectiveness reasons then the considerations which follow are: differential costs for different SENs; accountability of SEN resources; schools should be rewarded for 'adding value' rather than receiving funds for low attainment; and funds should be distributed to meet the needs of individual pupils. The issue of whether needs are best resourced *individually* (i.e. through statements and individual pupil SEN formula factors) or *collectively* (i.e. through a general allocation to schools to allow them to meet the needs of all the pupils in their area) is explored by Fish and Evans (1995, Chap. 8).

The purpose of allocating resources to raise educational achievement

If the purpose for allocating additional funding for pupils with SEN is to raise achievement then the goals to be pursued could be defined in different ways. These might be defined as an improvement in National Curriculum attainments or perhaps for a special school pupil the emphasis would be on the independence/self-help skills deemed to be necessary for life after compulsory schooling.

An important point is that resource policies are underpinned and guided by more fundamental ethical and value-based decisions concerning how *much* should be spent on *which* pupils in our schools (Dessent, 1987, p. 51). The phenomenon of 'resource drift' can occur whereby teaching or financial resources accorded to schools for SEN pupils drift over a period of time to other areas of the school's work which are perceived as having higher priority. The idea that children at the end of the continuum of need (e.g. those who have profound/multiple learning difficulties (PMLD)) require higher levels of individual attention would rarely be disputed. That they merit greater entitlement to teacher time and the available financial resources appears just within a society which expounds humanitarian ideals (*ibid.*, p. 55). This resourcing policy could be described as a form of positive discrimination although it is rarely conceptualised in this way by LEAs. However it does cause a conflict with the purpose of effectiveness. That is to say, some PMLD pupils will make very limited progress in terms of educational achievement during their compulsory education. The staffing levels allocated to these pupils would therefore appear to be more dependent on special care needs rather than SEN and have their roots in compassion and humanity (Pritchard, 1963).

In practice the principle of allocating additional resources for the purpose of raising the educational achievement of children with special needs has not been clearly distinguished from that of palliative care, compensation and positive discrimination. For instance OFSTED (1993, para. 42) reported that school development plans did not generally identify raising pupils' achievements as the central purpose of the establishments. Historically the provision of additional resources for children with special needs has been strongly associated with providing them with more attention from teachers and para-teachers in an attempt to develop and refine intervention strategies for individual pupils. Ainscow (1993) argues that regrettably much less attention has been paid to conceptualising what we are trying to achieve or the effectiveness of the interventions.

The purpose of compensatory resourcing

A different form of positive discrimination from the one described in the previous section has its roots in the Plowden Report (CACE, 1967) which itself was influenced by much of the anti-poverty legislation and programmes instituted in the USA during the 1960s (Silver and Silver, 1991). The conclusions of the Plowden Report recognised the growing body of educational and sociological research evidence of the existence of strong links between educational achievement and a variety of students' home background characteristics (Sammons, 1991). It was argued that schools in socioeconomically disadvantaged areas should be given extra resources because of the greater educational needs of their pupils.

Although, as Smith (1987) concedes, the educational priority area as proposed in the Plowden Report is now an outdated concept, the report still provided a major stimulus for the development of policies of positive discrimination in the distribution of educational resources and, in particular, the use of educational priority indices (EPIs). The school remained central to the distribution of extra resources because the Plowden strategy had recommended using the experience of school as a means of compensating children for their disadvantages. Teachers working in schools with a high level of disadvantage received an additional amount of money known as the 'social priority allowance'.

Further evidence for compensatory resourcing is provided from the Task Group on Assessment and Testing (National Curriculum TGAT, 1988). TGAT (*ibid.*, App. J, para. 1) noted the 'strong association between social background and educational performance of almost all types is one of the longest established and best supported findings in social and educational research'. The Audit Commission (1992a) quoted research (Gray *et al.*, 1984) which supports a correlation between the incidence of SEN, especially learning difficulties, and the level of socioeconomic privilege or deprivation in an area. Another indication of compensatory resourcing has already been mentioned in this chapter, i.e. the additional educational needs component of the SSA. This uses selected social factors as a reasonable proxy for the distribution of additional need (DoE, 1995).

The next section will examine the funding methods used by LEAs to provide for pupils with SEN but without statements.

Methods used by LEAs to fund additional educational needs

The first generation of LMS SEN formulae followed the guidance offered in Circular 7/88 (DES, 1988, para. 104) that the formula should be 'simple, clear and predictable' so that 'governors, head teachers, parents and the community can understand how it operates and why it yields the results it does'. A survey carried out in 1996–7 indicated that there are three distinct approaches to allocation which are currently being used by LEAs. These are:

- using simple broad indicators of social disadvantage;
- quantitative measures derived from tests of pupils' attainment and behaviour; and
- moderated professional assessment of individual pupils' needs.

A key distinguishing characteristic between these three approaches is whether the indicator of special need used for resource allocation is intended to predict accurately the incidence of special needs within each school or to identify individual pupils with special needs. An indicator of incidence is wholly consistent with the purpose of compensation for social disadvantage. Individual identification would be inappropriate for compensation funded at the level of school, area or community. The purpose of raising educational achievement could be served by a funding formula based either on incidence or identification, though an indicator which identified individual need would be preferable from the point of view of accuracy and hence effectiveness and accountability.

Analysis of LEAs' LMS formulae for AEN has shown that the majority of LEAs continue to use proxy measures of SEN, e.g. free school meals entitlement (FSME) (Marsh, 1997). Although the use of free school meals data is perhaps acceptable at a school level to predict the incidence of SEN, the relationship is much weaker at an individual pupil level. The correlation of FSME with a measure of pupil achievement on entry to school is 0.87 at a school level but falls to 0.20 at an individual pupil level (Marsh, 1995).

Many LEAs are reviewing their formula and have expressed their unease with using proxy indicators, preferring more direct measures, e.g. the use of professional assessments, standardised tests of educational attainments or the use of National Curriculum assessments (NCAs). This thinking is in line with the recommendations of the *Code of Practice on the Identification and Assessment of Special Educational Needs* (DfEE, 1994a) which suggests the adoption of a staged model of individual pupil assessment.

Table 5.1 The relationship between purposes, principles and methods of resource allocation

Purposes		Principles	Methods of resource allocation		
To raise educational achievement	Compensatory resourcing		Free school meals	Quantitative measures	Professional audits
	•	Simplicity			
•		Effectiveness		•	•
•		Needs responsive		•	•
	•	Equity	•	•	•
•		Efficiency		•	•
•	•	Cost containment	•	•	
•		Accountability			

Table 5.1 summarises by means of a matrix the relationship between the three methods of resource allocation and purposes and principles. If the main purpose of the LEA is for compensatory resourcing then the set of principles which will be supported are different from when the main purpose is to raise educational achievement. Free school meals can be justified as a proxy indicator of SEN, if the LEA considers that additional resources should be made available at a school level to compensate for social disadvantage experienced by pupils. However if the LEA's focus is on the pupil's entitlement and learning, then the other two methods of resource allocation for non-statutory special educational needs (NSSEN) which place an emphasis on individual pupil needs, would better meet this policy. Free school meals may be thought of as an indicator of incidence, quantitative measures can be either indicators of incidence or identification and professional audits are indicators of identification. An important point to note is that some principles or criteria are better 'delivered' by one type of SEN allocation system than another. For example free school meals is one of the best SEN indicators for meeting the principles of simplicity, objectivity, low administrative cost and cost containment. However FSME will rise in a recession and performs poorly with respect

to responsiveness to individual need. Educational tests and professional audits are better than FSME on a range of factors. The main difference is in the area of cost containment. Audit approaches, which include *Code of Practice* assessment stages, can be subject to 'identification inflation' which are more difficult to moderate than simple manipulation of test cut-off scores. Finally, methods of resource allocation are open to combined approaches. That is, a proxy indicator could be used to predict the numbers of pupils likely to be identified at stages 1 and/or 2 of the *Code of Practice* and educational tests/ National Curriculum assessments could be used to provide criteria for making a stage 3 assessment or deciding to make a statutory assessment (Marsh, 1996).

Conclusions

The funding of SEN is at the crossroads. Since the implementation of the Education Acts 1981 and 1988, LEAs have seen significant increases in the SEN budget. LEAs are now faced with the choice of attempting to control the amount of resources designated for supporting pupils with statements of SEN or accepting a 'demand led' budget. The bulk of the 'additional' money is being used to support pupils with statements in mainstream primary and secondary schools, where the numbers have more than doubled from 62,000 (0.8%) in January 1991 to 134,000 (1.6%) in January 1997. However the evidence suggests that the number of pupils educated in special schools (1.2%) has remained virtually constant during the same period (DfEE, 1997b). The continuing growth in the number of statements would appear, then, not only to draw disproportionate amounts from the general schools budget but also to divert attention away from inclusive policies aimed at reducing the special school population. The impact of LMS has meant that many mainstream schools have accrued additional resources from statements for 'their own' pupils perhaps at the expense of reviewing and adapting their approaches in order to achieve greater inclusion of pupils who would normally have been educated in a special school.

This chapter has proposed that a well designed funding formula can be an important allocation method for SEN, but it is still apparent that a radical rethink is needed about the system of statementing which is becoming too confrontational and adversarial. The system may even be restricting the prospects for improved inclusion practice by a concentration of attention on the 'increasing 2 per cent' in mainstream schools rather than on reducing the 'static 1 per cent' in special schools. The resources delivered by statements are becoming an inequitable method of ensuring that a child's special educational needs are met or whether the child has a greater chance of being educated in a mainstream school. Parental pressure groups are increasingly getting an unfair share of the limited resources available and perhaps damaging inclusive education options for other groups of parents who are not so articulate. The Independent Panel for Special Education Advice (IPSEA) have made a vigorous attack upon *The SEN Initiative* (Coopers and Lybrand/Society of Education Officers, 1996) and have viewed the issue from a children's rights standpoint. IPSEA claim that more resources should be found in order to ensure the protection of the child's special educational needs. It is not clear however why such a formal promise and contract, in the form of a statement, should be required only at a point where an LEA becomes involved in directing the provision (and often providing directly). Children have SEN at all stages of the *Code of Practice* and the argument is that they (or their parents) are entitled to as much reassurance as any others.

A high level of resource monitoring and evaluation should be administered by both LEAs and individual schools when resourcing SIE. Some thought also needs to be given to incentive schemes to encourage the inclusion of pupils from special schools. The challenge for LEAs and governing bodies as we approach the turn of the century is to develop inclusive education policies and formula funding arrangements for SEN which fully encompass the needs of all pupils with SEN, with and without a statement.

Suggested further reading

Galloway, D., Armstrong, D. and Tomlinson, S. (1994) *The Assessment of Special Educational Needs: Whose Problem?*, Longman, Harlow.

Lee, T. (1996) *The Search for Equity. The Funding of Additional Educational Needs under LMS*, Avebury, Aldershot.

Levačić, R. (1995) *Local Management of Schools*, Open University Press, Buckingham.

Marsh, A.J. (1997) *Current Practice for Resourcing Additional Educational Needs in Local Education Authorities*, EMIE, Slough (http://www.nfer.ac.uk/emie/emie3.htm).

References

Ainscow, M. (1993) *Towards Effective Schools for All. Policy Options for the Special Educational Needs in the 1990s*, NASEN, Stafford.

Audit Commission (1994) *The Act Moves on: Progress in Special Educational Needs*, HMSO, London.

Audit Commission (1997) *Local Authority Performance Indicators for 1995/6*, Audit Commission, London.

Audit Commission/HM Inspectorate (1992a) *Getting in on the Act. Provision for Pupils with Special Educational Needs*, HMSO, London.

Audit Commission/HM Inspectorate (1992b) *Getting the Act Together. Provision for Pupils with Special Educational Needs*, HMSO, London.

Burt, C. (1921) *Mental and Scholastic Tests*, P.S. King & Son, London.

Central Advisory Council for Education (CACE) (1967) *Children and their Primary Schools (the Plowden Report)*, HMSO, London.

Chartered Institute of Public Finance and Accountancy (CIPFA) (1995) *Education Statistics 1995–96 Estimates*, CIPFA, London.

Coopers and Lybrand/Society of Education Officers (1996) *The SEN Initiative: Managing Budgets for Pupils with Special Educational Needs*, Coopers and Lybrand/Society of Education Officers, London.

DES (1988) *Circular 7/88: Education Reform Act; Local Management of Schools*, DES, London.

DES (1991) *Circular 7/91: Local Management of Schools: Further Guidance*, DES, London.

DFE (1992) *Public Examination Results*, DFE, London.

DfEE (1994a) *Code of Practice on the Identification and Assessment of Special Educational Needs*, DfEE, London.

DfEE (1994b) *Circular 2/94: Local Management of Schools*, DfEE, London.

DfEE (1997a) *Excellence in Schools*, DfEE, London.

DfEE (1997b) *Excellence for all Children*, DfEE, London.

DoE, (1995) *Standard Spending Assessment Handbook 1995/96*, DoE, London.

Dessent, T. (1987) *Making the Ordinary School Special*, Falmer Press, Lewes.

Evans, J., Lunt, I., Young., P. and Vincent, C. (1994) *Local Management of Schools and Special Educational Needs. Final report to the Economic and Social Research Council (ESRC)*, Swindon.

Fish, J. and Evans, J. (1995) *Managing Special Education: Codes, Charters and Competition*, Open University Press, Buckingham.

Galloway, D., Armstrong, D. and Tomlinson, S. (1994) *The Assessment of Special Educational Needs: Whose Problem?*, Longman, Harlow.

Gipps, C., Goldstein, H. and Gross, H. (1985) Twenty per cent with special needs: another legacy from Cyril Burt? *Remedial Education*, Vol. 20, no. 2, pp. 72–5.

Goacher, B., Evans, J., Welton, J. and Wedell, K. (1988) *Policy and Provision for Special Educational Needs*, Cassell, London.

Gray, J., Jesson, D. and Jones, B. (1984) Predicting differences in examination results between LEAs, *Oxford Review of Education*, Vol. 10, no. 1, pp. 45–68.

Hill, D., Oakley-Smith, B. and Spinks, J. (1990) *Local Management of Schools*, Paul Chapman Publishing, London.

House of Commons Education Committee (1993) *Third Report. Meeting Special Educational Needs: Statements of Need and Provision. Volume II*, HMSO, London.

Knight, R. (1993) *Special Educational Needs and the Application of Resources*, EMIE, Slough.

Lee, T. (1992) Local management of schools and special education, in Booth, T., Swann, W., Masterton, M. and Potts, P. (eds) *Learning for All. 2. Policies for Diversity in Education*, Routledge, London.

Levačić, R. (1989) Rules and formulae for allocating and spending delegated budgets: a consideration of general principles, *Educational Management and Administration*, Vol. 17, no. 4, pp. 79–90.

Levačić, R. (1995) *Local Management of Schools*, Open University Press, Buckingham.

MacKinnon, D., Statham, J. and Hales, M. (1996) *Education in the UK: Facts and Figures*, Hodder & Stoughton, London.

Marsh, A.J. (1995) The effect on school budgets of different non-statemented special educational needs indicators within a common funding formula, *British Educational Research Journal*, Vol. 21, no. 1, pp. 99–115.

Marsh, A.J. (1996) *Criteria of Need. A Survey of Local Authority Policies and Practice*, Society of Education Officers (Special Needs Standing Committee), Manchester.

Marsh, A.J. (1997) *Current Practice for Resourcing Additional Educational Needs in Local Education Authorities*, EMIE, Slough (http://www.nfer.ac.uk/emie/ emie3.htm).

National Curriculum Task Group on Assessment and Testing (TGAT) (1988) *A Report*, DES, London.

Norwich, B. (1994) *Segregation and Inclusion. English LEA Statistics 1988–1992*, Centre for Studies on Inclusive Education (CSIE), Bristol.

OFSTED (1993) *Access and Achievement in Urban Education*, HMSO, London.

Pritchard, D.G. (1963) *Education and the Handicapped 1760–1960*, Routledge & Kegan Paul, London.

Sammons, P. (1991) 'Measuring and resourcing educational needs variations in LEAs' LMS policies in inner London', paper delivered at the BERA conference, Nottingham.

Scottish Education Department (SED) (1978) *The Education of Pupils with Learning Difficulties in Primary and Secondary Schools: A Progress Report by Her Majesty's Inspectorate*, HMSO, Edinburgh.

Silver, H. and Silver, P. (1991) *An Educational War on Poverty. American and British Policy-Making 1960–1980*, Cambridge University Press, Cambridge.

Smith, G. (1987) Whatever happened to educational priority areas?, *Oxford Review of Education*, Vol. 13, no. 1, pp. 23–8.

TES (1995) Statement system in danger of collapse, 3 November, p. 6

TES (1997) Special needs eat up London budgets, 31 January, p. 15.

Visser, J. and Upton, G. (eds) (1993) *Special Education in Britain after Warnock*, David Fulton, London.

Wedell, K. (1988) The new act: a special need for vigilance, *British Journal of Special Education*, Vol. 15, no. 3, pp. 98–101.

Wolman, J.M. and Parrish, T.B. (1996) *Escalating Special Education Costs: Reality or Myth?*, Center for Special Education Finance, Palo Alto, CA.

6

Markets, Managerialism and Inclusive Education

Len Barton

In this brief chapter I will, first, raise some general issues concerning the question of disability and in particular the essential features of a social model. Secondly, I will discuss the question of market-led ideologies and their impact on policy, provision and practice in education. This will involve an analysis of key features of what I am calling the 'new managerialism' within education. Thirdly, the question of inclusive education will be briefly explored. Finally, I will draw together some suggestions for future action.

A social model of disability

Within education generally and special education in particular, a form of psychological reductionism has had a powerful influence on policy and practice. From this perspective problems, needs, syndromes are individualised, defined, as well as explained in terms of a person's inabilities and/or attributes. This form of pathologising places an emphasis on, for example, cognitive factors, lack of motivation or interest and inappropriate behavioural and emotional states on the part of the individual.

In a discussion of Irish educational discourse McDonnell (1998) maintains that an essentialist view of the individual has been a pervasive ideology within education. Individuals are alleged to possess inherent characteristics and he contends (*ibid.*, p. 8): 'Pupils are defined in terms of the "amount" of "ability" or "intelligence" they are deemed to possess . . . and that failure and difficulties in education can be attributed to traits believed to be inherent in pupils themselves.' This type of perspective has been influential in many societies and has contributed to a culture of expertise and dependency, in which the definitions and decisions of professionals have become part of the disabling barriers that impact on the daily lives of disabled children and adults (Tomlinson, 1982; Skrtic, 1991; Oliver, 1996).

How we define disability is fundamentally important in that the assumptions involved will influence the ways in which we both understand and seek to address the question of inclusion. It will make a difference to our interactions and expectations of disabled people and to the degree of seriousness with regard to the profundity of the struggle involved in overcoming disabling barriers, including the extent of the changes required to the existing social and economic conditions and relations of a given society.

From a social model, disability is not a personal tragedy, an abnormality or a disease needing a cure. It is a form of discrimination and oppression in which patronising, sentimental, disenfranchising and overly protective attitudes and values legitimate and maintain the sorts of individualised pathologising that we previously referred to.

Disabling barriers of both an attitudinal and institutional form need to be identified, challenged and removed. Short and long-term strategies need to be worked out with regard to how, when and where particular actions for change are developed and implemented. The stubbornness of the disabling barriers and the difficulties of their removal must not be underestimated. Nor must they be perceived as overly deterministic and thus inhibiting the development of the necessary political action on the part of oppressed groups and their allies.

In an attempt to develop a comparative understanding of how and why negative attitudes are supported and changed, Coleridge (1993, p. 27) powerfully advocates that 'The negative response of most able-bodied people to disabled people is based mainly on ignorance: They assume that disablement is a catastrophe, and they fear it: fear creates awkwardness, avoidance and prejudice'. Not only does Coleridge emphasise the centrality of disabling barriers within society, including hostility, prejudice and discrimination but, importantly, he also highlights the extent to which the 'internal oppression' of a disabled person has to be dealt with involving 'a life long process of self-discovery, the discovery of a new identity' (*ibid.*, p. 28). How this is experienced and dealt with will also differ between those who were born disabled and those who became disabled at a later point in life.

This process of self-discovery involves 'all the agonies of denial, anger, and rejection' (Coleridge, 1993, p. 30) until the individual reaches a stage of acceptance. Nor is this a question of resignation but rather it 'involves a positive adjustment to the new identity, in which self-image and self-esteem are not impaired, but remain very much intact, they may even be enhanced' (*ibid.*).

In their writings disabled people recognise the importance of this experience of developing a sense of pride in who and what you are. David Hevey (1992, pp. 1–2) has most vividly captured this issue in his startling account of his own development:

> The second flash on this road to Damascus as a disabled person came when I encountered the disability movement. I had learnt to live with my private fear

and to feel that I was the only one involved in this fight. I had internalised my oppression. As a working class son of Irish immigrants, I had experienced other struggles but, in retrospect, I evidently saw epilepsy as my hidden cross. I cannot explain how significantly all this was turned around when I came into contact with the notion of the social model of disabilities, rather than the medical model which I had hitherto lived with. Over a matter of months, my discomfort with this secret beast of burden called epilepsy, and my festering hatred at the silencing of myself as a disabled person, 'because I didn't look it', completely changed. I think I went through an almost evangelical conversion as I realised that my disability was not, in fact, the epilepsy, but the toxic drugs with their denied side-effects; the medical regime with its blaming of the victim; the judgement through distance and silence of bus-stop crowds, bar-room crowds and dinner-table friends; the fear; and, not least, the employment problems. All this was the oppression, not the epileptic seizure at which I was hardly (consciously) present.

Before exploring the issue of inclusion we have attempted to identify some of the external disabling barriers and their impact on self-identity, representation, policy and practice. Both this account by Hevey and others by Coleridge we have previously included remind us of the crucial importance of how disability is defined, by whom, with what consequences. Both questions of inclusion and exclusion are ones in which disabled people, both individually and collectively, struggle over the power of naming. As we shall argue in this chapter, inclusion is concerned with the politics of difference and how it can be celebrated with dignity.

Marketisation, managerialism and education

Many societies have and continue to experience a radical restructuring of their educational systems. The grounds for such government interventions include the lack of acceptable standards of achievement within schools, the demand for more accountability and the need to be more cost-effective. These are often represented in crisis terms, especially when related to the position and performance of a society in the international competitive marketplace (Henig, 1994; Whitty *et al.*, 1998).

The extent to which education can be viewed as a market is a contentious issue, which has encouraged some analysts to maintain it is best conceived as a quasi-market (Le Grand and Bartlett, 1993). This does not detract from the significance of the recognition that markets involve winners and losers and as Dale (1997) so powerfully reminds us, they are always social constructions, never neutral and the state is always implicated in their framing and regulation.

The fundamental concern, therefore, surrounds the question of the governance of education and the roles of the state in this process (*ibid.*). This raises a number of serious questions, including:

- What is the best and most appropriate form of educational policy and delivery?

- How is education to be funded, and regulated?
- How are educational benefits to be allocated?
- Who and what is valued in educational institutions?
- How is performance to be assessed in institutional and individual terms (Ball, 1997; Dale, 1997)?

In seeking to engage with these concerns and discussing this in relation to the American context, Henig (1994, p. 4) maintains that 'The prescription is "restructuring" and the favoured way of bringing this restructuring about is to introduce market pressures into the process by which educational decisions are made'. This is very applicable with regard to our own society and, for example, by encouraging schools to compete for pupils, introducing new funding arrangements, providing opportunities for open enrolment, opting out, requiring the publication of league tables and establishing new forms of inspection, schools, it is alleged, will become more effective, efficient and generally improve their educational performance.

Supporting such developments has been the introduction of a form of business language in both official and everyday discourses by which we are encouraged both to think and talk about education. Key concepts include cost-effective, efficiency, performance indicators, quality assurance, accountability, unit of resource, output measures and income generation. In this context education is increasingly viewed as a private as opposed to a public good. Schools need to be more business-like and by investing them with more decision-making powers, the pressure is towards forcing them to become more marketable and seriously concerned with their reputations.

The values and priorities informing decisions over the purpose, delivery and outcomes of education are increasingly 'secondary to, and need to be subordinated to, budget considerations' (Angus, 1994, p. 89). Meeting the requirements of audit and assessment procedures in relation to visible performitivity has now become a perennial pressure.

In a discussion of the impact of marketisation on teachers and their work culture, Hatcher (1994, p. 41) perceptively notes that 'The management of the service is inseparable from the management of the workforce'. Central in this task is the headteacher whose role, relationships and practices have been subject to change as a result of government interventions. A significant aspect of this change relates to the time and energy that is being given over to questions of finance, buildings and external demands. Thus a strong separation is beginning to be established between headteachers and their staff as the former seek to engage with issues of 'corporate' image and effectiveness (Simkins, 1994).

Reinforcing the pressure on schools is a relentless barrage of criticism in which teachers have become the scapegoats for wider socioeconomic inequalities and difficulties (Phillips, 1996; OFSTED, 1996; 1998). One of the issues in a world of turbulent and continual change is the extent to which key participants such as teachers can own these developments. For Myres and Goldstein (1997) blaming schools, teachers and children for failing is a major outcome of the marketisation of education. Whilst not seeking to be complacent or lower their expectations with regard to schools and their achievements, they contend (*ibid.*, p. 117) that 'Naming schools as "failing", however, often has the effect of lowering morale and obscuring positive aspects. Public humiliation is not the best way to improve matters'. What is of crucial significance is that through a process of devolution and increasing competitiveness, the locality of blame is more clearly and sharply focused, it resides in and within the school. It is the cumulative impact of such changes which we have briefly outlined that has significantly contributed to the creation of a climate of fear, one in which low morale and anxiety within the teaching body are on the increase (Woods, 1995; Hargreaves, 1997).

Whilst the restructuring of education has been legitimated by an official rhetoric of choice, accountability and diversity, the changes have involved the significant transfer of control from the local to the central state. The outcome has been the establishment of an increasingly hierarchical and polarised system of education, in which existing inequalities between schools and in society at large have been exacerbated. Informed by market concerns a new value system and work culture have emerged within educational institutions. This has entailed the development of a new managerialism in which concerns over finance, public relations and markets are part of a more central interest, that of attempting to determine how staff think and feel about their work. In this context teachers are being significantly excluded from participating in substantive decision-making (Ball, 1997; Whitty *et al.*, 1998).

Management from this perspective is best understood not in terms of technical, skill-based procedural factors but rather as a set of relationships, a social and political process in which issues of power are central. Educational institutions like other social organisations are thus viewed 'as arenas of struggle riven with actual or potential conflict between members' (Ball, 1987, p. 19). Writing on the question of 'managerialism' Trow (1993) maintains that it takes two distinct forms, a soft and hard concept. It is the hard concept that is viewed as the major force at work in the British context and in particular that of higher education. He argues (*ibid.*, p. 3): 'The hard conception elevates institutional and system management to a dominant position in higher education; its advocates argue that higher education must be reshaped and reformed by the introduction of management systems which thus become a continuing force ensuring the steady improvement in the provision of higher education.' He continues (*ibid.*, p. 4) that one of the key reasons for this type of approach is 'the withdrawal of trust by government in the academic community, and in its capacity to critically assess its own activities and improve them'. Parallels can be drawn with the situation in schools and in further education, especially when there is evident mutual mistrust between the key participants in the change process.

Management is increasingly faced with the pressures to enhance their institutions' position in the marketplace and to intensify the drive for efficiency, effectiveness and quality outcomes. Schools, indeed all educational institutions, are to be run on a business-like footing. In a context of competition and selection, concerns over reputation and positions in the league tables mean that some children are going to lose out because they will not be seen as valuable or of the sort that schools want. Whilst there is no shortage of official rhetoric over opportunities and choice, managers now face having to make difficult and, at times, contradictory decisions (Grace, 1995; Menter *et al.*, 1997).

Viewing parents as consumers has given added support for the importance of socioeconomic factors and the cultural capital that this involves for the children concerned. Particular parents and their children will be viewed as more attractive in terms of contributing to the standing and reputation of a school. These dilemmas are vividly illustrated in the statement of a deputy head of a school that has a 'good reputation for special needs provision':

> Our intake has been very much special educational needs, difficult students – we are good at working with difficult students, we have a name for it. Now that is counter productive because if you get known out there as being good with difficult children you tend to draw difficult students. If we attract less able children our exam results are poor, our position in the league table is poor and we attract fewer able children the next year. It's that sort of downward spiral.
> (Bagley and Woods, 1998)

Apart from the deficit thinking reflected in the language describing these children, this statement illustrates the divisive, exclusionary mentalities that a market-led system of planning and provision encourages and legitimates.

Confirming this perspective, Vincent *et al.* (1996) examine the position and role of professionals in special education in a changing context. Depicting professionals as 'street-level bureaucrats' (Lipsky, 1980) they seek to identify the way in which professionals act as gatekeepers to relatively powerless groups. They maintain that by encouraging an individual deficit model, issues are depoliticised and decision-making procedures tend to be hidden. This dominant discourse has been able to offer little resistance to the influx of market-orientated values, especially those in the form of managerialism (*ibid.*, p. 486). They maintain (*ibid.*, p. 489) that within the local state 'Managerialism may help an eroded and fragmented local government system to appear to function more efficiently, but it will not, indeed, cannot penetrate below the surface to ask more fundamental questions about how best to arrange finance, and support the education

of all children'. Wider debates concerning equity, social justice, participation, citizenship are viewed as insignificant and remain largely
unaddressed.

Inclusive education

Inclusive education is not an end in itself, it is a means to an end, that
of establishing an inclusive society. Thus, the notion of inclusivity is a
radical one in that it places the welfare of *all* citizens at the centre of
consideration. It seeks to engage with the question of belonging and
solidarity, and simultaneously recognises the importance of the politics of
difference. Issues of difference and diversity are thus to be viewed in
dignified and enabling ways.

The emphasis is directed towards challenging and removing policies
and practices of exclusion. This includes the institutions and discourses
supporting such activities. In the pursuit of the removal of all disabling
barriers within a society, it is essential to establish a historical overview of
how disabling attitudes have been generated and maintained. This will
enable the focus of attention to be on those forms of discrimination that
have viewed individuals as 'other' and thus to be excluded and/or
treated as less than human.

It is essential that we recognise the significant differences between
'inclusion' and 'integration'. These are *not* interchangeable conceptions
and represent very different visions and perspectives with regard to education, society and the agenda for change.

Writing on the issue of inclusive education, Rouse and Florian (1997)
identify particular limitations of integrationist thinking. They contend
(*ibid.*, p. 325) that integration was 'too narrowly defined as placement,
without any regard to the quality of that placement' and that 'much
integration practice not only involved the relocation of pupils from special to mainstream [but] it also involved the transfer of many special
education practices'.

Criticisms of integration have also included its support of normalisa-
tion in which the emphasis was upon enabling the individual to fit into
society; that it was essentially concerned with assimilation and accommodation thereby providing a largely apolitical framework for change;
lastly, that it failed to address seriously the question and to challenge the
continuance of segregated special education (Barton and Tomlinson,
1984; Barton, 1995; Vlachou, 1997).

Inclusion is a process. Inclusive education is not merely about providing access into mainstream school for pupils who have previously been
excluded. It is not about closing down an unacceptable system of segregated provision and dumping those pupils in an unchanged mainstream
system. Existing school systems in terms of physical factors, curriculum
aspects, teaching expectations and styles, leadership roles, will have to

change. This is because inclusive education is about the participation of *all* children and young people and the removal of *all* forms of exclusionary practice.

Inclusive education is thus about responding to diversity, it is about listening to unfamiliar voices, being open and empowering all members. It is about learning to live with one another. The question of listening is a particularly important issue when applied to individuals and groups who have had their voice marginalised. So, for example, part of the criticism of disabled people has been over their lack of voice in relation to decisions affecting their lives. Thus, the importance of listening to disabled pupils is crucial. This is a demanding task particularly where there are limited forms of communication on the part of some children. But also because listening requires us not to talk. Given that teachers spend a great deal of their time talking it is not going to be an easy task. We as teachers are also poor listeners because we tend to ask questions to which we already have the answer(s). Yet the power of listening, as Ueland (1992, pp. 104–5, cited in Heyl, 1997) illustrates, is so crucial:

> Listening is a magnetic and strange thing, a creative force . . . When we are listened to, it creates us, makes us unfold and expand. Ideas actually begin to grow within us and come to life. When we listen to people, there is an alternating current, and this recharges us so that we never get tired of each other. We are constantly being re-created.

Through a sustained commitment to listening, mutual self-respect and dignity can be built up and trust established.

In a major government-supported examination of educational provisions for people with learning difficulties in post-school settings in England and Wales, the Tomlinson Report (FEFC, 1996, p. 4) seeks to challenge pathological approaches to disability and supports an approach which avoids locating 'the difficulty or deficit within the student and focus instead on the capacity of the educational institution to understand and respond to the individual learner's requirements.' Tomlinson introduces the notion of 'inclusive learning' in which the focus of attention is on how people learn and are helped to learn better.

Disabled pupils have historically experienced an insufficient match between how and what they need and want to learn and what is actually provided. Thus the report (*ibid.*, p. 33) maintains: 'Opportunities for participation, types of provision, curriculum content and delivery, assessment, accreditation and learning support do not match what these students require.' The report is quite scathing of the lack of understanding of the ways in which children learn and whilst recognising that teachers are significant in influencing how successful learning will be, it is extremely critical of those disabling assumptions that have historically influenced teacher education and practices within further education. These include (*ibid.*, pp. 32–3):

that disabled students are different from other students in the way that they learn.

that they are different in the amount they are capable of learning.

that they experience greater difficulty in learning than other students.

It is important therefore to recognise that, first, no child is ineducable and that disabled children are not less than human or an inferior species. Secondly, an individual's impairment, gender, race, sexuality and age should have no bearing on the right of a person to freedom, dignity and equity. All children are entitled to have a quality education. Thirdly, disabled children have experienced the disabling impact of low expectations and a lack of belief in their capabilities on the part of professionals including teachers. Lastly, there is an unacceptable gap between our declared commitment to the well-being of all children and the sorts of educational experiences we are providing in our schools today (FEFC, 1996).

Learning and relationships are at the heart of an inclusive project and these present us with some very challenging and fundamental questions, including:

- In what ways is inclusive education a human rights issue?
- How can schools create a welcoming environment?
- In what ways can we 'value' all pupils within school?
- What is meant by 'democratic participation' when applied to inclusive education?
- What conceptions of learning and the learner underpin practice within inclusive schools?
- What processes of evaluation can be put into place, in such a way that these serve the interests of learning rather than only – or principally – the interests of competitive credentialling? (CCE, 1995).
- How can we develop a positive view of difference and encourage community, solidarity?
- What strategies can be developed so that difference between students is recognised and catered for without excluding anybody from this entitlement? (*ibid.*).
- What does 'effectiveness' mean in relation to policy and practice?
- How are resources distributed internally within schools and why?
- What criteria will be needed to pursue and evaluate educational outputs in an inclusive setting?
- What form of management does inclusive education call for?

Underpinning these concerns is the significant question of the role of the state in the generation of inclusive policy and practice.

It is important to view such reports as Tomlinson (FEFC, 1996) and the recent green paper (DfEE, 1997) on *Excellence for all Children. Meeting Special Educational Needs* as containing a selection of ideas and interpretations and thus open to critical analysis. In relation to the issues that have been raised in this chapter, there are three reservations that need to be noted about both these very important documents. In my criticisms I will focus on the Tomlinson Report because it may well be the least familiar to the readers.

The first issue concerns the definition of disability within the report. Whilst there is clear evidence of an awareness of deficit approaches to disability, the report also raises criticisms about low expectations on the part of teachers and the limited, and in some cases, no opportunities of access into further education. However, there is no serious discussion about disability as discrimination and oppression. Part of this inadequacy is the result of a failure to address these issues in terms of a human rights approach. In this instance, the committee has not reflected the insights to be gained from the extensive publications by disabled people in the academic press as well as their own local coalition outlets dealing with this question.

A second issue is that of a questionable notion of 'inclusion'. For the report (FEFC, 1996, p. 5), there is an acceptance that provision will 'Sometimes . . . be a mixture of the integrated and the discrete. And sometimes, as in the specialist residential colleges, it will be discrete provision. We envisage a system that is inclusive and that will require many mansions'. Inclusion from this perspective involves allowing all forms of provision, including segregated, to exist in a well co-ordinated system. This is a very different view from those, for example, of the British Organisation of Disabled People, who maintain that inclusion is about eradicating all those previous forms of exclusionary policy and practice including segregated special education.

The last issue concerns the failure of the report to identify adequately and challenge critically those forms of policy and practice inspired by government interventions, which are *simultaneously occurring*, but which will significantly inhibit and frustrate the realisation of many of the recommendations of this report. It is a marked feature of the contradictory nature of policy developments that the FEFC should support a report of this nature, and at one and the same time be legitimating extensive changes that are in clear opposition to the idea of 'inclusive learning'. These include introducing a new funding formula with emphasis on value for money as a criterion of course provision, curriculum and development; the increasing emphasis on individualistic assessment-led learning; the establishment of a strong competitive feature of institutional life both within and across organisations; and a form of managerialism that is in stark contrast to the notion of an 'inclusive manager'.

The question of an inclusive society raises some of the most fundamental issues we can engage with. They ask us to consider what sort of a society we want, what is unacceptable about the present society we live in and what is the role of education in this process of change. It is imperative therefore that we seek to debate and dialogue with others over these serious concerns. In this context we must not confuse consultation with debate. The former is an increasingly powerful vehicle for social control.

Conclusion

In this chapter a principle has informed the analysis, which is the conviction that exposing the roots of discrimination and disabling barriers is a precondition to finding ways for their removal and our empowerment.

We have argued in this chapter that the ultimate objective is the realisation of an inclusive society of which education is a part. It is crucial in a society in which there is a relentless endeavour to create more efficient forms of production and control that we recognise and act upon the insights derived from the perspective so forcefully articulated by Brown and Lauder (1992, pp. 5–6), in which they maintain:

> The appeal to economic imperative as a rationale for educational reform should not obscure the fact that educational questions are *always social questions*, which invariably involve winners and losers. It is also important to note that decisions concerning the structure and content of education and training programmes are never simply technologically determined, but always involve a choice between alternative policies.

Historically mass schooling, as Brown and Lauder contend, has been influenced by a variety of competing interests and perspectives in relation to its purpose. Debate and dialogue over such matters need to be encouraged in an open and enabling context.

The sorts of changes that the creation of an inclusive society and educational system necessitates is not within the power of a single, charismatic visionary leader or headteacher. We are not advocating the necessity of a supra-human person. Nor can schools alone effectively engage with these demands. They need the support of government, parents, the community and the pupils.

Managing a school or institution on the basis of a commitment towards establishing a process of inclusion will involve several demands on the part of all the participants. First, they will need to be clear that the fundamental issues facing the school or department or institution are not mainly resource or technical issues, but rather, values and social questions. Why particular choices are made and on what basis will be the sort of questions that an open democratic management style will need to encourage. Secondly, they will need to recognise that they are all learners in this process, that they do not have all the answers, that they will need support and that they will make mistakes. Thirdly, they need to view conflict as an integral part of the change process and that finding ways of constructively engaging with such factors will be essential. Fourthly, they will need to support the centrality of staff development for all within the school which will require them to develop a clear, carefully planned, well resourced and monitored staff development policy. Without this no effective and lasting inclusive development will take place. Fifthly, managing for inclusion will involve a vision in which the 'good of the whole' will be viewed as an antidote to the excessive individualism of a system based on exclusionary mentalities. Re-examining the meaning and value of 'collaboration' and 'support' will be essential elements in the learning process of all the participants. Sixthly, ways of relating to all pupils in terms of high expectations and the nature of social interactions will be a perennial concern of the management of an inclusive practice. Lastly, making effective links with other schools and institutions will be essential in the struggle for community, sharing and solidarity.

These suggestions are not in any order of priority, nor is any claim being made that these are exhaustive of all the issues involved. What is being advocated is that given the stubbornness of the disabling barriers including the contradictory nature of government policies and the degree of political will to support such changes, there is absolutely no room for complacency. The well-being of *all* citizens is at stake.

Suggested further reading

Avis, J. (1996) The enemy within: quality and managerialism in education, in Avis, J., Bloomer, M., Esland, G., Gleeson, D. and Hodgkinson, P. (eds) *Knowledge and Nationhood*, Cassell, London.
Harber, C. and Davies, L. (1998) *School Management and Effectiveness in Developing Countries*, Cassell, London.
Oliver, M. and Barnes, C. (1998) *Disabled People and Social Policy: From Exclusion to Inclusion*, Longmans, London.

References

Angus, L. (1994) Sociological analysis and education management: the social context of the self-managing school, *British Journal of Sociology of Education*, Vol. 15, no. 1, pp. 79–92.
Bagley, C. and Woods, P. (1998) School choice, markets and special educational needs, *Disability and Society* (forthcoming).
Ball, S. (1987) *The Micro-Politics of the School. Towards a Theory of School Organisation*, Methuen, London.
Ball, S. (1997) Policy, sociology and critical social research: a personal review of recent educational policy and policy research, *British Educational Research Journal*, Vol. 23, no. 3, pp. 257–74.
Barton, L. (1995) Segregated special education: some critical observations, in Zarb, G. (ed) *Removing Disabling Barriers*, Policy Studies Institute, London.
Barton, L. and Tomlinson, S. (1984) The politics of integration in England, in Barton, L. and Tomlinson, S. (eds) *Special Education and Social Interests*, Croom Helm, London.
Brown, P. and Lauder, H. (eds) (1992) *Education for Economic Survival. From Fordism to Post-Fordism?*, Routledge, London.
Coleridge, F. (1993) *Disability, Liberation and Development*, Oxfam Publications, Oxford.

Consultative Committee on Education (CCE) (1995) *Tomlinson's Schools: Developing Effective Learning Cultures*, CCE, Malta.

Dale, R. (1997) Educational markets and social closures, *British Journal of Sociology of Education*, Vol. 18, no. 3, pp. 451–68.

DfEE (1997) *Excellence for all Children. Meeting Special Educational Needs*, HMSO, London.

FEFC (1996) *Inclusive Learning. Report of the Learning Difficulties and/or Disabilities Committee (the Tomlinson Report)*, FEFC, Coventry.

Grace, G. (1995) *School Leadership: Beyond Education Management*, Falmer Press, London.

Hargreaves, A. (1997) Rethinking educational change: going deeper and wider in the quest for success, in Hargreaves, A. (ed) *Rethinking Educational Change with Heart and Mind*, Association for Supervision and Curriculum Development, Vancouver.

Hatcher, R. (1994) Market relationships and the management of teachers, *British Journal of Sociology of Education*, Vol. 15, no. 1, pp. 41–62.

Henig, J.R. (1994) *Rethinking School Choice. Limits of the Market Metaphor*, Princeton University Press, Princeton, NJ.

Hevey, D. (1992) *The Creatures Time Forgot: Photography and Disability Imagery*, Routledge, London.

Heyl, B. (1997) Talking across the differences in collaborative fieldwork: unanticipated consequences, *The Sociological Quarterly*, Vol. 38, no. 1, pp. 1–18.

Le Grand, J. and Bartlett, W. (eds) (1993) *Quasi-Markets and Social Policy*, Macmillan, London.

Lipsky, M. (1980) *Street-Level Bureaucrats*, Russell Sage, New York.

McDonnell, P. (1999) *Integration in Education in Ireland: Rhetoric and Reality* (forthcoming).

Menter, I., Muschamp, Y., Nicholls, P., Ozga, J. and Pollard, A. (1997) *Work and Identity in the Primary School: A Post-Fordist Analysis*, Open University Press, Buckingham.

Mooney, T. (1997) Judge for yourself who should be named and shamed, *The Independent*, 9 October, p. 4 (education section).

Myres, K. and Goldstein, H. (1997) Failing schools or failing systems?, in Hargreaves, A. (ed) *Rethinking Educational Change with Heart and Mind*, Association for Supervision and Curriculum Development, Vancouver.

OFSTED (1996) *The Annual Report of Her Majesty's Chief Inspector of Schools*, HMSO, London.

OFSTED (1998) *The Annual Report of Her Majesty's Chief Inspector of Schools*, HMSO, London.

Oliver, M. (1996) A sociology of disability or a disablist sociology?, in Barton, L. (ed) *Disability and Society: Emerging Issues and Insights*, Addison, Wesley Longman, Harlow.

Phillips, M. (1996) *All Must have Prizes*, Little, Brown, London.

Rouse, M. and Florian, L. (1997) Inclusive education in the market place, *International Journal of Inclusive Education*, Vol. 1, no. 4, pp. 323–36.

Simkins, T. (1994) Efficiency, effectiveness and the local management of schools, *Journal of Education Policy*, Vol. 9, no. 1, pp. 15–33.

Skrtic, T. (1991) *Behind Special Education. A Cultural Analysis of Professional Culture and School Organization*, Love Publishing, Denver, CO.

Tomlinson, S. (1982) *A Sociology of Special Education*, Routledge and Kegan Paul, London.

Trow, M. (1993) Managerialism and the academic profession: the case of England, in *Studies of Higher Education and Research*, Council for Studies of Higher Education, Stockholm.

Vincent, C., Evans, J., Lunt, I. and Young, P. (1996) Professionals under pressure: the administration of special education in a changing context, *British Educational Research Journal*, Vol. 22, no. 4, pp. 475–91.

Vlachou, A. (1997) *Struggles for Inclusive Education. An Ethnographic Study*, Open University Press, Buckingham.

Whitty, G. (1997) School autonomy and parental choice: consumer rights versus citizen rights in education policy in Britain, in Bridges, D. (ed) *Education, Autonomy and Democratic Citizenship. Philosophy in a Changing World*, Routledge, London.

Whitty, G., Power, S, and Halpin, D. (1998) *Devolution and Choice in Education. The School, the State and the Market*, Open University Press, Buckingham.

Woods, P. (1995) *Creative Teachers in Primary Schools*, Open University Press, Buckingham.

Section 2

... to experience

7

Included From the Start? Managing Early Years Settings For All

ELAINE HERBERT

The LEA early intervention service

The early intervention home-visiting service, referred to in this chapter, subscribes to the Warnock philosophy of 'parents as first educators' of their children. This service, like many others in the UK, was set up in 1983 as a direct consequence of the Education Act 1981. Preschool children with a wide variety of developmental delays are referred to the service by professional or voluntary agencies or by parents themselves. Work with parents and their children takes place in their own home setting, the 'place where the child and family feel comfortable' (DfEE, 1994, para. 5:2) and involves devising activities in conjunction with members of the family to enhance the skills of both parents and children and to make assessment over time of the child's educational needs. Work with children builds on the crucial role of the adult. Thus adults who are well tuned into the child they are working with can bridge the gap (zone of proximal development) between what a child can do today in co-operation and what he or she might do alone in the future (Vygotsky, 1978). Careful records of the child's progress are maintained, evaluated and shared with parents. These assessments not only depend on information gathered in a one-to-one setting but also information from preschool group settings, such as playgroups and nurseries.

As the relationship with the family develops the sphere of reference broadens to encompass a recognition and acceptance of the families' concerns and aspirations for their children (Rouse and Griffin, 1992;

Carpenter, 1994). When the children enter their reception year the service ceases its involvement so the length of the involvement is dependent upon the age at which the child is referred. In the LEA, 84% of all children attend local nurseries on a part-time basis during the academic year in which they become four and they all enter reception classes in the September prior to their fifth birthday. For some children and their families, this involvement with the service may be for more than four years, for some it may be for less than two terms.

Early years and SEN

About this chapter

This chapter aims to address the issues and practicalities of the inclusion of young children with SEN in mainstream settings. Much has been written about the positive effects of including young children with SEN within mainstream classrooms (Barton, 1997; Lloyd, 1997). However, whilst many practitioners articulate their belief in 'inclusion', their practice serves to segregate and exclude.

This chapter identifies the role of professionals as managers/initiators and the need for a philosophy and ethos coming from senior management in order that practitioners at the point of contact with the children are supported by the surrounding network (Bronfenbrenner, 1979). In order to explore the issues in the early identification and assessment of young children, this chapter will look in depth at a case study of one child and reflect on the issues it raises. This individual 'story' highlights many of the issues relating to young children with SEN and their families.

It will focus on the issues of

- early identification
- medical diagnosis
- prediction of need
- role of the professional
- interagency collaboration
- partnership with parents and carers
- support and training of staff
- the nature of assessment
- differing forms of provision.

Early years and the Code of Practice for Identification and Assessment of Special Educational Needs

Being precise about what constitutes 'early years' is problematic as there is no single or official definition. Swann and Gammage (1993) contend there is no precise definition for the term but feel that there is increasing agreement that it encompasses ages 0–9. David (1995) points out that the

Children Act contains provision for children from birth to 8. For practitioners in schools, the term seems to refer to 3–7-year-old children; the time which is thought of as the 'infant years' and ends with Key Stage 1 assessment. For early intervention services, it may mean 0–5. For the purpose of this chapter the term 'early years' will relate to *the time from birth to 7 – the end of Key Stage 1 assessment* – the time which often marks the change from 'infants' to 'juniors'.

Special educational needs

Whilst it is difficult to define 'early years', 'special educational needs' in the context of 'early years' is even more troublesome. The recent green paper (DfEE, 1997, p. 12) acknowledges that 'the term "special educational needs" can be misleading and lead to unhelpful assumptions. It may suggest that children with special educational needs are a readily defined group, with common characteristics'. The *Code of Practice* (DfEE, 1994, p. 99) recognises that 'significant changes can take place in the progress of a child under five' and professionals who work alongside young children with possible SEN would give support to this statement. In this chapter, the definition will refer to a child for whom concerns were registered before his second birthday and for whom the LEA determined special educational provision.

The *Code of Practice* and under 5s

Section 5 of the *Code of Practice* (DfEE, 1994) deals specifically with the under 5s giving guidance for the 'assessments and statements for under fives'. The *Code of Practice* (*ibid.*, para. 5:1) recommends that LEAs should build upon the 'well established network of relationships and services' – social services, district health authorities, NHS trusts, family health authorities and the voluntary sector are named. The green paper (DfEE, 1997, p. 13) goes further in advocating an 'integrated approach . . . right from the start.' (p.13).

The *Code of Practice* (DfEE, 1994, para. 5:4) also states that when 'a child under two is referred to the LEA, it is probable that any special needs will have been identified by his or her parents, the child health services or social services'. During a child's first three years community health visitors often play a major role within families. This is particularly the case when there is concern about a child's development. The focus of health visitors' work is illness prevention, health promotion, identification of difficulties and liaison with other agencies. Their involvement begins when a baby is 21 days old – a reason why the majority of referrals for involvement by an early intervention team come from health visitors.

The *Code of Practice* (*ibid.*) also states that if a child is referred for assessment before the age of 2, he or she 'is likely to have a particular condition or to have a major health problem which has caused concern at an early stage'. Whilst this may be the situation in some referrals, 'general global delay' is often registered as the concern. This could now be expressed in the less offensive phrase from the green paper (DfEE, 1997), 'early signs of difficulties'.

As children grow older and begin to attend different forms of provision, 'all services providing for young children, such as playgroups and day care facilities or other provision run by social services, child health services or voluntary organisations should have information from the LEA on local procedures for the identification of special educational needs' (DfEE, 1994, para. 5:12, p. 101) This has been strengthened by the requirements of the Nursery Education and Grant Maintained Schools Act 1996, which ensures that if settings receive funding for 4-year-old children they must pay due regard to the Code. They cannot ignore it. Among other requirements, they must publish policies on their provision for children with SEN and ensure staff have the knowledge, skills and training to take early and appropriate action to meet special educational needs (DfEE, 1996). With the consent of parents (DfEE, 1994, para. 5:12–13) personnel from preschool settings also make referrals to early intervention services.

A case: the story of Steven

Steven was born prematurely, the second child of a long-term stable partnership. Initially his low birth weight and poor muscle tone caused concern among the medical personnel involved with the family. However, no medical diagnosis or intervention was offered and the family was assured by the family doctor that he would 'catch up after a poor start'.

The family's health visitor had made frequent visits to the family in order to maintain her overview of Steven's development. She was conscious of his 'hypotonia [floppy muscles], his sleepiness and his feeding difficulties' (notes received on the referral form). At the age of 10 months, with the family's permission, she referred Steven to the local early intervention home-visiting service, expressing her concern about his 'delayed global development and the family's wish for advice with activities to help with his development'. She also made similar referrals to the paediatric community physiotherapy service and the speech therapist. Whilst the family agreed to these referrals, they also served to increase their concern about the extent of Steven's difficulties and his future development.

Managing the early intervention
As a teacher on the early intervention team, I worked closely with Steven and his family on a weekly basis identifying learning objectives and planning a wide range of activities to reach these goals. Our partnership was both rewarding and stimulating as Steven's parents not only

extended suggestions I made but also devised their own activities tailored to coincide with his current interests. Through their involvement and observation they were able to use his strengths to overcome many of his difficulties. For example, at the time when Steven was learning to thread a length of clothes-line through tubing – not a favourite or easily achieved task for him as he experienced difficulties with manipulative skills – his parents had also observed that he was interested in digging for and finding worms in the garden. The difficulty with the threading sequence was overcome by using an uncooked piece of cannelloni being presented as a worm's house and the 'wiggly worm' clothes-line crawling through! The teaching notes indicate that his progress was good and he was responding to 'an informal play approach'.

The physiotherapist and speech therapist also visited the home working directly with Steven, giving advice to his family about continuing and extending the exercises between their visits. They realised that their suggestions were more specific than mine, focusing more precisely on particular areas of his development. Each of the professionals involved was aware that too much could be thrust upon the parents and it may interfere with the family dynamics (Carpenter and Herbert, 1997). Liaison proved difficult for the four different services providing support and advice. Some of the difficulties arose from the practical issues of location, making and maintaining ongoing contact with differing working hours; some from the deeper issues of service philosophy and management structures with differing perceptions of client needs and models of interaction. The personnel involved recognised these differences and in order to overcome them, regular but informal meetings were held in the family's home when the involvement was reviewed and changes were made in the light of the information gathered. Liaison was maintained and a plan was devised with the family with the aim of incorporating most of the activities into everyday life.

Medical diagnosis

At the age of 2, Steven was mobile, was making his needs known with single words, making his own choices and beginning to complete many tasks independently. During a routine visit to the hospital, the paediatrician, who had overseen his development since birth, suggested to Steven's parents that there may be a medical diagnosis for his poor muscle tone – he may have 'Praeder Willi syndrome'. This was a term they had never heard before and it frightened them. It was described to them by the paediatrician as 'a chromosomal disorder which results in obesity arising from obsession with food accompanied with a developmental delay' (information given by parents). Steven's physiotherapist was present during the diagnosis and it was at this point that she expressed her feelings that Steven may benefit from a 'more protected environment where he could receive a higher level of adult support'.

The immediate effect of this news and advice was that, despite their experiences with and involvement in his learning, the family's perception of his abilities and their plans for his preschool experiences changed significantly. They felt he may never achieve their hopes for him and that they should accept his limitations. For some time after, despite the reassurances of both the teacher and the speech therapist, they could only focus on his weaknesses. As a consequence of the medical diagnosis, the family decided Steven should attend a playgroup for children with SEN where they believed he would receive appropriate support for his needs and be within a sheltered environment.

Managing in preschool provision – playgroups
On four mornings of each week, Steven was collected and returned by minibus as this playgroup was outside his immediate neighbourhood and some three miles from his home. Little communication between parents and carers at the playgroup took place; mostly short verbal messages summarising his activities were given when he was 'dropped off'. Steven's parents made no contact with the parents of the other children either at the group or locally and this increased their feelings of isolation and difference within their community. Whilst Steven's mother maintained the friendships she had made with her older child, she made few contacts with Steven. Occasionally the family was able to make special arrangements to accompany him to the playgroup but they felt this was not encouraged by the staff. This was viewed as their time for respite. Sometimes they were grateful for this time, but often they would have liked the opportunity to participate, meet his friends and make contacts with other parents.

In the playgroup setting, he experienced high levels of adult:child interaction, often 1:1. My own observations were that his interactions with his peer group were limited as most of the other children attended irregularly and many were non-ambulant with little speech. The volunteers who staffed the playgroup were caring and motivated but untrained and the personnel changed each day. As a result, despite the good intentions of the helpers and my attempts to initiate change, no consistency of approach or expectation was achieved. There was a 'sympathetic acceptance of low achievement' (DfEE, 1997, p. 4). Steven soon learnt how to differentiate between the altering expectations and that he could get his own way.

Managing transition into mainstream settings
As with all other children within the LEA, Steven became eligible for a part-time place at one of the borough's nursery classes during his third year. Within each nursery the staffing ratio was one adult to ten children and at least one of the adults in the nursery was a qualified teacher.

The family already had experience of the local infants' school as their older child had attended. This school had a nursery class. Discussions with the family took place over a period of time about the advantages of being with a consistent peer group and the possibility of making an application to this neighbourhood nursery. Whilst the parents recognised the need for Steven to interact with a language-rich and physically active group, they were also apprehensive about how others would receive him and about the possibility that he may fail and be rejected by the school and community. At such a crucial time, it is the policy and practice of the early intervention home-visiting service not to put pressure upon the family, accepting that it is their right to make the decisions (DfEE, 1997). Close dialogue was continued with the other professionals in order that the parents were supported and did not receive conflicting or confusing advice. At this point there was no disagreement between any of the professionals as they all recognised that Steven needed the opportunity to function within a larger and less 'protected' group.

Steven's developing skills coupled with his increasing independence resulted in the parents' decision that a nursery place would be to his advantage and so they applied. They also included background medical information which they hoped would help the school in their decision and encourage them to accept him.

In preparation for this transition, the family was encouraged to allow Steven to attend a local playgroup for two sessions each week. The choice of group was made with the help of the children's department of the social services who suggested a local group known to have a positive attitude towards all children whatever their degree of difficulty. At the same time, Steven spent two sessions a week at the playgroup for children with special needs as his parents were still apprehensive and looked upon this as a 'safety net'. The professional felt that the lack of consistency in this dual provision was a difficulty but the parents' decision was respected.

The transition plan was achieving some success, Steven made progress in the community playgroup, became less dependent on the adult helpers, increased his social interaction with his peers and, above all, he loved being there – an obvious delight to his family.

Response of the school to the application

Upon receiving the application, the school's headteacher did three things:

1) Contacted me as the early intervention teacher – I reassured her that Steven was making progress in all areas of his development, was adjusting to the adult:child ratio in the local playgroup and would benefit from consistent contact with both adults and children possible at the nursery.
2) Made a brief visit to the 'special' playgroup where she and the nursery teacher observed Steven for half an hour, and talked to the staff – one of whom expressed her 'amazement' that the family was even considering sending him to nursery.

3) Visited the local library and looked up the syndrome in a medical dictionary, where she read that feeding difficulties associated with Praeder Willi syndrome usually arise between the ages of 2 and 4.

The net effect of these activities resulted in the parents' application being refused. The main reason cited was that the information about his 'condition' would mean the nursery teacher would have to 'change all routines to accommodate his voracious appetite and this would mean staff could never let him out of their sight and this would be to the detriment of the other children in the group'.

Lengthy discussions took place with the headteacher when the professionals involved explained that the nursery setting would enable Steven to access a curriculum considered developmentally appropriate for pre-school children resulting in a more realistic assessment being made of his educational needs (Herbert and Moir, 1996; David *et al.*, 1997). They also pointed out that the concerns they had registered were not apparent in the community playgroup and that advice and support both at home and in the nursery would continue. However, they were not prepared to reconsider their decision and the application was refused. The head-teacher felt that neither she nor her nursery teacher was adequately trained to help Steven. The professionals supporting the family felt the injustice of the decision but also recognised that if they challenged the decision, the prevailing attitude within the school would segregate and exclude Steven rather than include him (Barton, 1997).

The parents were 'devastated' with this rejection and felt 'bitterness' (parents' words) that in their openness they had shared information about Steven with the school which had resulted in him being rejected. Because of the close relationship the parents had with the services already involved, they were supported and encouraged to visit another nursery, one known to have a commitment by head, staff and community to equal opportunities for all their children. Due to the partnership developed with this school over a period of time, I was able with the parents' permission to share sensitive information with the headteacher, knowing that this would be used in a totally respectful way and would be accepted as in the best interest of the child.

During the family's first visit, the headteacher made time to sit and discuss the parents' concerns with them. She made it clear that she valued them as equal partners and did not belittle their anxieties. Much of the parents' apprehension was dispelled upon meeting the head and nursery staff – their positive attitude towards all children was obvious to the parents. The family made a further two visits to the nursery prior to Steven's entry in the September and this enabled them to approach the year with growing confidence. The nursery teacher also made a visit to Steven's home, as part of her normal practice of getting to know all the families and children before they enter her class.

Managing the nursery year

Steven entered the nursery with 29 other children. Initially he found many of the expectations of both the adults and children difficult. When individual attention was not given or when his wishes were not attended to quickly, he would throw himself on the floor and protest loudly. This behaviour was managed in the same way as would any inappropriate behaviour by any of the children. It did not become the focus of his difficulties. A large part of the nursery curriculum was devoted to enabling children to learn to accommodate to each other in their play and to accept adult attention as a group member. Steven too was encouraged to accept these limits on his behaviour. Collaboration between all the external support staff, nursery staff and Steven's parents enabled a consistency of approach and attitude both at home and at school.

One of the other children who joined the nursery at the same time as Steven was Carl. Carl presented as an earnest and articulate little boy who did not find the boisterous play of many of his peers easy to accommodate. Within the first term, Steven and Carl developed a friendship. Steven appeared to recognise and relate to Carl's mature, managing and articulate persona and Carl gained great self-esteem from finding himself able to act as Steven's special friend, guide and mentor.

Initially Steven was able to use 'tried and tested' play areas (sand at home, sand at nursery). Carl began to invite (perhaps order!) Steven to accompany him around the nursery. Thus both children were enabled to explore and experience all areas of the nursery curriculum to their mutual benefit. Although their friendship began as an exclusive one, gradually the confidence each gained through the support and companionship of the other enabled them slowly to include others in their play which eventually led to the acquisition of wide friendship circles amongst their peers (Herbert and Moir, 1996).

Steven did learn to wait his turn, to share his toys and co-operate with a given task or activity when his personal preference may have been in a different direction. The success was reflected in the formal report presented by the nursery teacher in the third term of his nursery year in request by all parties concerned for a statutory assessment of his educational needs:

> In terms of his social integration, Steven requires and is given no more individual attention than any other child in the nursery. It is felt that his high level of social integration and the good use Steven makes of this positive peer group should be taken into consideration when deciding any future placement.
>
> (Nursery teacher)

During this nursery year, I began gradually to reduce my intense involvement with the family and Steven in their home, recognising that the focus of his development had transferred to the school. The aim of early intervention must also be to empower parents and not to encourage or increase their dependence on professionals who work closely with them. The additional attention so often needed for a child with SEN can be problematic for a teacher who may have thirty other families to support simultaneously. Steven's nursery teacher made sure there was a constant exchange of information between home and school to support his learning either through direct contact or via the home–school book which they developed.

During the year Steven's parents spent time in the nursery where observations were shared, discussed and assimilated and they were, like other parents, given the opportunity to make relationships within the school. Whilst Steven had made good progress in the favourable adult to child ratio within the nursery, it was necessary to take into account that this would change in the reception class when he would become one of 26 children with one teacher. They were conscious not only of this changing adult:child ratio but also of the changes within the curriculum when he entered statutory education.

As the result of the information gathered from the ongoing assessment, both in the one-to-one setting at home and in the group setting at the nursery, Steven's current learning needs were identified. It was acknowledged by all concerned that in order to meet his needs he would require extra support for parts of the curriculum when he transferred to the reception year.

An educational review meeting was arranged when all the people who currently worked with the family were asked to draw up written reports on his progress. The presentation of reports at this meeting was only a summary of previous discussions. The family approached the meeting as fully informed and powerful participants, presenting their own report which accentuated their equivalent if different expertise (Wolfendale, 1989). Despite their knowledge both about the school and Steven's learning needs, there was no doubt that his parents approached this particular meeting with great anxiety. The outcome of the meeting was a unanimous decision that a referral for statutory assessment should be made to the education department.

As a result of the statutory assessment, a statement of special needs was drawn up which recommended that Steven should continue his schooling alongside his peers in the reception class with additional adult support. He was allocated a support assistant for two hours of each day to help with the development of his fine motor and his literacy and numeracy skills – areas identified within the assessment as requiring extra help.

Steven moved on with 25 of his peers from the nursery into the reception class in the September and the involvement of the early intervention service ceased.

The reception class
This was the first time in her short career that Steven's reception class teacher had had a child with a statement in her class. She was conscious that by choosing the inclusive option Steven's parents had accepted that

he needed to interact with his peer group and not become, once more, dependent upon adults. She was reassured by the head that it was not a scenario of success or failure and was given support to evaluate her own practice in a way which led her to believe that her established skills of providing a well structured and stimulating learning environment for all children were particularly relevant for Steven. She realised that it was her duty to attend not only to what was 'special' about Steven but also to what was 'ordinary' and that there was no mystique to analysing tasks. She was already doing this and making them accessible to all children, including children with learning difficulties.

This was also this particular teacher's first experience of working closely with another adult in her classroom. She realised that the support she and the assistant offered Steven should be managed in such a way that it neither interfered with group interaction nor prevented independent learning. They also felt that their expectations of Steven should be high and their approach should be consistent.

With the support of the headteacher, the special educational needs co-ordinator (SENCO) and the nursery teacher, Steven's teacher grew in confidence for although she identified and articulated that she would have high expectations for him, in practice these were not realised. She had to be reminded and supported when she felt that it was 'kind' not to expect too much when he had already demonstrated that he was capable of responding to identified targets. Surprisingly Steven's parents commented to the head on the teacher's growing confidence for they had been aware of her apprehension – an example of their confidence in the school to manage change.

During this time, Steven made progress with his 'academic' work and developed independence and self-confidence, forging friendships with a widening group of his peers.

Steven continued to receive both speech and physiotherapy at the local clinic. During this year, the consultant paediatrician informed the parents that his 'initial diagnosis may have been incorrect'. Steven's progress was not 'what he had expected'. The parents could not decide whether to be angry with the initial information – which they recognised had influenced many factors including their decisions about his preschool placement – or to be relieved.

At the end of his reception year, at his annual review it was recommended that Steven should move in to Year 1 with the same level of support.

Managing Year 1
The organisation of staff within the school ensured that Steven's class moved on to a strong and very able teacher, who had experience in diverse settings and of working with a wide variety of children with special needs. The combination of close liaison with the reception teacher,

the continuity of the classroom support worker and the confidence of the Year 1 teacher all worked together to ensure Steven's ongoing progress. The expectations within this class were consistently high, not only for Steven but for all the children. He responded accordingly. His work was carefully planned and differentiated where necessary with identifiable and achievable targets. Whilst his fine motor skills and number work continued to need and receive support, he had developed a growing interest and ability in reading. He was now among the more able readers in his class. There was no longer 'global delay' but Steven's learning difficulties were clearly identified and being addressed.

Information continued to be exchanged between home and school, although Steven was able to transfer much of this himself. In addition the teacher ensured that she maintained her own dialogue with the family, through informal contact and at the more formal parents' meetings and at the annual review.

Managing Year 2
Steven moved on to Year 2. His fine motor skills and his number work continued to need support and differentiation. The school and Steven's parents appreciated that the transition from infant to junior school may present difficulties but knew that they could not predict what these might be. They felt that he would continue to need the level of support currently in place but the changing curriculum may or may not present further difficulties. Ongoing communication and honesty ensured that the parents were active partners within the process. After their initial experiences they said they felt able to 'act positively and take risks' in Steven's best interests.

Steven's Key Stage 1 assessment results pleased not only his parents but also all the professionals who had been involved with him since his birth.

In the four years during which Steven was at the infant school, several other children with SEN had been included in its community with similar success. The school acknowledged that the community as a whole was enriched, giving opportunities for friendships to develop between children with a diversity of needs.

Discussion

Early identification and intervention

The *Code of Practice* emphasises at all points the necessity for the early identification of children with special needs. The purpose of any 'identification' should be 'intervention' which aims to accelerate the development of children. However, this 'identification' can also lead us to stress what is special and different about a child's development, forgetting 'ordinary' needs.

Any early intervention service, no matter in which setting it works, should have the family at its centre, seeing the child in the context of his or her environment, for children do not develop in isolation but are always in interaction with their surroundings (Gallimore *et al.*, 1989). We should never forget that whilst parents are 'the first educators of their children' they are first and foremost 'parents'.

Professionals must develop partnership with each family, built on a relationship of trust and respect for them and their child, recognising their equivalent if differing expertise and promoting a shared sense of purpose (Bastiani, 1989; Pugh and De'Ath, 1989; Wolfendale, 1989). This cannot be achieved in a short period of time but needs to be 'like a garden, constantly attended to and renewed' (Madden, 1994).

Steven's family were able to incorporate the activities into their every-day happenings (Ferguson and Mayer, 1991) but for some parents this will be more difficult and for many neither possible nor desirable. The ethos within any early intervention service should promote positive, not judgemental attitudes towards parents, accepting and working with the family *as it is*.

Activity 7.1

The green paper purports that the best way to tackle educational disadvantage is 'to get in early'. However, one concern which is often articulated by staff from early intervention teams – and was a factor in Steven's story – is whether this early identification may serve to accentuate the differences and that these may then be used to ex-clude rather than include children. Draw up two lists of five points, identifying the positive and negative effects of early identification.

How will the introduction of baseline assessment at 5 affect chil-dren with early learning difficulties? Will the findings help or work against them?

Whilst there is a wealth of innovative practice, the effects of early intervention have, as yet, not been systematically and extensively evalu-ated within the UK. However, there appears to be an agreement amongst professionals working in the field that parents who have been involved with such services have a clearer understanding of their children's style and rate of learning and have a more positive approach when provision is considered. Nevertheless, we have also seen from Steven's case study the negative effects of early identification and 'labelling' not only on Steven's family but also on professionals.

Medical diagnosis and resultant prediction

Despite the information about the progress in his development, Steven's parents and some professionals reacted to the diagnosis. Praeder Willi syndrome meant nothing to the parents but it disrupted their ability to anticipate his development. Also, society continues to perpetuate stereotypes and the grouping under labels 'encourages a false homogeneity in the perceptions of people' (Lewis, 1995). The first school's response was based on a snapshot assessment and limited information which may have been applicable to some children but was not evident with Steven.

Divisions in attitude among professionals can emerge with their differing approaches to the 'client' needs. Whilst health therapists appear to focus on areas of difficulties (the medical model), educationalists have a more holistic view of development (the social model). With Steven, this ensured that his 'treatment' did not become the focus of his intervention.

With young children, parents' experience of the education system may be limited and their reaction to the news that their child may have 'special needs' may be similar to Steven's parents' response to the medical label. Research has shown that parents value honesty from those associated with their children, but this must be based on measured information not on ill-informed prediction and incomplete data (Cunningham and Davis, 1985; Dale, 1996).

Alongside the issue of labelling and its effect on people is the other factor surrounding the status of the 'newsgiver'. Steven's parents and the first school adopted an unchallenging attitude towards the news given by the paediatrician who was seen as an expert. Whilst the paediatrician has been identified as the 'expert' within this study, information from other professionals can generate doubts about the value of our own information and knowledge.

Activity 7.2

A perceived imbalance of status can exist between professionals, often from the same discipline. What skills do we need to develop in our interactions to ensure that injustices are removed? Brainstorm ten suggestions, then rearrange them in the order of importance for you.

Interagency collaboration

The Children Act 1989, the *Code of Practice* (DfEE, 1994) and the green paper (DfEE, 1997) all reinforce the aim for services working with under 5s and their families to work together. Changes in the funding arrangements for 4-year-old children have meant that agencies have worked together to develop early years plans.

Families with preschool children encounter a range of professionals from different agencies. All those responsible for early childhood programmes profess to having issues of quality provision for families at the top of the agenda. However, constructive interagency work is difficult to achieve, as each organisation has its own culture, values, methods of training, staffing, language, aims, priorities, working hours and accommodation. These differences can combine to work against the needs of families. There is a tendency to guard territory and expertise. When families work with a wide range of professionals they may develop a close relationship with one of them and this person should be seen as the 'key' worker for that family, taking the role of co-ordinator and facilitator. However, this person needs to develop a sensitivity to the changing needs of families and that this may involve giving up 'territory' and transferring this role to a more appropriate individual or agency.

Professionals should also recognise that whilst they are there to offer support, their presence may also reinforce 'differences'. It is important that through intervention and support, families are enabled and empowered to make their own decisions and do not become increasingly dependent upon professionals.

Communication (either by telephone, letter or in person) and the development of good relationships take time and become increasingly difficult in a climate of purchaser–provider contracts. Steven's placements in both the community playgroup and the receiving school were the result of local knowledge and networks.

Networking and liaison take time to develop and can be affected by changes in personnel at all levels within the local structure. Unless such contacts are valued by managers, opportunities will be lost.

Contacts with parents

Throughout the case study it is possible to identify several styles of working and interacting with parents, ranging from the 'expert' to the 'consumer'. These differing ways of interacting with parents are clearly described and elaborated in Cunningham and Davis (1985), Hornby (1995) and Dale (1996). Within an early intervention service it is possible to respond to individual families and to develop close relationships. This is more difficult for schools to achieve with the pressures from the National Curriculum, and standard tests and tasks at Key Stage 1. Parents who have experienced the nurturing and supportive one-to-one relationships prior to school entry can find it difficult to adjust to the fact that they are one of many. This may also coincide with the time when they need extra reassurance and support.

Due to their relationship with the school, Steven's parents were confident that the school would manage the changes within the reception class; many parents, however, do not have the same confidence.

Activity 7.3

How can schools create time for parents who need extra contact and support? Make some brief notes suggesting ways in which this might be better achieved in the context in which you work.

Support and training for staff

The need for a rigorous programme of initial and ongoing professional and personal development was highlighted throughout the case study. Personnel from all areas stand out as needing initial training. But the process of ongoing development for all staff must be addressed. This needs to be resourced for whilst schools can develop their own 'packages' of in-house training, staff also need training from external agencies which extend opportunities for reflection and for developing strategies for reviewing practice objectively.

Teachers may need to acquire skills in managing other adults within classrooms. The reception teacher welcomed the skills of the support assistant but she had no prior experience or training for this aspect of her work. In Steven's case, it was with the help of a supportive headteacher that she accommodated to this role. This aspect of a teacher's responsibilities does not appear to be a feature of initial teacher training or to feature widely in INSET programmes but it is an area which needs to be addressed on a local and national level.

The role of the SENCO has been introduced and developed by the requirements within the *Code of Practice*. However, many SENCOs within infants schools also have responsibility for a class, with little or no time allocated for paperwork and for supporting young or insecure staff (Lewis *et al.*, 1996). They themselves may have received little training for the tasks which face them in their role as SENCO and in relation to the implementation of the *Code of Practice*.

Changes took place in 1997 within initial teacher training to ensure that newly qualified teachers have wider knowledge and a higher level of skills for meeting special educational needs. The green paper states that the government will 'encourage all teachers to develop further skills in curriculum planning, teaching and assessing pupils with SEN' (DfEE, 1997). However, whilst 'SEN training' continues to be seen as a separate issue – away from 'language and literacy' or 'numeracy' training – it will prevent us 'from listening to unfamiliar voices . . . and celebrating 'difference' in a dignified way' (Barton, 1997, p. 234).

Activity 7.4

Suggest three essential items in a school development plan which will ensure staff receive a rigorous and ongoing programme of professional development to support inclusive education.

How will all adults working with young children receive rigorous training?

In addressing Activity 7.4, you may have considered in-house and external methods of training; you may also have considered inter-agency 'trade-offs'.

The majority of adults who work with children under 5 are not qualified teachers, but have a range of other qualifications, many specifically related to early development (NNEB, BTech, NVQ, ADCE). They too require training but this is often difficult to access (Lloyd, 1997).

Role of supporting adult

Although the familiar arguments for sufficient funding to support children with SEN are not to be underestimated, all available funding is liable to be ineffective if the attitudes and aspirations of the professional adults are not committed to an inclusive philosophy (Clark *et al.*, 1995). Whilst both Steven's teacher and the support assistant subscribed to this philosophy they required support themselves.

Steven received help each day from a support assistant. The role of the supporting adult is a skilled job which requires a higher profile and a greater degree of training. The support needs to be given in such a way that an inseparable 'velcro' relationship does not develop between child and support assistant which would interfere with peer group interactions. This adult should be 'encouraging without fostering dependence and constantly preparing to depart' (Ball, 1994, p. 46).

There were 24,000 learning support assistants working in mainstream primary and secondary schools in January 1997. OFSTED have found that fewer than half of LEAs provide appropriate training for these staff.

Assessment over time

All teachers would acknowledge that children perform differently on different days at different tasks. From this case study it is possible to see the benefit of continuous assessment over a period of time. It is only by careful recording and evaluation that an accurate assessment can be made.

One difficulty encountered within the segregated playgroup attended by Steven was the lack of continuity and information. Whilst there are many concerns about the requirements within the desirable learning outcomes (DfEE, 1997), one positive outcome will mean that planning and record-keeping are assuming greater importance.

The *Code of Practice* recognises the changing needs for children under 5. Many of the professionals who knew Steven during his first two years were surprised (and delighted) by his developing skills as he grew older. With the advent of the desirable learning outcomes, the introduction of baseline testing at 5, the publication of Key Stage 1 results, the fight for scarce resources and the increased workload resulting from the *Code of Practice*, many professionals have voiced concern that there may be a large increase in requests for early statements. Schools may feel pressured in battling for resources to focus on a child's failures and not his or her successes (Barton, 1997).

Provision in early years settings

For Steven preschool provision took place in a variety of settings with differing adult:child ratios and with differing training and qualifications for the staff. Whilst many would argue that such diversity gives parents choices (DfEE, 1997), in reality no such choice is available (Pugh and De'Ath, 1989; David, 1992) and services for under 5s have been described as a 'disgrace' (Ball, 1994). The lack of co-ordination and the differences in training and status of educators within these sectors mean children have experiences of varied quality and central government policy can be crucial in the improvement and fuller provision of such services (David, 1993).

With the range of qualifications for workers in this sector, it is not difficult to understand Steven's parents' confusion. They believed that at the 'special playgroup' not only would he receive care but also that the staff were qualified to address his needs.

Activity 7.5

What information needs to be available in order that parents may make an informed choice about preschool provision? List five methods or ways of doing this.

As a result of the introduction of the now defunct 'nursery voucher' funding for 4-year-olds, more children are going into school at 4 (Pugh, 1996). The arrangements for funding have changed with local authorities working with other providers to develop early years development plans.

What impact do you think these changes will have on provision for preschool children with SEN? Could they lead to a more inclusive policy for children with SEN? Identify concerns and hopes in ten bullet points.

Partnership

One of the key themes throughout this case study has been that of 'partnership' in its many forms. Whilst many of the aspects of partnership have been explored in the preceding sections, it is important that we consider it separately.

Much has been written about 'partnership' with parents and it is a key factor within the *Code of Practice* (DfEE, 1994) and the green paper (DfEE, 1997). However, whilst there appears to be support for the benefits of partnership, central government policies and actions seem flawed by contradictions. The combined effects of legislation during the 1980s have meant the reduction and often axing of services for young children and their families. Competition is antithetical to the notion of partnership.

Parents may ostensibly have the opportunity to state preferences, but in effect they have no say over the allocation of resources, type of service delivery or teaching.

Competition for finite resources among services often leads to tensions at management levels which cascade to others. Although 'partnership' may continue between individuals, collaboration at service level becomes more difficult to achieve as territories become more defined and protected.

Partnership means different things to different people and can vary from home–school liaison and co-operation to joint agency planning: 'In short it is a means of establishing relationships in which both partners are respected and trusted, can communicate easily and clearly, and are working together towards the same end – a more effective and appropriate education for children' (Community Education Development Centre, 1988).

Throughout this chapter, we have seen how

- Steven and his family's needs changed and were addressed;
- the community, staff and children were influenced by his inclusion; and
- the response to a medical 'label' influenced professionals and parents.

Steven is an individual but this story was selected because over the years the issues within it have recurred regularly. The events in his case have highlighted both the strengths and weaknesses of working in collaboration with parents, other agencies and schools to ensure that young children have 'the best chance to develop fully' (United Nations, 1989, Article 6).

Acknowledgements

My thanks to the family within this chapter and to the professionals who are prepared to take risks in the interests of children.

Suggested further reading

Dale, N. (1996) *Working with Families of Children with Special Needs: Partnership and Practice*, Routledge, London.

Herbert, E. and Moir, J. (1996) Children with special educational needs – a collaborative and inclusive style of working, in Nutbrown, C. (ed) *Respectful Educators – Capable Learners: Children's Rights and Early Education*, Paul Chapman Publishing, London.

Hornby, G. (1995) *Working with Parents of Children with Special Educational Needs*, Cassell, London.

Lloyd, C. (1997) Inclusive education for children with special educational needs in the early years, in Wolfendale, S. (ed) *Meeting Special Educational Needs in the Early Years: Directions in Policy and Practice*, David Fulton, London.

References

Ball, C. (1994) *Start Right*, Royal Society of Arts, London.

Barton, L. (1997) Inclusive education: romantic, subversive or realistic?, *International Journal of Inclusive Education*, Vol. 1, no. 3, pp. 231–42.

Bastiani, J. (1989) *Working with Parents: A Whole School Approach*, Routledge, London.

Bronfenbrenner, U. (1979) *The Ecology of Human Development: Experiments by Nature and Design*, Harvard University Press, Cambridge, MA.

Carpenter, B. (ed.) (1994) *Early Intervention: where are we now?* Westminster College, Oxford.

Carpenter, B. and Herbert, E. (1997) Fathers: are we meeting their needs?, in Carpenter, B. (ed) *Families in Context: Emerging Trends in Family Support and Early Intervention*, David Fulton, London.

Clark, C., Dyson, A. and Millward, A. (eds) (1995) *Towards Inclusive Schooling*, David Fulton, London.

Community Educational Community Centre (1988) *Parents and the Education Reform Act*, Family Education Unit, Community Educational Community Centre, Coventry.

Cunningham, C. and Davis, H. (1985) *Working with Parents – Frameworks for Collaboration*, Open University Press, Buckingham.

Dale, N. (1996) *Working with Families of Children with Special Needs: Partnership and Practice*, Routledge, London.

David, T. (1990) *Under Five – Under Educated*, Open University Press, Buckingham.

David, T. (1993) Educating children under five in the United Kingdom, in David, T. (ed) *Educational Provision for our Youngest Children: European Perspectives*, Paul Chapman Publishing, London.

David, T. (1995) Issues in Early Childhood Education, *Journal of Educational Policy*, Vol. 10, no. 3, pp. 325–33.

David, T., Moir, J. and Herbert, E. (1997) Curriculum issues in early childhood, in Carpenter, B. (ed) *Families in Context: Emerging Trends in Family Support and Early Intervention*, David Fulton, London.

DES (1978) *Special Educational Needs: Report of the Committee of Enquiry into the Education of Handicapped Children and Young People (the Warnock Report)*, HMSO, London.

DfEE (1994) *Code of Practice on the Identification and Assessment of Special Educational Needs*, Central Office of Education, London.

DfEE (1996) *Nursery Education Scheme: the next steps*, HMSO, London.

DfEE (1997) *Excellence for all Children: Meeting Special Educational Needs*, HMSO, London.

Ferguson, D. and Meyer, G. (1991) *Ecological Assessment*, University of Oregon.

Gallimore, R., Weisner, T.S., Kaufman, S.Z. and Bernheimer, L.P. (1989) The social construction of ecological niches, *Journal of Mental Retardation*, Vol. 94, pp. 216–30.

Herbert, E. and Moir, J. (1996) Children with special educational needs – a collaborative and inclusive style of working, in Nutbrown, C. (ed) *Respectful Educators – Capable Learners: Children's Rights and Early Education*, Paul Chapman Publishing, London.

Hornby, G. (1995) *Working with Parents of Children with Special Educational Needs*, Cassell, London.

Lewis, A. (1995) *Children's Understanding of Disability*, Routledge, London.

Lewis, A., Neill, S. St-J. and Campbell, J. (1996) *Report on the Implementation of the Code of Practice in Primary Schools*, University of Warwick and National Union of Teachers, London.

Lloyd, C. (1997) Inclusive education for children with special educational needs in the early years, in Wolfendale, S. (ed) *Meeting Special Educational Needs in the Early Years: Directions in Policy and Practice*, David Fulton, London.

Madden, P. (1994) Paper presented to the international seminar on Partnership between Parents and Professionals in the Care of Children and Young People with Learning Difficulties, UMIST, Manchester.

Pugh, G. and De'Ath, E. (1989) *Towards Partnership in the Early Years*, National Children's Bureau, London.

Pugh, G. (1996) Evaluation of Nursery Vouchers: Lessons from Phase one, paper presented at The Institute of Education, London, October.

Rouse, D. and Griffin, S. (1992) Quality for the under threes, in Pugh, G. (ed) *Contemporary Issues in the Early Years: Working Collaboratively for Children*, National Children's Bureau/Paul Chapman Publishing, London.

School Curriculum and Assessment Authority (1997) *Looking at Children's Learning: Desirable Outcomes for Children's Learning on Entering Compulsory Education*, Nursery Education/SCAA, London.

Swann, R. and Gammage, P. (1993) Early childhood education . . . where are we now?, in Gammage, P. and Meighan, J. (eds) *Early Childhood Education: Taking Stock*, Education Now Publishing Co-operative, Ticknall.

United Nations (1989) *Convention on the Rights of the Child*, United Nations, New York.

Vygotsky, L.S. (1978) *Mind in Society: The Development of Higher Level Psychological Processes*, Harvard University Press, Cambridge, MA.

Wolfendale, S. (1989) *Parental Involvement: Developing Networks between School, Home, Community*, Cassell, London.

8

Inclusion, the Code of Practice *and the Role of the SENCO*

Caroline Roaf

Introduction

This chapter is being written at a time of rapid change for SENCOs. The ideas presented express my own attempt to make sense of the role as it takes shape around me in a large secondary school. In common with many other schools we have accepted the *Code of Practice* (DfEE, 1994) fully in principle, our policy is written and is reviewed annually, we have worked hard to develop user-friendly individual education plans and we monitor furiously. Towards the end of our five-year plan 'to have regard to' and 'work in the light of' the code, and after a recent inspection, we are pausing to take stock and prepare for the next review now planned to take account of imminent government initiative on SEN (DfEE, 1997).

While there are no substantial changes in the role itself, my experience is that the potential for change inherent in it has been dramatically increased. I found it difficult at first to identify what this could be attributed to. Certainly the code has given SENCOs permission to be assertive and fulfil their role as advocates for children. Its drafting and publication also coincided with the high profile given by the Salamanca Statement (UNESCO, 1994) to inclusive education, a term still relatively new in the UK. Nevertheless, many schools are working towards greater inclusion even though, in some localities, there is little encouragement to do so. The increased involvement of parents in their children's education and pressure from special interest groups are another factor. Finally, since the introduction of LMS, money has replaced staffing as the tool of management. This combination of a new philosophy, an enabling code, increased pressure from parents and special interest groups and new ways to access funding, has contributed greatly to the influence SENCOs can now exert in some schools. SENCOs in, for example, inclusive schools, tend to enjoy high status and influence policy and practice at senior management level. They negotiate budgets with their headteachers and governors, deploy resources flexibly and are less easily overwhelmed by the minutiae of the code's advice than their SENCO colleagues with low status. SENCO status has thus increasingly become an indicator of the status given to SIE. In this new phase what meaning do the terms 'special educational need' and 'inclusive education' have? How are the key elements in the SENCO role being interpreted and how might this role develop in the future?

SEN

A child has special educational needs if he or she has a learning difficulty which calls for special educational provision to be made for him or her. A child has a learning difficulty if he or she

a) has a significantly greater difficulty in learning than the majority of children of the same age
b) has a disability which either prevents or hinders the child from making use of educational facilities of a kind provided for children of the same age in schools within the area of the local education authority (Section 1).

This definition has been a source of debate and dissatisfaction since it was first used in the Education Act 1981. For some, it is dismissed (Audit Commission, 1992a; Thomas, 1995) with some derision as a 'non-definition'. For others it simply does not reflect the changes in thinking and practice which have taken place over the last fifteen years or so. Nor has it been effective in ensuring access to education for those most in need of it. A recent OFSTED report (1996, p. 39, emphasis added) even felt obliged, fifteen years after the 1981 Act, to include in its recommendations that 'All pupils with SEN *including those with behaviour difficulties* should be included on the SEN register'.

Fortunately, schools can extend the code's minimalist, deficit and potentially exclusive definition. Many schools now direct attention and resources towards, for example, students with specific talents, those in need of extra support and care because of their domestic circumstances or those at risk of exclusion. Our policy at my own school (Lord Williams's, Thame) states that we aim to meet the needs of any child requiring positive action to secure the educational outcomes of which he or she is capable. For us it is important to recognise both the diversity within the school population, and each child's individuality. Any one at any time might need special care and attention; some groups are habitually disadvantaged in the school system. None the less in order to distribute a finite resource equitably an agreed definition is needed. For some the Children Act 1989 (Sect. 17) is a useful starting point and has the advantage that it also applies to other local authority services:

a child shall be taken to be in need if –

a) he is unlikely to achieve or maintain, or have the opportunity of achieving or maintaining, a reasonable standard of health or development without the provision of services by a local authority . . .

b) his health or development is likely to be significantly impaired, or further
impaired without the provision for him of such services; or

c) he is disabled,

'development' means physical, intellectual, emotional, social or behavioural
development; and

'health' means physical or mental health.

Lack of clarity in the definition of SEN was considered by the Audit
Commission (1992a) to be one reason for the serious deficiences in the
way children with special needs were identified and provided for. They
recommended instead that there should be national guidelines as to when
a child requires additional help from the LEA and that these should be
drawn up with reference to the degree of children's need.They recommended (*ibid.*, para. 130) that they be 'specific enough to be useful but not
so tightly defined that they exclude those children who do not fit into
categories.'

In relation to children with EBD, the commission found that apart from
home tuition and some special units, 'provision is usually limited and
falls far short of giving these pupils access to a full curriculum' (*ibid.*,
para. 109). They also recognised (*ibid.*) that pupils who are excluded from
school do not necessarily have an emotional or behavioural disturbance:
'Some are disaffected from the schooling they are offered and some headteachers are reported to be anxious to improve the disciplinary image of
their school and hence are readier to exclude difficult pupils.'

The 1981 Act in fact promoted a term which has allowed schools to
be selective about whose needs they meet. As a consequence, schools
have learned to use a number of avoidance tactics. They can decide that a
child with needs does not have learning difficulties. Even if it is agreed
that there are learning difficulties, the school can still decide that meeting
them in an ordinary school is 'incompatible with the effective use of
resources' (Education Act 1981, Section 2). Since the 1981 Act definition is
repeated in the 1993 Act the problem remains.

Equally, lack of definition means that schools are free to improve on the
1993 Act and to create their own inclusive definition. Unless schools
identify needs against the broadest, most inclusive possible definition,
they will continue to fail some children. For example, the 1990s has seen a
marked rise in the numbers of young people recorded as truanting or
excluded (Graham and Bowling, 1995). These young people's needs do
not lend themselves easily to *Code of Practice* definitions and criteria and it
is no coincidence that a proportion lose contact with school altogether,
withdrawing themselves to the home or the street.

Establishing policy and approach in the inclusive school

The principles and definitions governing the education of children with
SEN have not appeared out of the blue. They are broadly comparable

with progress in relation to other disadvantaged groups. Originally, the phrase was used as the title of the Warnock Report (on the 'Education of handicapped children and young people' – DES, 1978). Since the mid-1980s, however, 'handicapped children and young people' have proved much less of a challenge to inclusion than some other groups. Children and young people with EBD and the children suffering extremes of poverty, who now make up 25 per cent of all children, today head the list of groups SENCOs struggle to include. The Education Act 1970 marks the first time that local authorities took responsibility for the education of all school-age children however severe their difficulties. The 1981 Act marks the right (not unqualified) of all children to be educated in mainstream schools. The 1988 Act entitled all children to the National Curriculum.

These developments have generated a variety of responses in terms of school ethos and organisation, one of which is inclusive education. Clark *et al.*'s (1995) recent gathering together of international opinion on this subject finds great diversity of interpretation springing from the general notion of inclusive schooling as an alternative to more traditional approaches to SEN. In the simplest terms, clearly spelt out in, for example, Stainback and Stainback (1990), integration expects students to change, or be 'supported' to fit the school. Inclusion expects the school to change to suit the child.

Activity 8.1

Collect two or three examples of SEN policy documents from schools in your area. How is SEN defined in them? Do the aims and values of these schools reflect integrationist or inclusive policies? What would you look for in a school promoting inclusive education?

For teachers in the UK, still struggling to promote integration, the notion of inclusive education poses many questions. Booth (1995) seems to suggest that inclusive education as an idea encourages teachers to develop creative and co-operative solutions to difficulties they would previously have shelved. If this is so, then gradually, as integration proceeds, schools can learn to be inclusive.

Key elements in the role of SENCO

The code's guidance on the role of the SENCO suggests that there is a general distinction to be made between its two main dimensions: activity at the level of the whole school and of the individual child. The challenge for the SENCO is to hold a balance between these two dimensions in the face of colleagues, parents and governing bodies who are not necessarily in agreement either in principle or in respect of individual children as to how this should be achieved. Since segregation and integration emphasise the individual and inclusion the whole school, much depends on the school's SEN policy and the skill with which the SENCO can articulate this.

These dimensions overlap, but of the seven areas listed in the code (para. 2.14) four are concerned with short-term positive action on behalf of individuals with whom the school is at present less effective. The remaining three are broadly 'whole school' concerned with long-term development, research and training, designed to help the school serve its community more effectively. These seven areas can be traced back to the seven identified in 1985 by the then National Association for Remedial Education (NARE, 1985), now National Association for Special Educational Needs (NASEN). An important difference between then and now has been that, formerly, SENCOs undertook more themselves of the work that today they encourage others to do. This has been the main thrust of 'whole school' SEN policies to the extent that some writers (Dyson, 1990) began to prophesy the demise of the SENCO altogether. However since then, the code appears to have affirmed the SENCO role. It is too early to be sure, but the evidence of the last ten years suggests that SENCOs, by encouraging others to do what was previously done by them, do not appear to have reduced their workload. No sooner has one challenge been accepted by classroom teachers than another is knocking at the SENCO's door. Clark *et al.* (1995) acknowledge that the momentum for change towards more whole-school activity has not stopped. Their recent research into innovative practice found, for example, that (*ibid.*, p. 84):

> innovatory schools . . . have ceased to think of special needs provision as something that either takes place outside the curriculum (and classroom) or is imported into classroom in the form of support teaching. Instead, they have come to see special needs provision as 'built into', or embedded, in the very routines that constitute ordinary classroom practice. In so doing they have considerably enhanced their ability to respond to all needs and characteristics.

In response to this they found that SENCOs were 'beginning to operate in an extended role which is not confined to the support of individual pupils with special needs. Rather s/he increasingly acts as promoter and facilitator of change in respect of teaching and learning issues as they affect all pupils' (*ibid.*, p. 72).

An extended role does not, however, sound like a static one, and moves towards inclusive education present a particular challenge. According to Ware (1995, p. 127), writing of the development of inclusive education in the USA:

> • Since its evolution in the 1980s, inclusive education has increasingly challenged the legitimacy of virtually every professional and institutional practice of twentieth century schooling. The structural implications of inclusive education are quite clear: it requires fundamental changes of the most basic structural

features of schools as organisations, that is, the very ways in which the work in schools is divided and co-ordinated among professionals.

It will be argued in this chapter that from research evidence, and personal experience, the role of the SENCO appears to be developing three main facets. These are organisation and management, research, and staff development and training. If SENCOs are to develop their role beyond the full implementation of the *Code of Practice*, they must be skilled in these areas.

Organisation and management

Effective co-ordination lies at the heart of the management role of the SENCO. The problems associated with co-ordination have been acknowledged in the business world for some time and some of this thinking has been applied to education (Handy, 1985). Dictionaries define co-ordination as: 'bringing parts into proper relation' and a co-ordinator as 'one who adjusts, settles, fixes, organises'. In my own job I have found this definition extraordinarily apt. 'Parts', whether these are resources or people or knowledge of the curriculum and legislation, or of external agencies, constantly need to be brought together, assembled and reassembled. SENCOs and their teams form an extensive network to achieve this. As a result of information exchange and liaison they 'settle, adjust, fix and organise' curriculum differentiation, classroom support, individual education plans and all the other aspects of the role already outlined. Co-ordination can be achieved through a number of different mechanisms but in the management of SEN provision, whether in a small primary or a large secondary school, team-building and networking will almost certainly feature (Bradley and Roaf, 1995).

Kanter (1984) suggests that the amount of co-ordination required in an organisation depends on factors such as the extent of specialisation in the organisation, the nature of the boundaries separating one from another and the willingness of specialists to communicate and work across boundaries. In big secondary schools there can be sharp differences in ethos and organisation, communication systems and professional behaviour between curriculum areas and between year groups. In primary schools this occurs between classrooms. Moving from one to another can represent a considerable change of culture. Co-ordination helps to solve these problems.

Research

Research activity among teachers seems to have increased to the point that it has become virtually a requirement, signifying a reflective teacher and learner (Ainscow, 1995). The level of expertise required, as new information about how the mind and brain work and new approaches to teaching and learning are discovered, encourages schools to promote research and development.

The code (para. 2.12) states that the governing body's report on its special needs policy

should demonstrate the effectiveness of the school's systems for

identification
assessment
provision
monitoring and record keeping
use of outside support services and agencies.

This in itself constitutes a major annual research and development task. From the minutiae of the code's advice and from the evidence of what SENCOs actually do, special needs team members now find themselves at the cutting edge of curriculum and staff development every day. At Lord Williams's, with learning support assistants (LSAs) supporting nearly 20 per cent of all lessons, there is a constant dialogue of inquiry, observation and assessment. This information contributes to the school's research and development programme supporting reflective teachers in a learning school. Learning support teams are well placed to carry out small-scale action research projects and to contribute to larger LEA or national initiatives and indeed encouraging research projects among their colleagues has become a strategy to help SENCOs fulfil the rest of their role.

Activity 8.2

There is a wealth of topics suitable for research in the area of SEN. Select one or two possible areas for research.

Staff development and training

In the past there was almost universal concern among special needs teachers about their status as effective classroom teachers. Over the years, they have gained credibility in the eyes of colleagues and headteachers. None the less the shift from teacher of children to adviser of teachers and trainer of LSAs is still likely to create unease. In primary schools this is less of an issue. Specialist support has always tended to come from peripatetic advisory teachers, and classroom teachers are accustomed to this role. Secondary schools have been less familiar with it and secondary teachers more inclined to be critical of the role played by a colleague not apparently teaching full time and seemingly protected from the rigours of the classroom. The *Code of Practice*, by emphasising the organisational, staff development and liaison role of the SENCO, has been instrumental in changing this perception and SENCOs have felt better able to assert their new role.

Acknowledges
Role being some non-teaching.
always up to the
school.

Recomm
SENCO 50% Teaching.

Curriculum differentiation

In practice, particularly since the 1988 Act, teachers have relied heavily on support teachers and LSAs to help them differentiate the curriculum and provide them with detailed background knowledge of the children in their classrooms. This has led to a wealth of initiatives which have been responsible for extensive staff development and have also helped to clarify the SENCO role for classroom-based colleagues. Examples are peer appraisal, team teaching, collaborative learning (Hart, 1992), mutual support and observation and the rapid growth of action research such as we have described. At Lord Williams's, differentiation has for some time now developed a life of its own within most curriculum areas. This marks a sea change in learning support activity and can be attributed to the effect of the introduction of the National Curriculum. Previously learning support teams spent much of their time designing appropriate curricula and tasks for students. Today the emphasis has changed. Differentiation is still needed but mainstream teachers are more likely to take on this responsibility themselves, looking to LSAs to help students reach appropriate levels of attainment. Instead other areas have been identified in the school development plan for learning support attention, notably underachievement particularly of boys, and behaviour management.

LSAs

LSAs are employed by schools in ever-increasing numbers and make a major contribution to the progress of students they work with. LSAs assemble knowledge of the curriculum and the students' and teachers' academic, social and personal attributes. They digest and reconstruct their impressions in a form which will help students progress. As SENCO, they are my eyes and ears, reaching, because of their special status, parts of the system I could not reach on my own. Their recruitment, training, deployment and support are time consuming and demanding but the implementation of the *Code of Practice* in many cases depends on them. They show a remarkable capacity for flexibility in approach and attitude in response to an ever-increasing diversity of need. But little is known about how they operate and what would help them to develop a sharper focus in their work. The role of the LSA is also changing rapidly. SENCOs now need their help to monitor the implementation of the code and to keep records and individual education plans up to date. Their need for professional development confirms even more strongly the SENCO role as trainer and adviser.

The SENCO role in primary and secondary schools

Although in principle schools need no longer recruit SENCOs from practising teachers, it would be unusual for them not to have teaching and/or teacher training experience. Other professionals such as advisory teachers, educational psychologists, education officers or education social workers could take on the role. In some cases this does appear to be happening where, for example, special needs is organised across a partnership of schools (Cade and Caffyn, 1995). In many primary schools the SENCO role is filled by the headteacher or deputy who may have little or no direct experience of special education. This is not necessarily a disadvantage, though it can be, since the main facets we have identified for the SENCO role (management, teacher training and an interest in research and development) are already elements in the headteacher role.

Research commissioned by the National Union of Teachers (Lewis *et al.*, 1996, p. 3) records some of the important differences in the effect of the code between primary and secondary schools:

> For example, in primary schols the predominant problem was that the position of the SENCO had to be added to a portfolio of responsibilities already undertaken by a classteacher (or by the headteacher). In secondary schools the predominant problem was of effective liaison across departmental structures in which there were priorities competing with the Code of Practice.

By contrast, secondary schools on the whole recruit SENCOs from existing support teachers who may find it difficult to shed their teaching role in order to develop their new role as resource manager and co-ordinator, researcher, adviser and teacher trainer. How far has the shift from segregation through integration to inclusive education been responsible for a shift away from a more specifically teaching role to the managerial, administrative and evaluative role advocated in the *Code of Practice*? In this chapter we have argued that status is increasingly an issue, and the need for managerial, administrative and research skills has raised the stakes significantly. SENCOs without these skills are likely to be sidelined and without the status will be frustrated.

The special needs register

According to the code schools should keep a register of children with SEN. This subject is potentially a philosophical minefield. In some schools the register might include almost everyone. Others may not want to distinguish between those who are on or not on the register. Is the register a record of the school's diversity or of its children's needs? What about children with specific talents? If the register is solely based on need does this reinforce deficit models of SEN? What effect does it have on parents to be told that their children are on the register? Meanwhile, as SENCO, I need some firm ground under my feet. I cannot hand out resources on a first come first serve basis, nor can I hand them over to the ones who shout loudest. In order to distribute resources equitably I need two kinds of information. First I need information about the demography of the school and its catchment area so that I can build up a picture of the diversity I might expect in the school. This will already tell me something about the kind of expertise I might need in the learning support team. Secondly I must find out which children need positive action in order to get the best out of school, and of these which are likely to require support beyond what the school can provide on its own. Both kinds of information are important. Being able to recognise differences and diversity helps one to recognise individual needs across a broad spectrum. Without this broad spectrum positive action tends to be directed narrowly, perhaps just to children with low reading ages. This may be very effective for some children but would leave others without resources. Our Lord Williams's register of students with SEN is derived from a much bigger data base recording information about the school population which might carry individual resource needs with it but need not. Examples would be the percentage of families without a telephone, the names of students enrolling in the school later than the normal entry time, the percentage of children entitled to free school meals, destinations of school leavers, examination results and so on.

With detailed information about the diversity of the student body schools are better able to respond effectively to individual needs as they arise. They can then plan appropriate provision and identify areas for development and preventative work. When external agencies such as educational psychologists and social workers, youth workers, psychiatrists, and specialists such as advisory teachers for particular groups, share in compiling the register it is likely to reflect the full range of need experienced by young people in the community. This information is an essential tool for research and staff development.

Funding arrangements and the advocacy role of the SENCO

Since the introduction of local financial mangement, getting and spending, accountability and value for money have become a central part of a school's role in relation to its students needing additional resources. The code makes it clear that 'provision for pupils with special educational needs is a matter for the school as a whole' (para 2.7). Individual schools must decide how the responsibilities for this will be divided. In practice as we know, headteachers sometimes take on the SENCO role themselves. This is possible because so much of the work can now, in principle, be covered by an efficient administrative assistant. Maintaining the register, overseeing the records, liaising with parents and external agencies, the co-ordination of provision and day-to-day oversight of policy are all tasks that a headteacher normally delegates. In schools where the role of SENCO and headteacher are played by different people much depends on the extent to which the headteacher delegates his or her management responsibilities for children with SEN. Limited delegation of management leaves the SENCO closer to an administrative assistant, often combined with a heavy teaching load. Extensive delegation brings the SENCO in line with other middle/senior managers.

It is important that headteacher and SENCO are clear about what responsibilities have been delegated. This is particularly true with respect to the funding arrangements to support children with special needs. SENCOs at the management end of the spectrum develop an understanding of what it costs to provide an appropriate service because fundamentally, effective provision for children with SEN depends on the acquisition and distribution of resources. This sometimes, though not invariably, means taking from some in order to give to others and can be contentious. Knowledge of the school's profile of need and the funds available helps to achieve a fair distribution of resources. Without this information the advocacy role of the SENCO becomes meaningless and it is only as a well informed advocate that SENCOs can appeal to an LEA for additional funds to support children with exceptional needs. Advocacy is also required within school to justify a necessary shift in resources, perhaps to move an LSA from one class to another, or to investigate achievement in relation to a particular curriculum area or group of students. SENCOs have to be able to respond rapidly to needs, however serious. Local finance can be a complex task requiring a certain amount of risk-taking. Close co-operation and trust between headteacher and SENCO are essential.

However there is a deeper significance to be attached to the simple question of whether or not a SENCO understands the working of a school budget. The Audit Commission (1992a, para. 137) expressed concern at the lack of incentives for LEAs to implement the 1981 Act: 'Funding mechanisms could be devised to create incentives for LEAs to succeed in meeting the needs of the least able pupils.' In order to justify a claim for funding special education either from the governing body in respect of the delegated budget, or from the LEA in respect of funds retained centrally, schools must prove that they can identify, assess and meet needs effectively. This is an important incentive. The sum of money allocated to the school by the LEA may not be very large, but a child's future in the school can depend upon it. SENCOs able to prove that their schools use additional funding effectively also prove that they can be trusted with more.

Consultation over funding becomes therefore a yardstick by which SENCOs judge the extent to which the management of SEN has been delegated to them. This in turn is a measure of the managerial style of the headteacher. Non-hierarchical management with 'flatter' structures operating through teams and networks depends on good communication systems and the free flow of information. These structures also encourage the creative thinking required of an inclusive school. Is the SENCO fully informed about the school budget and fully involved in discussions as to how funding is used or not? A SENCO's status in this respect reveals as much as do definitions of special need about a school's ethos and management style. In some schools this is not a problem. Everyone is informed about the budget and everyone has the opportunity to contribute in the discussions about its use. An unintended consequence of the current concern about budget cuts has been that governing bodies and headteachers have become more open about their financial management. SENCOs have benefited from this.

Monitoring, review and evaluation

The code outlines the information required in the governing body's report on the success of the school's SEN policy. In theory, if the management, research and staff development aspects of the SENCO role have been fully implemented this task should not be too daunting. But how in practice can this success be demonstrated? The code declares itself to be a living document. A school's SEN policy is no different. It sets out school aims and provides information about current practice and provision which constitute a set of success criteria. Some of these are benchmarks against which to measure improvement year on year. New elements can be introduced or withdrawn according to need as part of the whole-school development plan. SENCOs in inclusive schools will be anxious to establish how far special needs practice has become 'embedded'. How much information have classroom teachers absorbed about the diversity of their groups? Have they contributed to the individual education plans? How do classroom teachers, SENCO, special needs team members and external agencies communicate with each other? OFSTED is said to look for the fruits of effective co-ordination in the daily practice of each classroom teacher. Inclusive schools require success criteria which reflect the full range of individual need, evaluating matters such as attendance, improved staying-on rates post-16, raised student and parent expectations, measurable improvements in basic academic and social skills, reduced number of days exclusions, improvements in differentiation, teaching and learning methods. Criteria might also include reduced incidence of harassment and bullying, improved methods for recording achievement across a wide span of activity and increases in parent and student satisfaction.

Activity 8.3

Devise a set of success criteria to accompany the policies for inclusive education discussed earlier in this chapter.

The school in the community, the school as community

Booth (1995, p. 101) suggests that the trend towards inclusive schooling cannot be dissociated from similar moves in communities:

If we wish to create inclusive schools and the values on which they depend, what implications does this have for our views about inclusion outside schools? On the segregation of the elderly in homes and hospitals? Or on the inclusive labour markets and the regulation of poverty and greed?

This was recognised in the Salamanca Statement on 'Principles, policy and practice', agreed by representatives of 92 governments and 25 international organisations. It made large claims for inclusive education:

> regular schools with this inclusive orientation are the most effective means of combating discriminatory attitudes, creating welcoming communities, building an inclusive society and achieving education for all; morever they provide an effective education to the majority of children and improve efficiency and ultimately the cost effectiveness of the entire education system.
>
> (UNESCO, 1994, para. 4)

How is this to be achieved? School movements to promote integration and inclusion have been matched by community movements in the same direction, through parents' groups and pressure groups. Key passages in the code's advice concern school arrangements to work in partnership with parents, to take account of the wishes and feelings of children and young people and to work closely with other agencies. This advice brings the code in line with the Children Act 1989 and opens up new opportunities for SENCOs. Stainback and Stainback (1990) suggest that in a fully inclusive world, all community members would support each other and there would be no need for additional 'support' to come into classes. There will be times when difficult decisions have to be made between competing claims for resources, but closer working with local communities remains a precondition of inclusive education.

Conclusion

The SENCO role which emerged in response to the Education Act 1981 continues to evolve, developing new facets as it does so. Our study comes at an interesting juncture. It is not safe to make any predictions about the future role of SENCOs or the future of inclusive education. Academics are divided as to whether SENCOs have a future. Before the code, the idealists prophesied the role's demise, while realists foresaw a healthy future. The code cuts across both positions. It sets out tasks, roles and responsibilities but is not prescriptive. The code (Foreword) offers guidance to LEAs: 'It does not – and could not – tell them what to do in each individual case . . . much will depend on the schools' starting points.'

The code leaves it open as to who does what in its implementation, simply stating that 'a designated teacher' should carry out SENCO responsibilities. Tomlinson (1982) uncovered the vested interests of the special school system. Does the code protect the vested interests of the SENCO? If so will its implementation through SENCOs and special needs teams stand in the way of progress towards inclusive education? According to some it is taking long enough to overcome the vested interests of special schools. How long might it take to disband the newly entrenched SENCO? It is too early to say, though the innovative practice uncovered in the research of Clark *et al.* (1995) suggests that to avoid this accusation, SENCOs must continue to hand over their professional expertise and authority to colleagues.

If SENCO skills and resources are about equipping others to meet needs, what remains for the SENCO and what underpins the role? In this chapter we have suggested that management, research and staff development perform this function. More than other middle managers in schools, running year and faculty teams, SENCOs have learned to live with instability, uncertainty and change. They are the first to be affected by changes nationally, locally and at school level in relation to finance, the curriculum, the educational ideology and value systems of the headteacher and governors. To cope with these pressures SENCOs have had to search for ways in which to maintain their own sense of self-worth and purpose, while giving away the expertise which contributes to this. For many people working in SIE, one of the attractions of the job is its variety and unexpectedness. This is coupled with the freedom to work with others to promote the interests of children and young people, one of the world's largest and most disadvantaged minority groups. Advocacy, even at a whole-school level, still depends on the actions of individuals: 'Without creative personalities able to think and judge independently, the upward development of society is as unthinkable as the development of the individual personality without the nourishing soil of community' (Einstein, 1954, p. 14). The ability to think and judge independently, fostered through research and staff development, underpins movements towards inclusive education. Effectively managed co-ordination allows the information feeding the research and development, and resulting from it, to be put into practice quickly. SENCOs who can achieve this will be well placed to turn the code into the living document it aspires to be and will be able to revise it in the light of experience.

Suggested further reading

Butt, N. (1991) A role for the SEN co-ordinator in the 1990s: a reply to Dyson, *Support for Learning*, Vol. 6, 1 February, pp. 9–14.

Cade, L. and Caffyn, R. (1995) Family Planning for special needs: the role of a Nottinghamshire family special needs co-ordinator, *Support for Learning*, Vol. 10, 2 May, pp. 70–4.

Dyson, A. (1990) Effective learning consultancy: a future role for special needs co-ordinators, *Support for Learning*, Vol. 5, 3 August, pp. 116–27.

References

Ainscow, M. (1994) *Special Needs in the Classroom*, Jessica Kingsley and UNESCO, London and Paris.

Ainscow, M. (1995) Education for all: making it happen, *Support for Learning*, Vol. 10, 4 November, pp. 147–57.

Audit Commission (1992a) *Getting in on the Act. Provision for Pupils with Special Educational Needs: the National Picture*, HMSO, London.

Audit Commission (1992b) *Getting the Act Together*, HMSO, London.

Audit Commission (1994) *Seen But Not Heard: Co-ordinating Community Child Health and Social Services for Children in Need*, HMSO, London.

Bines, H. (1992) Developing roles in the new era, *Support for Learning*, Vol. 7, 2 May, pp. 58–62.

Booth, T. (1995) 'Mapping Inclusion and Exclusion: Concepts for All?', in Clark, C., Dyson, A. and Millward, A. (eds) (1995) *Towards Inclusive Schools*, London, Fulton, pp. 96–108.

Bradley, C. and Roaf, C. (1995) Meeting special educational needs in the secondary school: a team approach, *Support for Learning*, Vol. 10, 2 May, pp. 93–9.

Cade, L. and Caffyn, R. (1994) The King Edward VI family: an example of clustering in Nottinghamshire, *Support for Learning*, Vol. 9, 2 February, pp. 83–9.

Cade, L. and Caffyn, R. (1995) Family Planning for special needs: the role of a Nottinghamshire family special needs co-ordinator, *Support for Learning*, Vol. 10, 2 May, pp. 70–4.

Clark, C., Dyson, A. and Millward, A. (eds) (1995) *Towards Inclusive Schools?*, David Fulton, London.

Clark, C., Dyson, A. Millward, A. and Skidmore, D. (1995) *Innovatory Practice in Mainstream Schools for Special Educational Needs*, DFE, London.

DES (1978) *Special Educational Needs: The Report of the Committee of Enquiry into the Education of Handicapped Children and Young People (the Warnock Report)*, HMSO, London.

DfEE (1994) *Code of Practice on the Identification and Assessment of Special Educational Needs*, DfEE, London.

DfEE (1997) *Excellence for all Children: Meeting Special Educational Needs*, HMSO, London.

Dyson, A. (1990) Effective learning consultancy: a future role for special needs co-ordinators, *Support for Learning*, Vol. 5, 3 August, pp. 116–27.

Dyson, A. and Gains, G. (eds) (1993) *Rethinking Special Needs in Mainstream Schools: Towards the Year 2000*, David Fulton, London.

Dyson, A. and Gains, G. (1995) The role of the special needs co-ordinator: poisoned chalice or crock of gold?, *Support for Learning*, Vol. 10, 2 May, pp. 50–6.

Einstein, A. (1954) *Ideas and Opinions*, New York, Bonanza Books.

Graham, J. and Bowling, B. (1995) *Young People and Crime: Research Study 145*, HMSO, London.

Handy, C. (1984) *Taken for Granted? Understanding Schools as Organisations*, Longman for the SCCDC, York.

Hart, S. (1992) Collaborative classrooms, in Booth, T., Swann, W., Masterton, M. and Potts, P. (eds) *Curricula for Diversity in Education*, Routledge/Open University, London.

Kanter, R.M. (1984) *The Change Masters*, Unwin, London.

Lewis, A., Neill, S.R. St J. and Campbell, R.J. (1996) *The Implementation of the Code of Practice in Primary and Secondary Schools: a National Survey of the Perceptions of SENCOs*, Institute of Education, Warwick University, Coventry.

NARE (1985) *Teaching Roles for Special Educational Needs: Guidelines 6*, NARE, Stafford.

OFSTED (1996) *The Implementation of the Code of Practice for Pupils with Special Educational Needs*, HMSO, London.

Thomas, G. (1995) Special needs at risk?, *Support for Learning*, Vol. 10, no. 3, pp. 104–12, August.

Tomlinson, S. (1982) *The Sociology of Special Education*, Routledge and Kegan Paul, London.

Stainback, W. and Stainback, S. (1990) *Support Networks for Inclusive Schooling: Interdependent Integrated Education*, Brookes, Baltimore, MD.

Udvari-Solner, A. and Thousand, J. (1995) Effective organisational, instructional and curricular practices in inclusive schools and classrooms, in Clark, C., Dyson, A. and Millward, A. (eds) *Towards Inclusive Schools*, David Fulton, London.

UNESCO (1994) *The Salamanca Statement and Framework for Action on Special Needs Education*, UNESCO, Paris.

9

Interagency Work in the Management of Special and Inclusive Education

CAROLINE ROAF

Introduction

> He was offending while truanting from school. A mixture of the two. In the end we felt like tennis balls because Education said it was a social problem and Social Services said it was an education problem, and we were just going backwards and forwards from one to another.
>
> (Lloyd, 1994, p. 19)

This was how one 13-year-old's mother described her experience. In schools, when teachers find themselves in this situation they experience similar feelings of frustration. Long before being tossed into the inter-agency arena, young people in difficulty tend to be tossed first from one to another within school and within the education service.

When professionals and their clients need more than one service they need those services to work together. If this does not happen, the result is frustration, loss of confidence in the ability of agencies to work together and inactivity. Whatever resources are put in then tend to be wasted. The lapse of time caused by delays in the negotiation for assessment and resources means that, for some young people as they get older, difficulties increase. Then solutions become harder to reach and action when it happens is expensive and potentially damaging. Secure accommodation costs about £100,000 a year, a teenage pregnancy costs £40,000. Each crime committed by a young person costs society over £2,000. By contrast, resources devoted to youth work are relatively low. According to the Audit Commission (1996), costs rarely rise above £200 per head per year.

This chapter examines the relevance of interagency work to teachers and looks at some of the ways in which schools can respond to, and benefit from, co-operation with other agencies. It also looks at how schools themselves can co-ordinate their own provision more effectively.

Who loses out?

One recent study identified groups of young people who were not receiving appropriate support. These young people were:

- carers
- on the verge of criminality
- having mental health problems
- homeless
- out of school for any length of time
- experiencing education difficulties while being looked after by the Local Authority
- from families in stress
- experiencing delays in assessment or provision through the process leading to a statement under the 1981 Education Act.

(Joseph Rowntree Foundation 1995, p. 2)

Education is the front-line agency for children and young people. Among school pupils are young people experiencing difficulties such as these, some of whom fail to progress in their learning. Schools have a duty to educate them and to do so in co-operation with other agencies if this is needed in order for them to make progress (*Code of Practice* – DfEE, 1994). Schools as agencies are part of the problem but can also be part of its solution. How can this be achieved? The following case studies illustrate some of the issues to be considered.

Case studies

Ian

Ian is 14. His mother has been worried about her inability to manage his behaviour since he was about 4 years old. She asked for help on many occasions but recalls that the only help available at the time was intermittent and short lived. In school, over the years Ian has had many difficulties. His attendance is excellent but he suffers from very low self-esteem and has suffered long periods of bullying, from those who exploit the fact that it is easy to wind him up. He retaliates and gets into trouble for it. His home situation is now very difficult as he has been beyond his mother's control for some time and is involved in criminal activity. She has been living on her own with Ian and two younger children for some years. His father wants Ian to live with him. He exercises a different style of authority and believes that this will keep Ian's behaviour within reasonable limits. Although Ian has had some difficulties with reading and spelling in the past, it is his behaviour in class and towards his peers and his attitude to authority that prevent him from making progress in school. When he was 12 it was agreed that a multiprofessional assessment should be considered to ascertain the extent of his SEN, but there were long delays in this process. Since then his behaviour has become increasingly unpredictable and disturbing and he is now a danger to himself and others. At this stage the school, with help from the LEA, put together about £5,000 worth of additional support for Ian. This was provided in the form of individual sessions to help him with his written work, to build his self-esteem and confidence. LSAs were available to work with him in class and during social time. His tutor also worked hard to maintain links with home and to help Ian develop easier relationships with his peers and teachers. Even so he had a series of fixed-term exclusions for abusive and/or violent behaviour, which eventually resulted in a permanent exclusion. After further delay he is now on the roll of a special school but attendance is proving a problem.

Ros

Ros is 15. She has great difficulty in conforming to the school's code of behaviour. She hates school uniform and rarely wears it correctly. She also challenges teachers' authority and is constantly being sent out of lessons for disruption or failure to work. She is frequently in detention for a range of misdemeanours but rarely attends. She has a reputation as a bully and her behaviour is unpredictable. She is known to be a substance abuser. Links with home are extremely difficult to sustain since her parents live apart and neither want her. Ros reacts to this by staying with friends or more recently sharing in a squat. On her rare appearances in school, she never looks well. Although entered for a number of GCSEs and capable of good grades, Ros no longer attends school.

Neil

Neil is 13 and depressed. His mother died recently and he now lives with his father and grandmother. Relationships at home with the extended family and his father are extremely difficult for Neil to handle. His father is often away and his grandmother is an invalid. Neil is anxious about leaving his grandmother alone and is afraid she will either die or be unable to seek help in an emergency. He has begun to truant. He is expected to do very well in school and is beginning to feel a lot of pressure from his teachers.

Young people in situations such as these present teachers with a number of difficult issues to consider. The first concerns professional responsibility and boundaries. Who is responsible for what? How far can teachers go in their support of individual young people? How much discretion do they have? How proactive can teachers be? Secondly, what structures and communication systems exist to encourage professionals to co-operate? How useful is legislation in this area? Thirdly, what can parents and children expect? What are their rights and responsibilities and are they aware of them?

Classroom teachers in ordinary schools normally have limited experience of working with professionals in other agencies such as social services or health.

Problems faced by young people:
- Parents and young people with multiple needs have difficulty accessing appropriate agency provision because they require the services of more than one agency. No one agency has responsibility for co-ordinating services for this group.
- Parents and young people are not aware of their rights and responsibilities.
- Assessment is often delayed and different assessment routes and screening methods bring different perceptions of the problem and different resources. Substantive work done by other agencies may be put on hold pending the results of assessment by one service.
- Young people are defined by professional boundaries rather than by definition of their need. They therefore tend to be regarded as on the margin, or outside of, any one particular service provision.
- The special needs of young people from ethnic minorities are overlooked. When they need specialist support they find themselves outside mainstream agency provision.
- Young people get 'lost' in the system.
- Young people suffering from mental health problems are particularly vulnerable.

Problems faced by agencies:
- Each agency has different statutory responsibilities and may not always be clear about the limits of their responsibility. This can create difficulties in co-ordinating provision and developing a holistic care plan for a young person.
- Practitioners are unsure how their work relates to other specialist services.
- There is a lack of co-ordination when pupils transfer from one school to another and lack of continuity of approach to exclusions.
- Agencies find it difficult to agree joint procedures for action, for example, in cases where the education of a young person being looked after by social services is under consideration.
- Agencies often find it difficult to agree 'ownership' of the 'case'.
- Agencies do not hold the same information and have difficulty passing confidential information to one another.
- Each agency holds its own budget and few mechanisms exist for joint funding.
- Legislation has created additional barriers to interagency co-operation.
- If resources are involved (time and money) there may only be 'lip service' to co-operation.
- Different agencies have different responsibilities for young people at 16.
- Practitioners continue to feel threatened by, and anxious about, interagency collaboration. Where conflicts arise these are often attributed to personalities and individual agency difficulties rather than to the lack of a structure which would support and validate collaboration. There is little perception that effective joint working might alleviate the problems of the agencies as well as those of the young people.

By locating oneself mentally alongside the child who is experiencing difficulty and his or her family, in the community and at home, it is easier to examine how decisions by teachers and professionals in other agencies impact on the family life of young people such as we have described. Legislation now requires that services for children work together. It is obviously not the intention of the agencies and legislators that parents feel like tennis balls, passed from one agency to another, that members of one agency are unable to liaise satisfactorily with colleagues in other agencies or that children do not get the provision they are entitled to. Yet our case studies show how much young people and their families depend on a network of co-ordinated support within and between agencies, and how easily the lack of it leads to increases in, for example, young homelessness, exclusion from school or mental illness. To prevent this we need to look for ways in which interagency co-operation can reach back into schools since, in the first instance, young people at risk depend on support in a practical way from people close to them. These people, very commonly, are teachers.

Some recent legislation represents a timely attempt to bring policy-makers and practitioners closer together, and more closely in touch with young people and their families. Local authorities must now prepare children's service plans. These are 'the basis for delivering a truly effective service in response to the needs, and wishes of children and their families. They also provide a means for the creation of better integrated services and the best use of available resources' (Child Care Forum, 1996). They are expected to have clear, targeted and timed objectives related to outcomes which can be evaluated. Schools can make some important contributions to the development and execution of children's service plans but only if they can find a way of turning plan into action. Three possible approaches are suggested here.

First, schools can re-examine their concept of 'need' and work with young people, families and other agencies to establish agreed definitions and criteria. How do agencies know whose needs to prioritise? Is there agreement about this? Are their clients consulted?

Activity 9.1

This activity gives you an opportunity to reflect on your own experience of interagency work and to analyse some of the problems you have encountered.

Using the case studies above as examples, think of a young person (A) you have worked with that you would regard as needing the services of more than one agency. Draw up a brief pen portrait. Now think of another young person (B) to contrast with A. Using the list of problems, make notes on your experience of the differences in agency response and action between them.

Secondly, schools can build on their own strengths as institutions capable of listening and responding to the diversity of their students' needs and wishes. Thirdly, schools can take the initiative in forming local interagency liaison groups and networks to mobilise support for young people from other agencies and the community.

Definitions

In two of its reports, the Audit Commission stresses the importance of agreed definitions of the terms 'special educational need' (1992) and children in 'need' (1994):

> The first task is to define the 'needs' that authorities should be addressing and to target them accordingly. Some services are being offered to everyone when a selective approach would be more appropriate; but even targeted services may be provided unnecessarily. They may be imprecisely focussed, or miss those who need them most because they are focussed inaccurately. Authorities must also identify 'risk indicators' in order to guide targeted support accurately to where it is most needed.
>
> (Audit Commission, 1994, para. 42)

Schools are now required to produce their own policies on SEN in which they must provide detailed information about their provision and practice. They must also report annually on the success of the policy and explain how resources have been allocated. Many schools also have an equal opportunities policy. Taken together, these documents help schools respond to the diversity of their students at the level of both policy and practice. They are useful as a reference point when deciding whose needs to target. Much depends therefore on how needs are defined. In some schools attendance problems or EBD have been regarded as either disciplinary matters or non-educational issues. Support from the school has not necessarily been forthcoming. In other schools definitions of 'need' include these difficulties, and resources have been directed towards them.

However, from our case studies it is clear that despite well intentioned legislation, targeted support for those most in need of it does not necessarily follow. In the example which opens this chapter, the boy is offending while truanting. How does this accord with the definitions of 'need' used in the relevant legislation? The likelihood is that this boy's 'needs' would not be regarded as 'educational' in terms of the Education Act 1993. He would not then be entitled to additional support from the LEA. Under the Children Act 1989 he might be defined as a child in 'need' on the grounds that 'a reasonable standard of health or development' (Sect. 17) could not be ensured 'without the provision for him of services by a local authority.' However, the local authority might decide that this boy's needs were low on their list of priorities. He would get very little, if any, support unless something happened to precipitate a crisis.

Although schools can do little on their own in situations which have reached crisis point, they have a very significant role to play at earlier stages. However, they can only play this role if they choose to redefine the relative and potentially exclusive definitions of SEN used in the Education Act 1993, to include the full range of needs which might be expected to arise among their community of students. This means recognising the diversity of their students, becoming more proactive on their behalf and more alert to the possible risks they can be exposed to which would affect their educational opportunities. If professionals start with the intention of identifying and assessing children's needs holistically, then developing definitions and criteria which are agreed by all parties and can be used across all the relevant agencies should be a priority.

Interagency liaison

Interagency work in relation to children and young people has been discussed and recommended for at least a generation in a range of reports from Kilbrandon (1964), Plowden (CACE, 1967) and Seebohm (1968) to Utting (1991) and the Audit Commission (1994). Recent legislation continues to recommend it. Extensive research on a number of other groups of people requiring local authority services (for example, Arnold *et al.,* 1993) likewise concludes that the recipients of these services would benefit if the agencies providing them worked together more effectively. However, this assumption has been questioned in some quarters. Who benefits from such collaboration?

Interagency work has, for some writers, been construed as complex and difficult, time consuming and hard to sustain (Webb, 1982). Others challenge this view on the grounds that lack of co-operation leads to increased distress and community dysfunction. They point to increasing concern in some well publicised and politicised incidents about public security and the failure of community care to protect the public in cases where, for example, a person suffering from schizophrenia commits a murder. A number of reports also demonstrate the immense personal risk and/or huge expense which can be incurred as a result of the failure to co-operate. This triggers particularly urgent concern in relation to children and young people (Parsons, 1994). Others again consider that interagency work helps the agencies by focusing on systems and management rather than on helping the children and their families (Hallet and Stevenson, 1980). Joseph Rowntree Foundation (1995, p. 1) on the other hand, found that alleviating agency problems was an important part of alleviating those of the young people: 'Practitioners continue to feel threatened by and anxious about, interagency collaboration. Where conflicts arise these are often attributed to personalities and individual agency difficulties rather than the lack of a structure which would support and validate collaboration.' A further argument sometimes raised is that if each agency did its job properly and was properly resourced then there would be no need for interagency co-operation. This argument tends to gain support at times of financial constraint. When individual services are being severely cut they have great difficulty fulfilling their roles within an agency, let alone in relation to clients regarded as marginal to their service or requiring help from another, equally straitened agency. To make a contribution to an interagency service may then be regarded as putting the whole service in jeopardy. None the less the main weight of the evidence is that failure of the agencies to co-operate has been a key factor in the failure of services to meet needs.

While studies successfully identify causes, and tragedies are frequently attributed to the failure of agencies to co-operate, solutions have proved elusive. There have been some notable exceptions. In relation to child sexual abuse, legislation and government guidance (DoH/DES, 1991) followed the Cleveland Inquiry. Although the problem has not gone away, these children and young people's difficulties are now acknowledged and systems have been put in place to ensure that policy is put into practice. Other groups have received less attention. New forms of difficulty for children and young people, identified as social circumstances, change and become more complex, and require flexible, well co-ordinated services able to respond to needs quickly. Can interagency structures and communication systems be devised to bring this about? If so, how might they be initiated?

Activity 9.2

Turn to the readings by Riches (1988) and Riley (1992). In these articles the factors prohibiting or promoting interagency work are explored in some detail. They also examine the different levels of co-operation required to achieve integrated services more responsive to users' needs.

Working with others: key elements in collaboration

Recognising the existence of successful models

Models of co-operative working have been operating within agencies for some time (Higgins and Jaques, 1986). But practitioners and policy-makers have failed to recognise that effective *intra*-agency models can be adapted for *inter*-agency use (Hambleton *et al.*, 1995). These are now emerging between agencies (Elmore, 1987; Arnold *et al.*, 1993).

In the personal and social services these models are designed to bring focused support to people who without them would risk 'falling through the net' of agency provision. They tend to have certain characteristics in common. In general they appear to focus on the client group at three levels, through:

- senior management *policy and planning groups;*
- middle management *teams;* and
- formal *networks* operating informally and open to all.

Effective models are solution focused and encourage creative thinking. Through them professionals can be challenged to overcome agency boundaries, professional jealousies and vested interests and consider more collaborative ways of working.

Teams and networks

Kingdon (1982) notes that teams and networks are both essential in providing a balanced package of care to most individuals but emphasises that there are important distinctions between them. Teams consist of small groups which share common tasks, similar values and hold distinctive knowledge and skills. In the personal and social services they tend to work with the client group to secure long-term planning, individual case management and preventative work. Teams typically take referrals from others, and either manage these themselves or act as 'network brokers' among other agencies or groups to secure the resources needed to maintain the individual within the mainstream network of support. Some cases are managed entirely by the team, others may require no more than fairly lightweight liaison. Much of the team's efficiency is secured through effective co-ordination, communication and information exchange. There is often an emphasis on research and staff development.

Networks, by contrast, consist of a range of people with different knowledge and skills who may meet infrequently, yet who work on a common task when the occasion demands (Muir, 1984). Through their regular meetings, networks discuss issues raised by members in the course of their work. Networks rarely have power but can be highly influential through the information they feed back up through the system to senior policy-makers and managers. Lloyd (1994) found that membership of the Oxford Adolescent Network of agencies working with young people in difficulty was around 70. A small number of these were regular attenders and others attended if the topic for discussion interested them or was one they could contribute to or gain from. Networks of this kind perform an essential function in helping practitioners at all levels to support each other, to share information, identify gaps in provision and to make the most of the resources they have.

Increasingly, service users, among them young people, are being consulted over service provision. Schools have an opportunity to play a part by enabling direct consultation with children and young people through the curriculum and through, for example, assemblies and school councils.

In this way every teacher can begin to contribute to the interagency planning process.

Policy and planning

Teams and networks function most effectively when fully supported by policy-makers and strategic planners, including local authority elected members. In some local authorities, joint strategy-making bodies have been set up for this purpose. Without commitment to co-operation at this level, interagency project teams run the risk of being short lived. An effective network and its associated team have the ability to identify future areas for research and development. This information can be built into the overall strategy, provided there is a group dedicated to this. A strategy group is particularly important because of the key decisions which are taken at this level about the use and distribution of resources. Holterman (1996), in a study into the benefits and costs of increasing investment in children, proposes a range of policies which would benefit children and young people in the UK. She concludes (*ibid.*, p. 10) that 'Taken as a whole this package can be seen as a coherent programme for change: each part has its own rationale and the parts are mutually consistent'. Joint strategy groups are needed to achieve these programmes.

Co-ordination and training

Teams and networks cannot achieve their potential without effective leadership, network broking and co-ordination. This requires attention to the communication systems used in an institution or community. It also requires access to reliable, up-to-date information about the legislation governing each agency, the cultural and ethical beliefs of participating agencies and their working methods. At a practical level, keeping up-to-date knowledge of each agency's resources is also important. Higgins and Jaques (1986, p. 5), in their study of training for teamwork in healthcare, considered that 'The increasing focus on human behaviour in relation to life difficulties, and on people as human beings rather than on their specific characteristics as owners of diseases or social or legal problems, leads to a recognition of what individual professions have in common rather than what divides them'.

Training for interagency co-operation has become an increasingly important part of the team leader's co-ordinating function, on their own account to help them understand the complex world in which they operate, as well as to help them train others. Training also helps agencies understand the level of co-operation that already exists between them. These levels may range from co-operation through collaboration to merger, each one presenting different training needs and carrying with it different expectations as to likely outcomes (Lloyd, 1994). Riley (1992) concludes that as unification is rare, even greater co-ordination is required. Increased specialisation also increases the need for co-ordination as has the proliferation of non-statutory voluntary sector workers now employed by many of the primary care agencies. These workers are often employed on part-time contracts in short-life projects and depend on networks and co-ordination to make the most of their work and the resources they command. Just as teams need co-ordination to help their members achieve more than they could on their own, so do groups of policy-makers.

Activity 9.3

In two related articles, Gill (1989) and Maginnis (1989) trace the development of Lothian's Regional Youth Strategy. Since then a number of other local authorities have adopted similar strategies for similar reasons. The articles are very clear about the obstacles confronting those who promote interagency strategies of this kind. They are equally clear about what they hope the strategy will achieve. In many areas some elements of a youth strategy already exist. Try to identify these in your own area and consider how they might be developed further.

The school's role in interagency work for children and young people

For education, as for health and social services, interagency co-operation is no longer an option. The *Code of Practice* (DfEE, 1994) for the identification and assessment of SEN advocated an interagency approach to the framing of individual education and care management plans and this has been further endorsed by the green paper *Excellence for all Children* (DfEE, 1997).

Although progress towards more effective interagency working is, as we have seen, hindered by lack of a common language and local structures to implement legislation collaboratively, schools can help by developing their policies and definitions of 'need' in collaboration with the agencies they work with. Less easily resolved is the tension, touched on by Riley (1992), between 'care' and 'education' and between educational and non-educational provision. In British society, it is unclear as to whether these are regarded as distinct or a unity. Either way the care element tends to be controversial, neglected and underfunded. In implementing the Education Act 1981, LEAs have developed arrangements to ensure some redistribution of resources which are then directed to individual children with special needs. In health and social services money does not follow children in the same way and no mechanisms have yet been formulated to ensure the matched funding which would have been such a help to the Ian of our case study and his family. Without inter-agency funding strategies, coherent interagency planning which would bring about the integration of care and education is hard to arrange. As a consequence more children and young people truant, are excluded or otherwise fail to benefit from education than would otherwise be the case.

Riley's (1992) discussion highlights this tension in relation to provision for the under 5s. It is no less acute for older children and teenagers. Ultimately, during childhood and adolescence, the school, even more than the family, becomes the locus of interagency activity. Schools are then faced with a dilemma. If they accept their interagency role, they also accept some responsibility for care as well as education. If they do not (and are not selective in their intake) they risk poor exam results and a rise in truancy and exclusions. In the past it was easier than it is now to ignore this. Legislation has heightened awareness of this dilemma and made it more apparent than previously that how schools co-ordinate their own resources and promote effective interagency co-operation is an ex-tremely important part of the way in which they assert the entitlement to education for those who are most likely to be denied it.

School models of co-operation

One of the ways in which schools gain the support they need from other agencies for the care of their students is by developing effective support structures within school. Many schools already operate very successful models to support young people which mirror almost exactly the models of co-operation we have just described. Prominent in the model (and variously labelled) are special needs/learning/curriculum/pupil support teams. Where these are based in centres which act as a 'holding bay' between home, or the street, and the classroom, young people can receive immediate support from skilled staff with time to listen. Support teams are able to co-ordinate resources from within the school and are in the best position to mobilise additional resources from other agencies or the local community and to act as an entry point for them. This model dis-plays the same features of the team, network and policy group that seem to be effective elsewhere in promoting co-operation across professional and agency boundaries. This is as important in the microcosm of the school as it is in the community.

In the school model, the strategy group is represented by the senior management team and governing body and has overall responsibility for policy and development and oversight of the team's activities. Finally, the network can be identified in the school model in the interagency liaison meetings many schools operate to co-ordinate support for young people in difficulty.

These are some of the similarities of approach between school models and community models. Interagency models of this kind are now emerging in a number of local authorities. Research into these shows that they share some characteristics of good practice which will be very familiar to special needs/learning support teams. These are:

- Formal commitment and support from senior management, and from politicians to practitioners.
- Formal and regular interagency meetings to discuss ethical issues, changes in legislation and practice, gaps in provision and information sharing, at all levels, to develop short and long term strategies.
- Common work practices in relation to legislation, referral/assessment, joint vocabulary, agreed definitions, procedures and outcomes.
- Common agreement of client group and collective 'ownership' of the problems, leading to early intervention.
- Mechanisms to exchange confidential information.
- Frameworks to collate data and statistical information across the agencies to inform all practice including ethnic monitoring.
- Monitoring and evaluation of services in relation to interagency work.
- Joint training in order to understand each other's professional role.

(Joseph Rowntree Foundation, 1995)

The benefits will likewise be familar. For individuals, the model provides support enabling them to remain in school if attendance is at risk, or return to school if they have been out for any length of time. Continuity of support is also guaranteed. Because the team can tap into the community networks, it can plan, together with other agencies, packages of support extending beyond the school day for young people with complex needs. Their short and long-term development can be considered as can their need to acquire greater self-esteem and confidence to help them make positive relationships with adults and their peer group.

The role of the SENCO

SENCOs, in implementing the code, now assume a key role in linking with other agencies. In reality, the extent of this involvement is likely to depend on a variety of factors such as the attitude of governors and headteacher, the school's admission policy and its definition of SEN. SENCOs are too often beleaguered. They tend to be caught between a school ethos which may be solely fixed on educational goals regardless of the range and complexity of individual need, and the demands of the code and the Children Act. SENCOs can find themselves in a very difficult position, trying to promote an inclusive philosophy in an exclusive market economy (Ball, 1995, p. 75). Schools which allow SENCOs or others to cross the divide between school and community, perhaps through close links with the youth service or local projects concerned with young people, or as members of interagency liaison groups/ networks, will be better able to put together the flexible education programmes which are needed in order to maintain some young people in mainstream education. SENCOs also tread a thin line between the 'care' and 'education' aspects of the school. Without a structure designed to integrate these aspects children and young people cannot easily be supported in the holistic way which makes sense to them and their families.

Conclusion

Interagency co-operation can help schools secure educational entitlement and improved life chances for all their students but requires formal structures and systems to make the most of local resources and expertise. Hambleton *et al.* (1995, p. 75) found that

> there is a whole range of collaborative activities: some of which have been clearly thought out at the beginning and others which have grown in an organic way. It is important that the vehicle of collaboration is fit for the purpose intended. This will require budgets, objectives, roles, structures and processes to be clearly defined; occasionally it will require joint arrangements to be time limited. All of this will require clear definition and clarity of purpose.

SENCOs and the teams they lead are now responsible for liaising with other agencies and have much to contribute to our understanding of interagency co-operation. Schools should recognise this and endorse the further development of effective interagency models in their communities.

Suggested further reading

Gill, K. (1989) A context for joint practice, in Gill, K. and Pickles, T. (eds) *Active Collaboration: Joint Practice and Youth Strategies*, Intermediate Treatment Resource Centre, Glasgow.

Maginnis, E. (1989) Lothian Region's youth strategy: a political perspective, in Gill, K. and Pickles, T. (eds) *Active Collaboration: Joint Practice and Youth Strategies*, Intermediate Treatment Resource Centre, Glasgow.

Riches, P. (1988) Working together for whose benefit?, *Children and Society*, Vol. 3, pp. 270–8.

Riley, K. (1992) Provision for the under fives: bringing services together, in Booth, T., Swann, W., Masterton, M. and Potts, P. (eds) *Policies for Diversity in Education*, Routledge/Open University, London.

References

Arnold, P., Bochel, H., Brodhurst, S. and Page, D. (1993) *Community Care: The Housing Dimension*, Joseph Rowntree Foundation, York.

Audit Commission (1992) *Getting in on the Act. Provision for Pupils with Special Educational Needs: The National Picture*, HMSO, London.

Audit Commission (1994) *Seen but not Heard: Co-ordinating Community Child Health and Social Services for Children in Need*, HMSO, London.

Audit Commission (1996) *Misspent Youth . . . Young People and Crime*, HMSO, London.

Butler-Sloss, Rt Hon. Lord Justice E. (1988) *Report of the Inquiry into Child Abuse in Cleveland 1987*, HMSO, London.

CACE (1967) *Children and their Primary Schools (the Plowden Report)*, CACE, London.

Child Care forum (1996) Meeting Children's Needs for the 21st Century, *Child Care forum*, Issue 10.

DfEE (1994) *Code of Practice on the Identification and Assessment of Special Educational Needs*, DfEE, London.

DfEE (1997) *Excellence of all Children: Meeting Special Educational Needs*, HMSO, London.

DoH/DES (Welsh Office) (1991) *Working Together: A Guide to Arrangements for Inter-agency Co-operation for the Protection of Children from Abuse*, HMSO, London.

Elmore Committee (1987) *Support for Difficult to Place People in Oxford*, The Elmore Committee, Oxford.

Gerwirtz, S., Ball, S. and Bowe, R. (1995) *Markets, Choice and Equity in Education*, Open University Press, Buckingham.

Gill, K. (1989) A context for joint practice, in Gill, K. and Pickles, T. (eds) *Active Collaboration: Joint Practice and Youth Strategies*, Intermediate Treatment Resource Centre, Glasgow.

Hallet, C. and Stevenson, O. (1980) *Child Abuse, Aspects of Inter-professional Co-operation*, Allen & Unwin, London.

Hambleton, R., Essex, S., Mills, L. and Razzaque, K. (1995) *The Collaborative Council: A Study of Interagency Working in Practice*, LGC Communications, London.

Higgins, P.M. and Jaques, D. (1986) Training for teamwork in health care, *Higher Education Review*, Vol. 18, no. 2, pp. 5–19.

Holterman, S. (1996) The impact of public expenditure and fiscal policies on Britain's children and young people, *Children and Society*, Vol. 10, no. 1, pp. 3–13.

Hornby, S. (1993) *Collaborative Care: Interprofessional, Interagency, Interpersonal*, Blackwell, Oxford.

Joseph Rowntree Foundation (1995) *Multi-agency Work with Young People in Difficulty, Social Care Research Findings 68*, Joseph Rowntree Foundation, York.

Kilbrandon Report (1964) *The Report of the Committee on Children and Young Persons in Scotland*, Scottish Office, Edinburgh.

Kingdon, D.G. (1992) Interprofessional collaboration in mental health, *Journal of Interprofessional Care*, Vol. 6, no. 2, pp. 141–47.

Lacey, P. and Lomas, J. (1993) *Support Services and the Curriculum*, David Fulton, London.

Lloyd, C. (1994) *The Welfare Network: How Well does the Net Work?* Occasional Paper, Oxford Brookes University School of Education, Oxford.

Muir, L. Teamwork, in Olsen, M.R. *Social Work and Mental Health*, pp. 168–76, Tavistock Press, London.

Parsons, C. *et al.* (1994) *Excluding Primary School Children*, Family Policy Studies Centre, London.

Seebohm Report (1968) *Report of the Committee on Local Authority and Allied Personal Services*, HMSO, London.

Solity, J. and Bickler, G. (1994) *Support Services: Issues in Education, Health and Social Services Professionals*, Cassell, London.

Utting, Sir W. (1991) *Children in the Public Care*, HMSO, London.

Webb, A. (1982) Strained relations, *Social Work Today*, Vol. 13, no. 42, pp. 10–11.

10

The Future of Support Services: Issues for Management

MARTIN DESFORGES

Introduction

This chapter considers some of the problems caused by recent changes in the educational system that concern SEN, and it attempts to identify the key issues that need to be addressed by managers of support services to ensure delivery of an efficient high-quality professional service, within the context of a system working towards inclusive education.

The Education Act 1981, based on the Warnock Report (DES, 1978), acknowledged the principle of integrating pupils with SEN into mainstream schools. Although it provided no extra finance to help this process, it gave LEAs new and important functions to provide a broad range of services to meet individual special educational needs. However, the 1986 and 1988 Education Acts as well as the Education Act 1993 contain clauses that reduce rather than enhance the probability of pupils identified as having SEN being integrated into mainstream schools, particularly the clauses which make it more difficult for LEAs to fund support services. Although the recent green paper *Excellence for all children* (DfEE, 1997) attempts to address some of the issues which appear to be working against inclusive education, the mechanisms for ensuring adequate funding for the maintenance, development and training of a comprehensive LEA support service for pupils with SEN are not clear.

In recent years the crucial debate in special education has moved from issues of how to achieve integration to how to bring about a system of inclusive education, where as of right all children will be educated in mainstream schools, whatever their educational needs. This debate has started to clarify the dilemmas faced by support services in the variety of roles they assume within the education system. Do they support individual pupils enabling them to survive within a classroom and curriculum structure which fails to meet many of their learning needs, or do they support schools and LEAs in their efforts to develop an appropriate curriculum and pedagogy, differentiated at a classroom level, which would meet the educational needs of all pupils? Offering classroom teachers support which allows them to continue working in ways which are inappropriate for some pupils in their classroom is hardly likely to motivate those same teachers to adopt new working methods which will lead to the inclusion of pupils currently segregated.

There is a fundamental contradiction between support teaching as a strategy for change, working towards inclusive education, and support teaching as a way of protecting classroom teachers from the pressures of change. The key management issue is to develop policies and working practices which enable support staff to meet the aim of inclusive education so that those with SEN have access to regular schools which can accommodate them within a child centred pedagogy capable of meeting all their learning needs. This chapter explores these dilemmas, and considers how support services might adapt to meet the new role of progressing towards inclusive education.

Historical development of support services

Prior to the publication of the Warnock Report (DES, 1978), LEAs provided a peripatetic teaching service to assist pupils with particular difficulties. The most common provision was remedial education with specialist teachers withdrawing pupils from class to help improve literacy skills. This work was done with individual pupils or in small groups elsewhere in the school or at a local remedial reading centre. Provision for pupils with mild sensory or physical impairments was often arranged on a similar basis. These services had a variety of organisational frameworks. Some were part of the child guidance or educational psychology service, with educational psychologists as line managers. Some were remedial teaching services attached to segregated special schools or remedial reading centres. Some were autonomous services with their own management structure, organised as part of the central services of the LEA. The main task of these teachers was seen to be direct work with individual pupils or small groups, and as the 1989 HMI report notes (DES, 1989), it was often carried out in poor-quality accommodation such as corridors, school halls or medical rooms.

Educational psychology services go back to 1913, when the first educational psychologist was employed in London to devise a fair way of allocating pupils to the limited number of places in segregated special schools. It was not until the 1930s that child guidance clinics became common outside London, and during the 1960s an increasing number of LEAs established separate educational psychology services. The main thrust of this work was individual casework. By the 1970s most of these services were moving from clinic-based work to more direct work in and with schools. One important consequence of this move was a focus on preventative work, with in-service and project work with schools or across LEAs, and a reduction in the time spent on casework.

The Education Act 1981 was the first piece of legislation that stated the role of educational psychologists in the assessment of pupils with learning difficulties, and the Act made it mandatory for LEAs to obtain psychological advice as part of the multiprofessional assessment of SEN. With this statutory role, casework began to assume greater importance in terms of time allocated to it. This trend accelerated in the late 1980s when, under the Education Reform Act 1988, LEAs had to delegate over 85 per cent of their budgets directly to schools, and were less able to retain comprehensive support services.

During the 1980s, in response to the growing pressure for integration of pupils identified as having disabilities and learning difficulties, both primary and secondary schools began to adapt their curriculum and teaching to meet better the needs of individual learners. Many LEAs developed advisory support teams able to provide a broader range of help than that given by remedial reading teachers. In some areas this led to the growth of SEN advisory and support services of the kind recommended by the Warnock Report.

This post-Warnock view of support services stressed the importance of whole-school policies aimed at ensuring that every class and subject teacher was able to deal with SEN in mainstream classrooms. The new role of the learning support teacher was to advise and assist in differentiating the curriculum and to engage in co-operative classroom teaching. These changes are reflected in the concepts and language used by professional groups and in, for example, the journal of the National Association of Remedial Teachers, where the term 'remedial education' became 'support for learning'.

In this brief historical review it is important to note that the educational reforms imposed by central government through a programme of legislative change in the late 1980s did not address special education directly. The first drafts of the National Curriculum, with its age-related norms and stages of assessment, clearly failed to account for those pupils with SEN. Whilst government policy was highly prescriptive for mainstream education, DES (1989) Circular 22/89, Assessment and Statements of SEN, London: DES which replaced DES (1983) Circular 1/83, Assessment and Statements of SEN, London: DES in its guidance on implementing the Education Act 1981, had little to say on the role of support services, and its message was advisory rather than directive. Although it was specific about the need to consider integrated placement in mainstream schools, it had no guidance to offer on the nature of support services that might be needed to help make integration a reality for a greater proportion of pupils with SENs.

Throughout the 1980s the support teacher role had been further developed to include consultancy work with individual teachers and whole school staff, moving even further from the direct teaching role. These new roles and models of working were criticised by many (e.g. Moses *et al.*

1987), and there was evidence that many support teachers continued to use withdrawal teaching as a major strategy, despite their belief that this was no longer regarded as an effective intervention by significant others in the education system.

Duffield *et al.* (1995) set out to explore these beliefs and working practices amongst support teachers in Scotland. They used the five key aspects of the support role identified by the Scottish Committee for staff development in education:

1) Consultation and collaboration with class/subject teacher
2) Development of a differentiated curriculum
3) Direct teaching or co-ordinating services for individual pupils
4) Contributing to whole school policies on learning support
5) Staff development in relation to learning support

They sampled 10 per cent of the support teachers in Scotland and asked them to rate these five aspects of their role from most important to least important. The percentage rating of each aspect in order of prime importance is given in Table 10.1. Clearly, direct teaching, either through cooperative work in class or individual tuition, was seen as the main task for support teacher.

Table 10.1   Aspects of a support teacher's role in order of importance

Aspect	Of prime importance (%)
Co-operative teaching	44
Consultancy	23
Individual teaching	20
Staff development	<4

Activity 10.1

If you are a support teacher, do a one-term diary analysis using the categories in Table 10.1 to summarise the pattern of your own working practices. At the end of the term ask yourself if you are happy with the pattern. If not, in what direction would you like to change?

If you are working in a school, interview the support staff working in your school to get information on how they spend their time in your school, using the same categories. Do you think this is the most efficient working pattern?

If neither of the above applies to you, interview someone working in one of these roles to discuss these topics.

As the notion of support developed, the numbers of unqualified non-teaching assistants working with pupils with SEN began to grow. Clayton *et al.* (1990) found an increase of 380 per cent in Wiltshire between 1983 and 1989. Goacher *et al.* (1988) report that 77 per cent of LEAs recorded a significant increase in number of non-teaching assistants supporting pupils with SEN. Despite this growth, neither the 1989 HMI survey of support services nor the NARE report (see Lorenz, 1992) mention this development, and it remains an area much in need of research. What are the range of support tasks that can adequately be carried out by un-qualified, and often untrained support assistants? How can managers know whether use of support assistants is an efficient use of financial resources?

Activity 10.2

Find out about the following, and make some field notes:

- How many non-teaching assistants support pupils who are experiencing difficulties in your school?
- What tasks do they perform?
- What training do they get?
- What evidence is there that they are able to carry out the tasks allocated to them?

If you are a support teacher, do you carry out any tasks that could be done by a non-teaching assistant? What are those tasks?

Reduced role of the LEA

By the end of the 1980s the growth of support services in England and Wales had come to an end, with a greater central government emphasis being placed on school autonomy, and the role of the LEA being reduced. Diamond (1993) lists some of the factors at work that curtailed powers of LEAs to retain large central services. First, legislation required that 85 per cent of the LEA budget had to be delegated to schools by December 1993. Delegation of budgets to schools, both mainstream and special, increased the autonomy of schools and reduced the role of the LEA. Given the administrative tasks LEAs have to perform, together with the services that must be centrally retained (educational psychology and education social work services), there is little scope for LEAs to fund comprehensive support services working across the full range of SEN. If this were to be done, it must be done in co-operation with schools who are prepared to use some of their budgets to purchase such services from the LEA rather than from other providers. Secondly, the mechanisms for allowing schools to become grant maintained reduce the amount of money available to LEAs, thus increasing the difficulties. Thirdly, there is a trend for education departments to merge with other departments – such as social services, leisure, libraries and museums – with the result that each part of the education department, including support services, must compete with other local government services for financial support.

The educational reforms introduced through legislation in the past decade brought into being conflicting trends. Although schools were given increased autonomy at the expense of LEAs (e.g. in financial management, employment issues), in other areas central government increased its own control – through imposing a National Curriculum and its associated assessment procedures in which it took control of much of the curriculum, that was traditionally seen as an area of teachers' professional expertise. More recent developments suggested that the next attack would be on pedagogy, with the government urging which particular teaching styles should be used (such as whole-class learning rather than small groups focused on differentiated tasks). The introduction of the 'literacy hour', which specifies the types of tasks that should be used, is one example of this trend. This increased politicisation of education has had a profound effect on special educational support services. A further trend has been the introduction of concepts and vocabulary from free-market economics: competition, customers, customer care, total quality management, etc. These concepts are replacing the previous notions of public service, duty, clients, professionalism and professional ethics. All these changes have meant that support services must reconsider their purpose and place within the education system, with the obvious concomitant management implications.

In this new climate the core task for LEAs within the field of special education is to ensure that pupils with SEN receive an effective service by developing a partnership with both schools and parents. The Audit Commission emphasises the creation of client–contractor relationships between schools and LEAs. The LEA specifies the funding available for all pupils with SEN, both statemented and non-statemented. It has the responsibility to develop effective systems of accountability to ensure targeted money reaches client groups and achieves specified objectives; to monitor the use of funds for non-statemented pupils with SEN; and to ensure the accountability of support services. LEAs also have a role (largely through their psychological services) to help schools with the early stages of the *Code of Practice* in identifying, assessing, providing specialist support and monitoring pupils with SEN. They also have a crucial role in stages 4 and 5 of the *Code of Practice*.

Meaning of support

Dyer (1988) explored the significance of changing terminology in SEN and found that 'support' was the word most commonly used in the 1980s. He charts its use back to the help and guidance that was provided in class for pupils with sensory impairments, and suggests that the support model was broadened to take in other difficulties. He considered that it was a way of asserting the rights of all pupils to a common education, even though they may be having more difficulties in making progress than many of their classmates. He found confusion over whether the word was used to describe activities aimed at working with individual pupils, at helping class teachers, or both. He suggested four different levels of support, with a variety of activities that might be used to provide it (Table 10.2).

Table 10.2 Levels of support and associated activities

Type	Activity
Pupil	In-class teaching, withdrawal teaching
Teacher	Team or co-operative teaching, consultation, analysis, observation, advice
Curriculum	Advice, planning, materials
School organisation	Consultation

This framework of support is similar to that developed by Duffield *et al.* and, like Duffield, does not consider the different professional roles that may be involved. It is interesting to note that the *Code of Practice* suggests that three main aspects of SEN which should be addressed by support services are identification, assessment and intervention in the form of individual educational plans. None of these activities is cited in the models of support Dyer (1988) and Duffield *et al.* (1995). It is as if the activities of identification and assessment are not problematic, and have already taken place before the involvement of support services. A number of studies have raised the issues of identification and assessment with respect to gender (Malcolm and Haddock, 1992), race (Desforges, 1995) and socioeconomic factors (Gray, 1992). Differential referral on the basis of any of these variables calls management into account in terms of the equable allocation of resources and over issues of values: why is it that so many black parents resist referral to SEN support services and resources whereas middle-class parents pursue resources to meet the needs of their dyslexic children? (See Desforges, 1997.)

Activity 10.3

Look at the SEN register in your school (or, if you are a support teacher, look at the register in one of the schools on your patch). Analyse the register in terms of gender and ethnicity at each of stages 1–5. Are there any imbalances when you compare this with the make up of the school? What issues arising out of this analysis do you think the school should consider?

Legal background: the role of support services in SEN

Under the Education Act 1981 parents had rights of appeal to the Secretary of State, who often took many months if not years to come to decisions on individual cases. The 1993 Act, and the *Code of Practice* arising from it, however, suggests that central government wished to distance itself from the day-to-day implementation of policy whilst, at the same time, retaining control by specifying to a high level of detail what professionals and LEAs should do. Instead of appeals to the Secretary of State, special tribunals now adjudicate in cases of dispute between parents and LEAs. Rather than helping schools implement the 1993 Act, the *Code of Practice* provides a set of procedures against which the tribunal can decide whether the LEA has fulfilled its functions under the Act.

The code states that its purpose is to help schools and LEAs obtain the best value from the financial resources and expertise available for children with SEN, from those who need a little extra help to those with more serious learning difficulties. It states: 'there is a continuum of special educational needs and [that] such needs are found across the range of ability. It recognises that the continuum of need should be reflected in a continuum of provision.' Booth (1995) is sceptical of this notion of a continuum of provision, and poses some interesting questions for managers who are trying to develop such a continuum. Perhaps the strangest aspect of the legislation is the continued use of the tautological definition of 'SENs' first used in the Education Act 1981.

Paragraph 9 of DfE (1994) Circular 6/94, The Organization of Special Educational Provision, London: DfE, refers to the responsibilities of LEAs, which includes the management and availability of support services, and the importance of LEAs producing clear and coherent authority-wide policies for special educational needs.

Part 2 of Circular 6/94 deals specifically with support services and their role in helping schools identify, assess and make appropriate provision for pupils with SEN: 'Schools should understand how they may secure access to support services and know the terms on which they will be available. It is equally important that LEAs should be able to assess the demand for support services.' It states that support services include 'equipment, materials, staff support or technical or professional expertise used for the identification and assessment of, or making special educational provision for, pupils with special educational needs within the meaning provided by section 156 of the Education Act 1993'. Interestingly, the *Code of Practice* (para. 2.58–2.60) is rather narrower in its view of support services, including only specialist teachers, advisers or teachers with knowledge of information technology for pupils with special educational needs, and educational psychologists. It makes no mention of non-teaching assistants, child care assistants or special needs assistants, nor does it include special equipment.

The circular lists examples of tasks that may be carried out by support services as:

1) Advice to teachers (teaching techniques, strategies, classroom management, curriculum materials).
2) Support to curriculum development for children with SEN.
3) Identification, observation and assessment of individual pupils.
4) Use of technology, including IT for pupils with SEN.
5) Direct teaching and practical support for classroom teachers.
6) Professional development of teachers working with pupils with SEN and the development of the school's policy on SEN.

The legislation clarifies the powers of LEAs to supply SEN support services. Under Section 162 (para. 67) of the Education Act 1993, LEAs may supply such services 'for the purpose only of assisting governing bodies in their duty to ensure that appropriate provision is made for pupils with SEN'. Since 1 April 1995, however, educational psychology services have been mandatory exceptions to the delegation of support services, and funding for this service may not be included in schools' budget shares. Paragraph 78 suggests that LEAs should also retain centrally 'low incidence SEN support services, notably those for pupils with visual, hearing and speech and language impairments', but it falls short of making these services mandatory exceptions.

Delegation of funding for support services

There are clear tensions in the advice given in the circular between the central government wish for LEAs to delegate as large a share of finances as possible to schools and the desire for LEAs to retain responsibility for ensuring schools have access to a comprehensive support system for meeting SEN. Part 3 of the circular deals with this co-ordination of provision. It states that LEAs' special needs policies should set out arrangements for the management and availability of support services, and for monitoring the performance of these services. It suggests that LEAs should provide full and clear information to all schools in their area about their provision of support services, and should regularly review that provision. This should ensure LEAs are aware of schools' requirements, are able to make service-level agreements with schools, and are able to maintain services that are staffed and equipped at a level that will efficiently meet demand.

However, if funding for support services is delegated, schools are free to purchase the service from any source they choose, not necessarily from the LEA. They could choose to use services from the voluntary or private sector, or from another LEA. Paragraph 77 states that 'the Secretary of State envisages that funds for SEN support services can be included in budget shares where schools would welcome the opportunity of seeking such advice from sources other than their own LEA'.

Paragraph 80 acknowledges the difficulties posed by this, and accepts the need for clear service-level agreements, specifying scope, quality, duration and cost of the services provided. It goes on to suggest that the length of such agreements should be for no more than three years, and for many agreements a shorter period will be appropriate. These constraints will be returned to when we consider the management implications later in this chapter.

Despite the difficulties noted above, the circular concludes that 'this will ensure LEAs are fully aware of schools requirements, are able to conclude service level agreements with schools, and are able to maintain services that are staffed and equipped at a level which will efficiently meet demand'. This may well turn out to be a pious hope rather than a reality arising out of appropriate financing and training of a centrally retained support service that has a clear view of how to match task to method.

The green paper *Excellence for all Children* (DfEE, 1997) acknowledges the difficulties with present funding mechanisms. It raises the question (*ibid.*, p. 91): 'What needs to be done for the new LMS arrangements to support effectively the responsibilities of both schools and LEAs for the SEN provision at stages 1–3 of the Code?' The paper notes that many LEAs already delegate to schools the funding for all or most SEN provision at stages 1–3, and expresses the view that such delegation is to be encouraged because it reflects school responsibilities under the *Code of Practice* and 'allows schools to take their own decisions about purchasing additional support, whether from their own LEA, SEN services from other agencies, including other LEAs, or from the private sector' (*ibid.*).

Despite this support for the autonomy of individual schools and for encouraging market forces to operate, the paper (*ibid.*) also 'recognises the arguments for retention by LEAs of some funding to support pupils at stages 1–3. Retention can ensure the maintenance of high quality LEA services, particularly for low incidence needs with which schools may be unfamiliar'.

A further dimension is the recognition of the particular difficulties faced by the new small authorities created by the reorganisation of local government, which may be unable to meet the needs of pupils requiring very specialised provision. One suggested solution is for regional planning, so that education, social services and health departments, together with the voluntary and independent sectors, work in partnership to 'encourage cooperation and specialisation in SEN support services' (*ibid.*, p. 58). It is hard to see how these conflicting perspectives can be reconciled, but the creation of mechanisms which encourage interagency working and allow the funding of comprehensive SEN support services will be of vital importance if inclusive education is to be developed.

The *Code of Practice*

Circular 6/94 is clear that SEN support services can play an important role in helping schools identify, assess and make special education provision for pupils with SEN (see Diamond, 1995). The major task is to establish the new roles of schools, support services and LEAs under the legislation, and to consider how support services can help schools improve the way they meet the special educational needs of their pupils while, at the same time, enabling schools to develop greater 'ownership' of special educational needs.

Diamond (*ibid.*) summarises the duties of LEAs as making clear

1) what is available from support services;
2) how they may be accessed by schools; and
3) on what terms support is available – free at point of delivery via centrally retained funding, or costed via service-level agreements or 'buy-back' arrangements.

LEAs have an obligation to consult with schools to consider the demand for support services schools will require. Although schools and their governors are primarily responsible for identifying, assessing and making provision for stages 1–3, they can use the support that has been considered necessary to help them in this task.

It is at stage 3 that the role of support services becomes more prominent, with the SENCO sharing responsibility for the child with external specialist services. It is important that support services are clear, to themselves and to schools, about what they can offer in terms of identification, assessment and intervention or provision to help the pupil with SEN at stage 3. As Diamond (*ibid.*) points out, the definitions of aims and objectives and how these relate to the broader aims of the LEA's policy in relation to SEN are critical. If LEAs have support services simply to fulfil minimum statutory duties for pupils with statements, the preventative role will be lost, and the percentage of pupils put forward for statements may increase considerably. *Excellence for all Children* (DfEE, 1997) states that it wants changes which enable LEA support staff to spend more time working with children in school, and helping teachers improve their skills in meeting the needs of children at stages 1–3 of the *Code of Practice*.

At stage 4, the LEA seeks advice from a variety of professionals in education and health. The advice of educational psychologists must be obtained for this multiprofessional assessment, and support teachers may often contribute to this advice.

At stage 5, where the LEA stipulates the level of support needed to meet the SEN described in the statement, and if the pupil is to be educated in a mainstream school, support teachers or non-teaching assistants are usually the main sources of support stipulated in the statement.

Key management tasks

Given the new climate and relationship between schools and LEAs described above, managers of support services need to define the role they have in enabling schools to meet the SEN of all their pupils through the operation of the *Code of Practice*. This can only be done within the context of the LEA plan for special needs. A number of key issues must be addressed:

1) What time and expertise will be devoted to preventative work in the form of in-service training, advisory and consultative work? How can the support services help schools meet the needs of a greater proportion of pupils such that they *never* reach any of the stages of the *Code of Practice* (some writers refer to such pupils as stage 0)? How can they support schools and teachers to develop a differentiated curriculum able to meet the educational needs of all pupils?

2) What does the LEA require of support services in terms of involvement at stage 3, and at stage 4 in reaching a decision on moving to a multiprofessional assessment? Will support services be involved in moderating criteria for stage 3 interventions and for moving to stage 4?

3) To what extent will support services be used as the named resource in the statement to meet the special educational needs of the individual? What part will they play in the LEA's statutory duty to monitor the educational progress of pupils with statements (particularly in terms of the annual review and helping the LEA meet its obligation to ensure the provider has delivered what the LEA wanted to purchase)?

Excellence for all Children (DfEE, 1997) seeks to develop national and local programmes to support increased inclusion, and sees LEA support services as having a crucial role in helping mainstream schools meet an increasingly complex range of special educational needs as inclusive education develops.

These decisions can only be made within the framework of the LEA plan for SEN and will be influenced by the support service managers' role within the broader SEN management structure. Much will depend on the proportion of special needs finance that has been delegated to schools rather than retained centrally by the LEA. A crucial element will be the roles of the different professionals in the support services – psychologists, teachers, non-teaching assistants, and the allocation of budgets to each. To what extent and for what purposes will non-teaching assistants be used? How will these groups relate to each other in terms of shared responsibilities and role differentiation? What management structures will best support collaborative working, minimising the risk of role confusion or conflict, overlapping job descriptions and inefficient use of resources?

Responding to the issues: Children First

Children First, Nottinghamshire's policy for pupils identified as having SEN, stresses corporate, not competitive, planning. Consultation with mainstream schools about moving towards greater inclusion of pupils who have disabilities or learning difficulties emphasises the effective use of existing resources, better co-ordination of support services, proper attention to training, and a planned programme of incremental change. An increase in finance for this programme was agreed by switching money from out-county places to support individual placements in local schools. The county retained centrally a range of special needs resources (support teachers, support assistants and special school teachers engaging in a mainstream support role). These resources are targeted (using mainstream support groups consisting of area administrators, area inspectors, educational psychologists, special needs support managers and mainstream headteachers) to those pupils with the most significant needs, as well as supporting schools to include children with SEN. A key principle in resource decisions has been the targeting of support to the greatest need. Several schools have moved to a position of more corporate response to children with SEN. Area mainstream support groups have been able to allocate blocks of support to families or pyramids of schools, with schools making more decisions about priorities (Barber *et al.*, 1992).

In 1993, however, the prevailing ethos that then emanated from government to make schools competing businesses, to try to distinguish school and LEA responsibilities along the purchaser/provider split, together with increased parental powers to request statutory assessment, worked against the development of the corporate co-operative planning inherent in the Children First policy (Gray and Dessent, 1993).

Possible roles for support staff

Within such a structure, support staff could have a number of different roles, and these are identified below.

An advisory role for pupils at stage 1 and 2 of the code

The aim of this role would be to improve the knowledge and skills of school-based staff to enable them to identify, assess and devise interventions in the form of individual educational plans. This would involve in-service work for all or part of school staffs to provide area-based or authority-wide training for SENCOs. It would also involve issues of differentiation of the curriculum to achieve a better match between the needs of pupils and classroom tasks and activities. Differentiation becomes increasingly problematical when central government and the OFSTED chief inspector push the notion of whole-class teaching as the efficient way for schools to operate. In large schools, setting or streaming is an option; in smaller schools it is not. Setting and streaming also raise the fundamental issues of the reliability and validity of the assessments used to form the groups, which often ignore uneven rates of development and may cause pupils to live down to the reduced expectations of lower sets or streams.

What little information there is suggests that few schools have trained or qualified SENCOs, implying a huge need for this type of professional development work with teachers. It also raises questions for the support services themselves. Do support service staff have the necessary skills and experience to carry out this work, and what are their own training needs to help them carry out these tasks?

Activity 10.4

Carry out an audit in your school of special needs qualifications and the experience of all staff. Include attendance at short courses. If you are a support teacher, do this in one of your schools. What are the implications for the training plan for the school?

Note: This activity may require careful judgement and tact on your part. You are strongly advised to explain the purpose of your inquiry to the staff and to seek their support in advance.

Lack of training is particularly acute with non-teaching assistants. Here we have unqualified staff taking on the job of helping pupils with significant learning difficulties in mainstream classrooms and working with pupils that qualified teachers may have been unable to work with in a satisfactory way (see Lorenz, 1992; Thompson and Baskind, 1995).

Consultancy work with schools will help schools develop their own expertise and planning in these areas. Since the change in teachers' conditions of service to include five school-based training days, there is evidence of a fragmentation of training opportunities for teachers, with reduced emphasis on longer courses of full-time post-experience study and an increasing use of a one-off, half or one-day school-based course on a specific topic.

An intervention role with pupils at stages 3–5

Intervention would mean direct work with pupils in identification, assessment and intervention, and sometimes as part of the additional resources named in the statement. These are the more traditional tasks of support staff and have been subject to powerful critiques (e.g. Dessent, 1987; Gray, 1992; Booth, 1995). Increasing the amount of support managed outside mainstream could demotivate and deskill mainstream teachers who feel that someone else has responsibility for their difficult pupils. On the other hand, little or no outside provision could make mainstream schools and teachers more motivated to meet such needs and, by reducing the size and role of support services, the financial savings so made could be added to mainstream budgets.

Further, the incentive of extra finance for mainstream schools for each statemented pupil means an incentive to maximise the number of pupils put forward for statements. As support staff must be involved in assessing whether the criteria from the *Code of Practice* are being met and must contribute to the multiprofessional assessment, so even less of their time is available to help schools intervene to move pupils forward. If schools could be persuaded to meet a greater range of special needs without recourse to statements, more resources would be available for teaching rather than supporting the administrative procedures of statementing. Dessent (1987) develops this thesis, and Gray (1992) describes how one LEA has tried to operate such a system.

The LEA officer

Here the role of the support worker is to monitor the education of pupils on statements in mainstream schools, to help monitor schools' overall policies in the field of SEN, and to identify pupils according to the criteria set out in the *Code of Practice*.

These different roles can cause difficulties where one individual has to carry out more than one role at any one time. Let us imagine an educational psychologist working to help a school support a pupil with learning difficulties. An individual assessment is carried out, and an individual educational plan drawn up. The class teacher is helped to differentiate the curriculum, appropriate materials are introduced and progress is monitored. However, both the class teacher and parent feel that the progress is too slow, and demand a formal assessment. The psychologist feels that the intervention has not been given long enough in order to judge its success. As LEA officer the psychologist has to switch roles and offer advice on whether the criteria have been met to move to stage 4. Neither teacher nor parent will see this as a balanced and independent judgement. If the case does go to formal assessment, the parent may no longer trust the judgement of the psychologist, seeing the psychologist as supporting the interests of the LEA rather than those of the pupil and parent. This is particularly so if the assessment of needs does not coincide with the views of any one of these parties. In these cases there are several different clients – the pupil, the parent, the teacher and school, and the LEA. All may have different perspectives on the problem, and it may be difficult if not impossible to reconcile them. How can management structures help to clarify these role conflicts, and help the individual support worker deal with the ambiguities inherent in the situation outlined above?

Training needs of support staff

In order to carry out these new roles of consultant, adviser and trainer working with mainstream teachers, support staff themselves need training. The 1989 HMI survey of SEN support services (DES, 1989) indicated that fewer than half the services surveyed had received any training for the new roles. The reason for this was not simply due to lack of resources but to lack of forethought and planning. Even in those LEAs committed to training support staff few had developed expertise in the areas of general advisory work, curriculum development and the structure and processes of school management. In only a very few LEAs had the work of these newly formed support services been co-ordinated with other schools advisory services (subject curriculum support), and too often schools were getting conflicting advice from different services. The general picture was one of fragmentation, with the various services that offered consultation or advice lacking common objectives. *Excellence for all Children* (DfEE, 1997) notes that fewer than half LEAs provide appropriate training and continuing professional development experiences for support staff. It notes the need to review the arrangements both for initial specialist training for teachers taking on a support role in the field of SEN and for providing a programme for continuing professional developement for staff already in this role.

Garner (1996) raises issues of training and professional development across the whole field of special education. He found that almost half the teachers of pupils with severe learning difficulties have no specialist knowledge or training. He notes serious difficulties in covering basic special needs issues in initial teacher training courses, mainly due to lack of time. Many newly qualified teachers are unfamiliar with their responsibilities under the *Code of Practice*, and have received little or no training on the various special needs they are bound to meet in their work as classroom teachers. Although every school must appoint a SENCO, there is no nationally agreed standard of knowledge or skill they should have, nor any agreed form of training. Most have little or no formal training for the role, and are given little time to carry it out.

It is against this background that support services are operating, and careful planning is needed to ensure support staff have the knowledge, skills and resources to help staff in schools develop knowledge and skills in the area of SEN, and at the same time ensure common frameworks with other advisory services to ensure schools are getting congruent advice from these different sources. The management tasks are clear, and there is a need to develop supervision and appraisal systems which help identify the continuing professional development needs of staff and to use these to set service training goals in order to give training a high priority.

Working within the new culture: problems with market forces applied to SEN

Bowers (1995) offers an extended critique of the difficulties caused by attempts to operate a market forces model of SEN. He starts with the premise that the market forces model assumes that what was wanted in education would thrive and expand, whereas that that was not wanted would wither and disappear. Joint Audit Commission and HMI reports (1992a; 1992b) argue that LEAs should see their role as a client, with the schools as contractors. LEAs will purchase services from the providing agencies – schools. With the funding of most units and resourced provision for pupils with SEN being delegated, and with the widespread practice of delegating funding for statemented pupils, there has been a significant move to this purchaser role on the part of many LEAs. The *Code of Practice* reinforces this, with the LEA being seen as the final reviewer of the school's attempts to meet the needs as described in the statements.

However, the situation is not that simple. If the LEA (as purchaser) alone could decide on what it needs to buy from mainstream schools, there would be a reasonably close fit to market forces. However, if parents are also given a role in the purchasing of services, they may ask for more resources than there are finances available to purchase them. Whilst the LEA has a global strategic and resourcing function for all SEN pupils in its authority, parents have more specific preoccupations with their own children. Legislation gives parents the right to be involved in the process of what services should be purchased for their child, and they are often supported by powerful voices from pressure groups in the voluntary sector. As Bowers (1995) notes, many of the voluntary organisations offering advice, support and advocacy for parents have a vested interest in the outcomes. Many are themselves providers with their own special schools (often expensive residential institutions) and they need pupils with fees paid by LEAs. They also offer consultancy to schools and training for teachers on a commercial basis.

This tripartite tension between provider schools, purchaser budget-holding LEAs and parents with raised expectations of individual rights supported by voluntary bodies is clearly too complex to be understood within simple market economics. Central government has recognised this in many aspects of its drive to privatise publicly owned utilities. It has provided for a regulatory body to arbitrate on some of the dilemmas raised by the introduction of market economics into new areas. In the case of SEN, the *Code of Practice* allows for independent tribunals to act as the final review body in cases where parents are dissatisfied.

For special needs support services the picture is even more complex. At first these were to be purchased by schools, and funding for them (apart from educational psychological services) could be delegated to schools. The *Code of Practice* gave increased prominence to these services as a necessary part of the code's later stages. LEAs now, however, act as providers of some services free to schools at the point of use, and other services are offered to schools on a fee-paying basis. If budgets for support services are delegated to schools, there is a clear temptation, and obvious benefit, to schools if they move straight to getting the educational psychologist involved, bypassing the services they need to pay for at the point of delivery. Resisting, and explaining the reasons for resisting, these pressures will take up educational psychologist time and may cause unnecessary conflict, making it more difficult to sustain harmonious working relationships with schools.

A final complication is that, under both the Education Acts 1993 and 1994, LEAs bear ultimate responsibility for the effective education of pupils. It is unlikely that they would be absolved from that duty because the provision is made by a locally managed or grant-maintained school.

For all these reasons the management of the special needs budgets in LEAs is fraught with difficulties. At least two chief education officers have lost their jobs because of a failure to prevent large overexpenditure in the area of SEN. The *TES* of 12 April 1996 reported an overspend in East Sussex of 820 per cent, the county having budgeted for 100 statements in the year, but in the event having funded 920. Bowers (1995) gives a number of other examples of specific difficulties caused by this particular model of market economics. As Vincent *et al.* (1994) write: 'This market oriented culture sits uneasily with the traditional benevolent humanitarianism of special educational professionals.' Although *Excellence for all Children* (DfEE, 1997) acknowledges the dilemma in terms of the balance between delegation of SEN funding to schools versus retention by the LEA, and between competitive tendering versus co-operation to provide comprehensive support services across regions, it does not suggest how to resolve these tensions. There is a clearly stated goal: 'No matter where a pupil lives and whatever their needs, an appropriate level of support is available' (*ibid.*, p. 54), but no mechanism is proposed to ensure this happens.

Educational values and SEN

The major reforms in education which have taken place over the past ten years have been based on a clear set of values underpinned by the notion that competition is a powerful way of improving standards. Competition between schools has been encouraged by publishing league tables of National Curriculum results, attendance figures and results in public examinations. By giving parents the theoretical choice of naming which school they would like their child to attend, it was assumed that some schools would attract many pupils and expand, whilst some would be undersubscribed and would reduce in size or close.

Recently, both the right and left of the political spectrum have tended to denigrate the achievements of schools and encourage a simplistic view of educational aims and methods, centring on 'back to basics', whole-class teaching and the improvement of standards. The liberal values of realising the personal potential of all individuals and of allowing for a variety of outcomes by which educational success would be measured – social, emotional and spiritual – have been rejected. In such a climate those who do not achieve according to the set narrow criteria are a burden to the school and prevent it from reaching its goals. It might be suggested that, in such a system, there would be an increase in the number of pupils identified as having SEN and who require segregated provision, and that more pupils would cause management problems because of their behavioural or emotional needs and would hence be permanently excluded. It comes as no surprise, therefore, that there is evidence that all these things have been happening in recent years (e.g. Norwich, 1996).

Clearly the value system reflected in recent central government policy supports a view that competition between schools functioning as autonomous units will drive up educational standards as defined by such crude criteria as exam results or attendance figures, taking little account of school catchment features. In such a climate there is a diminishing role for LEAs and, in July 1996, the Secretary of State for Education suggested that the percentage of the budget delegated directly to schools should increase to 95 per cent. If this comes about what is the future for SEN support services? What are the implications for support staff? How can LEAs involve themselves in countering these developments and once more assert the rights of all children to be educated in mainstream schools?

The New Labour government elected in May 1997 committed itself to inclusive education, a reduction in the numbers of pupils with statements and a rapid rise in standards in basic attainments. We have already witnessed the impact that judging schools on a narrow range of attainments in basic subjects has on driving up both exclusions and the number of pupils put forward for statements. Lindsay and Thompson (1997) deal at length with the dilemmas faced by parents and professionals when their value systems are challenged by policy that creates tensions within the education system. Is there the political will to face up to some of these tensions and to help create mechanisms that will improve the possibilities for inclusive education by ensuring the existence of appropriate support services for pupils with SEN?

Conclusion

Much of the literature on SEN management focuses on structures – special schools or integrated resources, structures of support services, the ways in which support teachers relate to psychologists, the creation of area teams or the maintenance of unitary LEA services. This chapter has tried to focus on functional issues, and it is only when these have been addressed that we can look at the range of structures which would enable these functions to be carried out efficiently.

References

Audit Commission/HMI (1992a) *Getting in on the Act*, HMSO, London.

Audit Commission/HMI (1992b) *Getting the Act Together*, HMSO, London.

Barber, P., Gray, M. and Hickling, M. (1992) The Hucknall Families in *Special Children*.

Booth, T. (1995) Continua or chimera?, *British Journal of Special Education*, Vol. 1, no. 21, pp. 21–4.

Bowers, T. (1995) Touched by the invisible hand, *Support for Learning*, Vol. 3, no. 10, pp. 104–11.

Clayton, T. (1993) Welfare assistants in the classroom – problems and solutions, *Educational Psychology in Practice*, Vol. 8, no. 4, pp. 191–7.

DES (1978) *Special Educational Needs: Report of the Committee of Enquiry into the Education of Handicapped Children and Young People (the Warnock Report)*, HMSO, London.

DES (1989) *A Survey of Support Services for Special Educational Needs*, DES Publications, Stanmore.

DfEE (1994) *Code of Practice on the Identification and Assessment of Special Educational Needs*, DfEE, London.

DfEE (1997) *Excellence for all Children: Meeting Special Educational Needs*, DfEE, London.

Desforges, M. (1995) Assessment of special educational needs in bilingual pupils, *Schools Psychology International*, Vol. 1, no. 16, pp. 5–18.

Desforges, M. (1997) Ethnic minority communities and values in special education, in Lindsay, G. and Thompson, D. (eds) *Values into Practice in Special Education*, David Fulton, London.

Dessent, T. (1987) *Making the Ordinary School Special*, Falmer Press, Lewes.

Diamond, C. (1995) How to get the best from your 'flexible friend', *Support for Learning*, Vol. 2, no. 10, pp. 63–9.

Duffield, J., Brown, S. and Riddell, S. (1995) The post-Warnock learning support teacher: where do specific learning difficulties fit in?, *Support for Learning*, Vol. 1, no. 10, pp. 22–8.

Dyer, C. (1988) Which support? *Support for Learning*, Vol. 1, no. 3, pp. 6–11.

Garner, C. (1996) *Professional Development Needs to Meet Special Educational Needs*, SENTEC Flash Ley Resource Centre, Hawksmoor Rd, Stafford ST17 9DR.

Gray, J. (1992) Resourcing for integration of children with special educational needs, *Educational and Child Psychology*, Vol. 4, no. 9, pp. 19–24.

Gray, P. and Dessent, T. (1993) Getting Our Act Together, *British Journal of Special Education*, Vol. 20, no. 1, pp. 9–11.

Lindsay, G. and Thompson, D. (eds) (1997) *Values into Practice in Special Education,* David Fulton, London.

Lorenz, S. (1992) Supporting special needs assistants in mainstream schools, *Educational and Child Psychology,* Vol. 4, no. 9, pp. 25–33.

Malcolm, L. and Haddock, L. (1992) Making trouble – get results, *Educational Psychology in Practice,* Vol. 2, no. 8, pp. 97–100.

Moses, D., Hegarty, S. and Jowett, S. (1987) Meeting special educational needs: support for the ordinary school, *Educational Research,* Vol. 2, no. 29, pp. 108–15.

Norwich, B. (1996) Special needs education or education for all: connective specialisation and ideological impurity, *British Journal of Special Education,* Vol. 2, no. 23, pp. 100–3.

Thompson, D. and Baskind, S. (1995) Using assistants to support the educational needs of pupils with learning difficulties, *Educational and Child Psychology,* Vol. 12, pp. 46–57.

UNESCO (1994) *The Salamanca Statement and Framework for Action on Special Needs Education,* UNESCO, Paris.

Vincent, C., Evans, J., Lunt, I. and Young, P. (1994) The market forces? The effects of local management of schools on special educational need provision, *British Educational Research Journal,* Vol. 20, pp. 261–77.

Section 3

Response

11

Managing to Include? Rights, Responsibilities and Respect

CATHY NUTBROWN

It is a privilege to contribute the final chapter to this book and to reflect on issues of management in inclusive education, from the 'outside'. I say the outside because though I write as someone who has – among other things – taught, 'managed' a teaching team, and 'included' children with SEN into mainstream settings, I do not consider myself expert in either *management* or *inclusive education*. So, I should perhaps offer some justification for my presence in this book in general, and for why I should presume to write this final reflective chapter in particular. It is this. My teaching experience and philosophy lie in early education, my early experiences of teaching young children are the cornerstone of my current work in early education, in literacy, in assessment and in children's rights. Those who know the work of early childhood educators know that nursery education at its best *is* inclusive education. There will be few nursery teachers who, in the past two or three decades, have not:

- included children with learning difficulties in their nursery classes;
- prioritised the allocation of places in order to include children with particular needs;
- carried out individual observations and diagnostic assessments;
- discussed with parents how best to meet their children's needs;
- managed their settings in order to enable *all* children equality of access to a differentiated curriculum; or
- liaised with numerous professionals and agencies who serve children with learning difficulties.

For many nursery teachers the issue of additional support for children with SEN rarely arose. It was often the case that children with particular needs were included with their peers in the nursery setting. In cases where it was thought that children may need additional support for their *future* learning the process of writing a statement of need began in preparation for the time when children were about to move on to compulsory education. More recently some early years teachers have taken on the role of SENCO in their schools and all teachers of young children have a role in the implementation of the *Code of Practice* (discussed in Chapter 8 by Caroline Roaf).

This chapter, coming at the end of a collection written by experts in their fields of management and inclusive education, pays tribute to early childhood educators who have, for decades, developed practices by which they have *managed to include* young children with SEN in mainstream settings as a matter of course. They did so because that was the most obvious practice and because children were entitled to be educated within their own local communities. Inclusion might not always have been successful for children, parents or staff – doubtless more professional development opportunities and fuller knowledge would have improved opportunities offered to some children – but fundamentally, inclusion – rather than exclusion in a special unit, special school or no provision at all – was in most cases the first option.

Managing to include?

This book brings together many key issues and ideas pertinent to the management of inclusive education, including:

- principles of *special education* and *educational management*;
- the move from *special* to *integrative* to *inclusive* education;
- the legacy of history in the management of special education;
- managing learning, curriculum policy and effective teaching practice;
- issues of funding and resourcing inclusive education;
- the ability of schools to include young children;
- the role of SENCOs;
- the implications of the *Code of Practice*;
- the role and future of support services; and
- interagency working.

The many issues, challenges, obstacles and opportunities highlighted by earlier authors in discussing the issues above seek to respond to the question: But how *do* schools and teachers *manage to include*? In the opening chapter, Peter Clough reminded us that attitudes pervade management. Indeed the attitudes, preconceptions and others' interpretations of children's needs and dispositions are factors which teachers must manage in order to teach appropriately.

There can be times when inclusion can almost seem effortless, where all that is to be managed is another unique child beginning in the education system. Such cases are often preceded with information from other professionals, including medical practitioners – who hold their own attitudes and presumptions. Elaine Herbert, in Chapter 7, demonstrates how medical diagnosis may not always be a reliable predictor of children's achievement and how teachers' openness to find out about children as people and individuals provides an important key to inclusion. Such was my own experience of Rachel:

I recall the day I visited a nursery class and met Rachel, a beautiful child, just three years old with blonde hair and deep, grey eyes who walked with her own distinctive speedy, childlike bounce. I was immediately struck by her bright personality and her long, long fine fingers, so delicate and so deft as she threaded tiny beads onto a thread to make herself a necklace. Before she began at the local nursery class her teacher was told by the health visitor that Rachel had cerebral palsy, that she wore callipers and – at times – 'demanded much attention'. Her teacher told me:

'When Rachel first began at nursery we all had a tendency to rarefy her. We had all read the notes about her and met her just once when she visited. We had this idea of a 'precious child' who needed much care and who might need extra and special attention. At first we all tried to cushion her from danger. But Rachel sought out danger! We do admire her, she is exceptional, she amazes us. She is special in that she just does everything and we really don't need to think about her any differently to the other children. She needs none of our special attention – she can fight her own corner.'

Her teacher talked about how, when she read the health visitor's notes she wondered 'What three year old doesn't at times "demand much attention"?' Rachel was always smiling, rarely angry, always energetic and included *herself* with others in her nursery class with ease.

But inclusion is not always so easy, so naturally achievable or so painless, as Martin's story will tell:

The special needs support teacher told the teacher in charge of the nursery class at a community infant school that she was working with a boy called Martin who was autistic. The teacher had a vague idea of what this meant, believing that he could be anywhere on a continuum of particular patterns of behaviour. The special needs support teacher was keen that Martin should attend his local nursery. The nursery teacher had clear and specific reservations – not rooted in negative attitudes, ill informed preconceptions and others' interpretations of children's characteristics or their needs, but grounded in her concerns for the current management of the nursery where she worked. She told the support teacher that she felt this was not the place for Martin and explained her reasons. She said that she was happy for Martin and his mother to visit the nursery but that she thought this nursery, full already with vulnerable children who had such particular needs grown out of poverty, ill-health and other forms of deprivation, was not the place to try to include a child who was likely to need stability, consistency and routine. The teacher knew that the support teacher thought she was making excuses, being obstructive, needed persuasion, more information. She asked the teacher if she would meet Martin and his mother. And so the teacher at the school arranged a time when Martin and his mother could visit the nursery with the support teacher.

It was a bright June morning. All was well, many children were playing outside in the sunshine, it was a settled beginning to the day and everything was calm. Martin was just four years old. He was blonde, with deep blue eyes – distant. He found the coloured bricks of interest and settled to play with them for a while. The nursery teacher talked with his mother, learned about her only son. Martin's mother talked about her beautiful little boy, how all was fine until just before his second birthday, when he stopped his lively chatter, insisted they always walked to the shops the same way, that he always ate the same food, always wore the same clothes. As the woman talked to the teacher she shed no tears, but the teacher knew she was crying.

The nursery teacher said that Martin was welcome but, though she knew it would likely hurt his mother, she added that this nursery was not an easy place for children. She talked gently about the difficulties of many children who attended and how there would be days when routines would be broken, when several children cried for the whole session, and when the calm of this June morning would be replaced by chaos. The teacher knew that Martin's mother thought she did not want him. Nothing could be farther from the truth, but the teacher knew that this place was not the place for Martin.

Martin was admitted, for five mornings each week, He was admitted by a teacher committed to the principle of *inclusion*, but he was admitted to a nursery ravaged by staff conflict, where people would not *be* managed and – because of their own needs – could not always successfully manage themselves. Martin was admitted to a nursery full of children with damage and dislocation in their lives – physical and sexual abuse, overwhelming poverty, disproportionate ill-health, numerous wet beds, and no end of broken hearts.

Martin stayed for two weeks. Each day his teacher talked with his mother. Each day she told her what Martin had enjoyed, and of the struggle he had with his peers in the nursery. There were many troubled children in Martin's company, and though Martin was interested, and bright and he was *able*, the nursery *dis*abled him. In that setting he was not being included in a calm, ordered society. He was not a member of a predictable community, he was appended into a community of children and adults in chaos.

After two weeks Martin left. His teacher hoped he had not been harmed, but she knew the harm it had caused his mother. Martin went to a nursery a few miles away which had a special unit for children with special educational needs and which worked to include children from that unit into mainstream classes once they had become established in the school community.

Martin's story suggests that we should not include everywhere, any-where, at any cost, and that there are times when settings are unable to include children with particular needs until the needs of those settings too have been addressed. Elaine Herbert, in Chapter 7, describes the case of Stephen where one headteacher refused to admit him into the nursery. If the setting could not include him, her decision (though perhaps not her reasons) might have been correct. What is needed in such schools is appropriate professional development and management support for headteacher and staff in order to move those educational settings on to develop their educational culture as a less exclusive and more inclusive community.

The struggle to achieve *truly* inclusive education has been exacerbated by such problems as:

- inadequate funding;
- increasingly centralised control of curriculum;
- prevailing attitudes of society towards disability;
- lack of action on human rights in general and children's rights in particular; and
- lack of adequate and funded professional development for teachers and others.

These issues and the effort to overcome them have been described by earlier contributors. But there remains a question. Is it a case of *just about* managing to include, or is inclusive education being managed *with success* to the benefit of all children and society?

Rights, responsibilities and respect

Binding together the contributions in this book must be a consideration of three fundamental issues: rights, responsibilities and respect. These three must permeate discussion of management for inclusive education and deserve some kind of endword here.

Considering rights

In December 1991 the UK government ratified the UN Convention on the Rights of the Child. It addressed children's rights to protection, freedom from discrimination, survival and development, security in family life and the right to participate in matters concerning them. Three years later in the first UK government report on progress on implementation there was a failure to acknowledge any need to change, improve, reconsider, monitor or resource any legislation, policy, or practice (Lansdown, 1996, p. 2). A non-governmental report from the UK Children's Rights Development Unit (Lansdown and Newell, 1994) offered the UN committee a more critical analysis of the UK implementation of the convention which prompted criticism of many aspects of government policy both in relation to the rights contained in the Convention and the lack of procedures in place to implement the Convention in the UK.

Though the UN convention as a whole has relevance, for the purposes of the issues under discussion here there are two articles of the convention which are worth attention. Article 23 asserts the right of children with 'disabilities' to 'enjoy a full and decent life, in conditions which ensure dignity, promote self-reliance, and facilitate the child's active participation in the community'. In short, Article 23 charges governments to include *all* children in their own local communities. Article 29 addresses education in general, stating that education should be directed to 'the development of the child's personality, talents and mental and physical abilities to their fullest potential'. Articles 23 and 29 taken together assert the rights of all children to be educated to their potential, within their own communities.

Those who argue against children's rights sometimes do so on the basis that rights mean responsibility and children should not be burdened with responsibility so therefore cannot be endowed with rights. This is nonsense, an excuse created in order to block progress on fundamental issues of humanity. As Peter Clough asserts in the opening chapter, because the balance between needs and rights can be difficult to achieve, and because there can be tensions between the rights of one child and another, this is no reason to refrain from seeking solutions. Where children have special educational needs, adults must sometimes take for them the burden of responsibility whilst they also recognise – and teach children about – their rights.

Lansdown (1996, p. 10) writes: 'The Convention provides the basic tools for analysing and evaluating practice. The task is now in the hands of every adult living or working with children to translate those tools into fundamental changes in the reality of children's lives.' This responsibility lies as much with those who *manage* in order to *include* as it does with policy-makers and purse-holders.

Children's rights are the responsibility of everyone, not simply of the government of the day. Every educator, every manager, has a responsibility to work within a framework of children's rights and they can do much on a day-to-day basis to support, extend and uphold children's rights. The signalled intention of the government in 1997 to incorporate the European Convention on Human Rights (ECHR) into UK domestic law was welcomed, along with warnings that all the Principles of the UN Convention on the Rights of the Child still need to be implemented and should not be overshadowed by the move on human rights (Gunner, 1997). Reviewing benefits and limitations of the ECHR as a tool for enhancing children's rights, Lansdown (1998, p. 21) suggests that the incorporation of the ECHR into UK law is

a step in the right direction. But for children, it is not enough. We must therefore welcome this commitment on the part of government as progress towards the ultimate goal of societal recognition of children as holders of human rights. But we must also continue to argue for a commitment to full implementation of all the principles of the UN Convention of the Rights of the Child, in law, in policy and in practice.

Such a commitment to children's rights – in law, policy and practice – would have a profound effect on the management of inclusive education and the opportunities it could lead to in moving from policies to effective inclusive experiences.

Taking responsibility

Children's rights in and to education cannot be realised unless and until those who teach – and those who manage *for* teaching – accept that they all have a responsibility *towards* children and power they can use *for* them. The *nature* of those responsibilities might well differ but those whose work involves the business of learning have inescapable obligations to children – to facilitate their learning and nurture their future potential as individual citizens.

Teachers' responsibilities include creating appropriate learning climates for the children they teach – that is to say, the physical surroundings and emotional climates in which children are *disposed to learn*, as well as the *content* of that learning. As Felicity Armstrong discusses in Chapter 4, the freedom of teachers to be creative and develop innovative individual practices to the benefit of pupils with individual and specific learning needs has been severely curtailed by increasing central control. However difficult the task, it still remains the responsibility of teachers, schools and government to ensure that *all* children have the experience of education which enables them to learn and develop to their fullest potential. This means:

- the creation of *enabling environments* where children who may require – at times – a different kind of teaching to help them realise their own potential, are recognised as full participants in their school community;
- remaining prepared to challenge policy which does not readily translate into effective experience for children;
- teachers also work in *enabling environments* where they receive new opportunities – through professional development – to develop their own thinking and practice; and
- headteachers receive the support they need to manage their schools in ways which facilitate teachers and pupils to give their best to learning.

In schools throughout the UK there are fresh examples daily of what can be accomplished when adults turn their responsibility from the rhetoric of *policy* into the reality of *experience* and manage their teaching in ways which enable all children to reach their own unique potential. It will also be possible to find situations where the opposite is true, where policy and practice are divorced and where children do not always reap the benefits of working in tune with adults who can fulfil their responsibilities, where children are not *taught*, but are *schooled* in ways which do not include them in their learning or address their specific needs.

Taking responsibility requires much of policy-makers, headteachers and teachers. It requires them to scrutinise their work at every turn, to examine their organisation, their curriculum, their resources, their security, their relationships with parents, their use of support staff, their assessment processes. The list is probably endless. Teaching *is* an onerous responsibility and deserves to be recognised as such by government, LEAs, headteachers, teachers themselves and parents. Taking responsibility is never easy, but it can be done with experience, with recognition, with knowledge and with love. Recognition of such great responsibility must be accompanied by appropriate levels of support as and when needed.

Creating a culture of respect

What might it mean to create a *culture of respect* in education? What does *respect* mean in terms of children's learning? This is a question that requires an individual response of conscience, of being and of intellect. It might be sufficient here to say that *respect* is not about being 'nice'; it involves more integrity than that. Showing respect means being clear, honest, courteous, diligent and consistent. Respect for children is a disposition that can nurture the capabilities in children which will help them to learn. Respect for children will enable adults (teachers, parents, researchers, inspectors, psychologists, doctors, government ministers, local policy-makers) to fulfil their responsibilities towards children. Respect is a disposition that enables those who work with – and for – children to fulfil the most demanding of their responsibilities.

*Dis*respect is not necessarily malicious – it can often be born of naiveté, and sometimes manifests itself in strange and unexpected ways. I recall working with a group of early years teachers on an LEA INSET course. We were discussing ways of managing what we called 'difficult' behaviour. One teacher described her experiences of admitting Rosie, a 3-year-old with Down's syndrome. She talked about her anticipation of a demanding child who would need much attention, and of her surprise – having met and worked with Rosie – at how 'easy' it was to include her in all that happened; she found no 'difficulty' at all. But this honest and open contribution from a young teacher was met with 'advice' from another course participant (who had never met Rosie). She offered: 'Down's Syndrome, I know about Down's Syndrome, I've worked with lots of them. You can train her out of that affection and the kissing. Don't ever reward it. Don't ever offer her your cheek . Don't kiss her back or offer her hugs. You can train that out of her.' Rosie's teacher was visibly stunned. She responded to what she heard with courage, and said:

Rosie's affection is part of Rosie. What right do I have to attempt to change her? Her hugs and her kisses are her, part of her relationship with other adults and children. Loving and holding and kissing are part of being with Rosie – not always – but often. I teach Rosie – but I won't try to change what *is* Rosie.

Creating a culture of respect in education means valuing children for who they are. It means accepting and respecting what they bring, nurturing what they can do, anticipating what they might need and offering the best we can in order to enhance new thinking, new doing and new learning.

Respect for learners gives educators the courage to assert that they want the kind of education for *all* children which enables them to pursue their own goals and to recognise their own unique achievements.

Being and believing – a message for those who *manage* . . .

I began this chapter by acknowledging the real privilege allowed to me in contributing to this collection of thinking and experience. I have said what I have to say, and this book represents a desire, a willingness and an ability to explore and discuss the outstanding issues of managing *for* inclusive education *for all children*. But at the end of the day, when teachers and headteachers go home, when schools are locked and then policy-makers return to their own lives, it is parents who put their children to bed, who share their sometimes wakeful nights and who know uniquely their needs, joys, pains and abilities. This book can conclude in only one way, so this final chapter ends with the words of parents who seek what is right for *their* children:

Let our children be

Please allow our children to be. To be just as they are.
Being is essential, it is about identity, about existence.
Being is the essence of ourselves.
Our children have the right to be.

Please welcome difference. Difference teaches us about ourselves and each other.
Do not allow your fear of our children to spoil the opportunities they offer and the gifts they bring.

Please acknowledge our children's humanity. Do not treat them as less than human.

Please try to accept that our children are ordinary children.
We are not interested in your labels for them.

Please try to accept that we do what we believe is best for our children. This is no different from the majority of parents.
When we do not share your perceptions of our children, understand that we recognise the labels you give to us, also.

Please recognise your power. Think very carefully about the messages you give when you talk to us about our children and their futures.

Please recognise that we are tired of our children being treated as the property of professionals.
Do not tell us to be patient. Our children are children now.
If their time is wasted they do not get it back. Understand our anger if you tell us you know what is best for them.

Please understand that we love our children very much.
This may be difficult for you, since you perceive them as defective.

Please recognise we are on a journey.
We are travelling towards a point in the future where all children are of equal value.

Please understand that we are absolutely serious when we talk about the need for change.
We will not accept present discrimination.
When we say all children must be included, we mean all children.
All does mean all.

(Murray and Penman, 1996)

References

Gunner, A. (1997) Children's rights = human rights?, *Children UK*, Vol. 15, Winter, pp. 12–13.

Lansdown, G. (1996) The United Nations Convention on the Rights of the Child – progress in the United Kingdom, in Nutbrown, C. (ed) *Respectful Educators – Capable Learners: Children's Rights in Early Education*, Paul Chapman Publishing, London.

Lansdown, G. (1998) The European Convention on Human Rights: implications for children in the United Kingdom, in *Children in Scotland 1998: Children's Rights = Human Rights? An examination of Human Rights Standards and their Capacity to Promote and Defend the Rights of Children*, Children in Scotland, Edinburgh.

Lansdown, G.and Newell, P. (1994) *Agenda for Children*, Children's Rights Development Unit, London.

Murray, P. and Penman J. (1996) *Let Our Children Be*, Parents with Attitude, Sheffield.

Index